# RAHUL
### A BIOGRAPHY OF
# DRAVID

**The Nice Guy Who Finished First**

An author, screenwriter and anchor, **Devendra Prabhudesai** (b.1976) has worked across sectors—from working with the Police to rehabilitate victims of crime to planning and executing some of the biggest cricketing events in India in the recent past. He was Manager—Media Relations and Corporate Affairs, at the Board of Control for Cricket in India (BCCI) from January 2008 to July 2015.

He designed and scripted India's first 'Heritage Cricket Walk' for HopOn India in 2017. He was Guest Editor of 'The Rock,' a special issue on Rahul Dravid that *India Today* brought out in 2006. 'The Nice Guy Who Finished First' was originally written in 2005. It was his second book.

'As the mentor and guide of the future generations of Indian cricket, Rahul is invaluable as he is known to tell them the importance of playing for the country and the responsibility that comes with the honour and privilege of being able to live the dream. That cricket doesn't owe them anything and they are the ones that owe everything to cricket. God bless him and more strength to his shoulder.'

– Sunil Gavaskar

'There was no doubt about Rahul's class even in 1996. He had the ability, the sincerity and a penchant for adapting to the challenges posed by international cricket. I could only see him getting better. An individual starts to stagnate the day he refuses to acknowledge that he has some shortcomings that need to be worked upon. Rahul was not so good in ODIs at the start of his career and that cost him his place in the team. I remember calling him when he had been left out of the ODI side in the late 1990s. I told him that he could either view his omission as a setback or as an opportunity to improve. We all know which of the two options he chose. He worked hard and made himself an outstanding limited-overs player. He never sought short-cuts.'

– Sachin Tendulkar

'Maintaining one's position at the peak becomes easier if one is able to re-focus on the next ball, the next challenge. Fear is an emotion provided by nature for our protection. It cannot disappear totally. It has to be overcome and the challenge faced. Only two types of people are totally fearless. One, you find in the graveyard and the other, you find in a mental asylum. Rahul is someone who takes decisions and accepts responsibility for the same. That is the hallmark of a champion. Losers tend to look elsewhere. He is an ideal role model for anybody who wants to reach the top in his / her chosen profession.'

– Late B.P. Bam, Sports Psychologist

One of the most overused words in the cricketing dictionary is "great", because there are very few players in any country who quality. It is, in any case, a subjective view and all of us are limited by the number of players we have seen over the years. When judging earlier players, we have to take the word of people we trust, who have, in fact, seen them play. My view of Indian batsmen is that there have been a lot of very good ones, some able to play in all conditions, some best when playing on their own pitches.

'I believe there are three "great" Indian batsmen and I put them in order of appearance on the Test scene—Sunil Gavaskar, Sachin Tendulkar and Rahul Dravid. Tendulkar and Gavaskar have given me many days of great enjoyment and Dravid in recent times has played some wonderful innings. Attributes common to all three are courage and clear thinking and an ability to carry the attack to the opposition by keeping a step ahead of the bowlers.'

– Late Richie Benaud (2005)

Also By The Same Author:

*Winning Like Sachin; Think & Succeed Like Tendulkar* (2018)

*Hero: A Biography of Sachin Ramesh Tendulkar* (2017)

*SMG: A Biography of Sunil Manohar Gavaskar* (2009)

# RAHUL
## A BIOGRAPHY OF
# DRAVID
## The Nice Guy Who Finished First

**DEVENDRA PRABHUDESAI**

RUPA

Published by
Rupa Publications India Pvt. Ltd 2005, 2010, 2019
7/16, Ansari Road, Daryaganj
New Delhi 110002

*Sales centres:*
Allahabad Bengaluru Chennai
Hyderabad Jaipur Kathmandu
Kolkata Mumbai



Photo credits: Kamal Julka, Pradeep Mandhani, *Deccan Herald*, Sanjay Jagdale, Devraj Raut, Rajesh Shah and the author.



ISBN: 978-93-5333-311-9

First impression 2019

10 9 8 7 6 5 4 3 2 1



Printed at Parksons Graphics Pvt. Ltd., Mumbai

*To my grandparents*

Dear Ssapan,

Good luck to you as you move onto the next stage in your life.

Without a doubt, you will continue to have success in all areas

May success be with, always. Wishing you good luck.

- Anush

22/1/2020

# Contents

Standard Bank
Standard Bank
Standard Bank

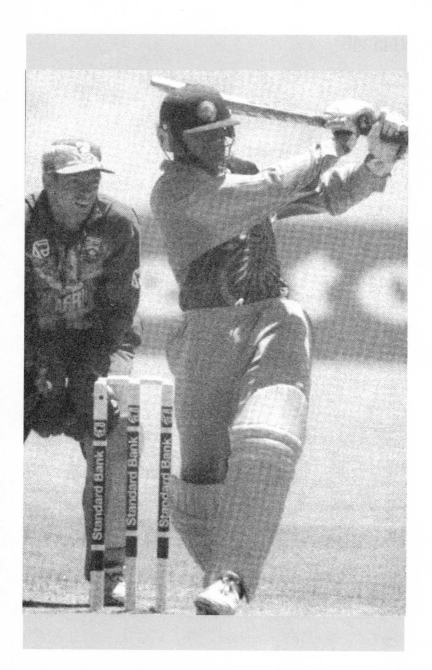

# PREFACE

Walter Reginald Hammond represented England in 85 Tests and scored 7,249 runs at an average of 58.45 in a glorious career that stretched from 1927-28 to 1946-47. These were stupendous figures, but unfortunately for him, whatever he did, his Australian contemporary Donald Bradman did better.

In an international career that began in 1928-29 and culminated in 1948, Bradman scored 6,996 runs from only 52 Tests. He scored seven more hundreds than Hammond and averaged the small matter of 99.94 runs per Test.

Cuthbert Gordon Greenidge, a destructive opening batsman from the Caribbean, scored 93 and 107 on his Test debut against India at Bengaluru in 1974-75. That marked the beginning of a remarkable career. He amassed 7,558 runs from 108 Tests at an average of 44.7, inclusive of 19 hundreds and 34 fifties, in a career that ended in 1991. However, he was unable to command the adulation he deserved for the simple reason that his career coincided with that of a cricketer named Isaac Vivian Alexander Richards, who made his debut in the same Test as he and ended his career a few months after he did. 'King' Richards scored 8,521 runs from 121 Tests at an average of 50.23. He crossed hundred 24 times in Tests and outshone nearly every batsman of his era.

Gundappa Raghunath Viswanath was rated highly by cricket-lovers throughout his international career, which spanned the period from 1969-70 to 1982-83. His batsmanship won India many a memorable match at home and overseas in the 1970s and early 1980s. He scored 6,080 runs from 91 Tests at an average of 41.93. However, his teammate and brother-in-law Sunil Gavaskar scored 1,305 more runs and 12 more centuries, averaged 53.51 from 85 Tests and rewrote the record-books in the same period. Gavaskar played international cricket till 1987 and became the first batsman to break the 10,000-run barrier in Tests.

The game of cricket goes by several rules, some written, others unwritten. One of the unwritten ones is that cricketers tend to find it difficult, if not impossible, to emerge from the shadow of a contemporary or teammate who happens to be bestowed with that special title: 'Legend'.

But as is the case with every rule, there have been exceptions. Cricket-lovers of the new millennium had the privilege of watching and following an exception that was glorious, to put it as mildly as possible.

Rahul Sharad Dravid spent the first few years of his international career in the shadows of the legendary Sachin Tendulkar, his much-loved teammate and former captain, a deity of the masses and darling of the media.

As the years passed, Rahul overcame several hurdles, some technical, others mental, to carve out a niche of his own. His tools were the same as Tendulkar's: self-belief, a passion for hard work, unwavering determination, and a fierce commitment to his team's cause.

Rahul was one of the primary catalysts in the transformation of an 'under-performing' group of individuals into a competitive, fighting unit, in the first decade of the new millennium. His services to Indian cricket did not end with his retirement as a cricketer.

This is his story.

Devendra Prabhudesai

# Introduction

*The Nice Guy Who Finished First* is the remarkable story of Rahul Sharad Dravid. It tells the tale of an individual who succeeded in his chosen profession because of his ardent faith in the five Ds—Dedication, Discipline, Determination, Devotion and Desire.

The updated version of the biography reconstructs the incidents and events that contributed to making Rahul Dravid one of the greatest cricketers to have played the game. It is a tribute to an epitome of grace and humility, and a role model who refused to rest on his laurels, always lived in the 'here and now' and did whatever he could do to achieve long-term solutions rather than short-term fixes. He remains as committed to the quest for perfection in his present incarnation as Coach as he was as a Cricketer.

Rahul Dravid's moments of triumph are described in the biography, as also his trials and tribulations. The book narrates the epic battle, one that he eventually won, to break free of the stereotypes that haunted him in his early years at the international level. His efforts to emerge from the intimidating shadows cast by some teammates and contemporaries are illustrated in great detail. The book highlights the physical, mental and of course, technical attributes that have elevated Rahul to legendary status.

In this honest endeavour to recount the story of Rahul

Dravid from his formative years to the present day, the author is assisted by reminiscences from his mentors, seniors, teammates and even opponents, all of whom witnessed the making of a cricketing legend from close quarters. Then, there are the photographs, some of the best ever, which showcase the genius of a legend.

It is an engaging, absorbing and succinct read.

# 1

## TAKING GUARD

20 June 1996... The English and Indian cricket teams lined up on either side of the wooden gate that separates the playing area of the Lord's Cricket Ground from the Members' Enclosure. The second Test of the 1996 series between the two countries was the final international assignment of Harold 'Dickie' Bird, one of cricket's most revered umpires. The players' 'Guard of Honour' brought the spectators to their feet and tears to Bird's eyes. Among the players saluting the veteran umpire was a young man with stars in his eyes.

It was a time of turmoil in Indian cricket. The campaign to win the World Cup earlier that year had ended amidst a shower of stones and bottles at Kolkata during the semifinal against eventual winners Sri Lanka. The selectors responded to the loss by dropping Manoj Prabhakar and Vinod Kambli, two of the team's prominent players, from the squad for the next tournament, a tri-series at Singapore. While Prabhakar's omission came as no surprise after his annihilation by the Sri Lankans in a league encounter of the World Cup, the swashbuckling Kambli's axing was widely condemned. He was a popular member of the side and cricket-lovers didn't take too kindly to the claims made by 'inner sources' that he had been punished for his 'indiscipline'. The furore over his omission completely obscured the news of the inclusion of a twenty-three-year-old Bengaluruan named Rahul Dravid.

'Rahul was always a good listener and learner, serious and dedicated. He would reach the nets earlier than any other player and have a knock with the ballboys before the practice session began. I don't remember him missing a single practice session,' recalls illustrious Indian wicketkeeper Syed Kirmani, under whose leadership the seventeen-year-old Rahul made his debut in first-class cricket in a Ranji Trophy encounter against Maharashtra in the 1990-91 season. In his very first innings, the teenager scored 82 and helped his team reach a total of 638. Javagal Srinath then rocked the strong Maharashtra batting line-up with figures of 7-93 and Karnataka took the decisive first-innings lead.

Rahul's early elevation to first-class cricket was a consequence of the transitional phase that Karnataka cricket was going through at the time. Quite a few stalwarts who had served the state and in some cases, country, with distinction, had bowed out in the recent past; G.R. Viswanath, Roger Binny and Brijesh Patel, to name just three. Their absence was obviously being felt. Kirmani returned to Karnataka after a brief stint with the Railways to take over the captaincy and mentor the next generation of players. He was complemented in this endeavour by the Karnataka selectors, who experimented with youth and ended up unearthing as many as four special talents who went on to do the state and country proud—Javagal Srinath and Anil Kumble in 1989-90, and Venkatesh Prasad and Rahul Dravid a year later. While Srinath and Kumble had debuted under Binny's leadership, Kirmani was Rahul and Prasad's first first-class skipper.

Rahul made it to the first-class level five years after he first attended a cricket coaching camp—the KSCA (Karnataka State Cricket Association) camp conducted by former first-class cricketer P.S. Viswanath. Rahul caught the eye of coach Keki Tarapore, who became his guru. Under Tarapore's tutelage, Rahul went on to do exceptionally well in local and regional Under-13, Under-15 and Under-17 competitions. Then came the call from the state selectors.

Rahul followed up on his 82 on his Ranji Trophy debut with an innings of 134, his maiden first-class hundred, in his second Ranji fixture, the 1990-91 quarterfinal against defending champions Bengal. It turned out to be a controversial game that Karnataka lost despite scoring 791-6, due to the dubious 'Quotient Rule', which was to Indian cricket in the late 1980s and early 1990s what the infamous 'Rain-rule' was to the 1992 World Cup. Teams suffered in some cases, benefited in others, but quite unlike the rain-rule, some teams managed to 'manoeuvre' the quotient rule far better than others, Bengal being one of them. That game also provided Rahul with his first view of another talented teenager who contributed 74 to Bengal's score of 652-9—Sourav Ganguly.

What distinguished Rahul from others in the same age-group was a sound technique, coupled with a prodigious hunger for runs. He began the 1991-92 season with 126 in Karnataka's first Ranji engagement against Goa, and 128 in the next clash against Kerala. His run-hunger and technical proficiency impressed G.R. Viswanath, who was closely attached to the state side as selector and manager in the early 1990s. The maestro attributes Rahul's success to his cricketing origins and attitude. 'Playing regularly on matting wickets, especially in the initial stages of one's career, makes the batsman a better back-foot player. The advantage of being a back-foot oriented batsman is that he gives the impression that he has plenty of time to play a stroke. Moreover, executing shots square of the wicket comes quite naturally to those who nurture their cricketing dreams on matting. Of course, one still has to work hard, and Rahul was an extremely diligent cricketer. It did not take him too long to establish himself as a frontline batsman in the Karnataka team after his brilliant debut,' Viswanath, who like Rahul had played all his early cricket on matting, told this author.

In the same season, Rahul was appointed captain of an Under-19 Indian team for a series against a team of youngsters from New Zealand. The responsibility brought out the best in him. He guided India to a thrilling 12-run win in the first 'Test' and a draw in the second. His innings of 116 in the second 'Test' at Mumbai was his first hundred against a team from overseas. The Indian boys took the 'Test' series 1-0 and won the one-day series 2-1. Rahul made an impression not only with his brilliant batting and canny captaincy, but also for his deceptive bowling. He bowled thirty overs of off-spin in the three one-day games and bagged five wickets for 99 runs.

A year later, on the eve of the 1992-93 Ranji pre-quarterfinal against Madhya Pradesh in Bengaluru, Viswanath told the visiting captain, one of his former India teammates from Mumbai, who was now leading MP as a 'Professional', to 'watch out' for the boy.

'There has been a touch of class in everything that I have

seen Rahul do since that first meeting,' says Sandeep Patil, who went on to become Rahul's first 'coach' in the national team. 'When I saw him in 1992-93, there seemed to be a streak of arrogance in him, which is not such a bad thing. But there was a touch of class even in that arrogance! He was supremely confident of his abilities.'

Rahul's sequence of scores in the 1992-93 Ranji Trophy prior to that game read 54, 37, 200*, 56*, 55, 79 and 9. The double hundred, the first of his career, came against Andhra Pradesh, and delighted Viswanath as much as it did Rahul.

> 'I was longing to watch a long innings by Rahul, and he obliged with that performance against Andhra. I was immensely happy for him, and convinced that he had it in him to make it big.'
>
> —G.R. Viswanath

Patil, a great admirer of Viswanath's, needed no further endorsement of Rahul's talent than the maestro's words, but the teenager provided conclusive proof of his skills by scoring 89 in the first innings. In the second innings, Karnataka needed 238 to win when Rahul came in to bat at 48-2. Patil decided to tempt the youngster to go for the big shots by bringing the field in. He succeeded when Rahul succumbed to the bait, giving a catch to mid-on when he had scored only seven. Madhya Pradesh won that game by only five runs, and Patil believes that it was Rahul's dismissal that turned the match.

There were some impressive performances in 1993-94 as well. Rahul's 93 for the Rest of India in the Irani Trophy fixture against Punjab earned him the praise of Sanjay Manjrekar, his captain for that game.

Twelve months later, Rahul scored 132 in his second Irani Trophy encounter, this time against Manjrekar's home-team Mumbai. Scores of 67 and 148 for South Zone against Central Zone in the Duleep Trophy resulted in a call-up from the national selectors for the final two matches of a limited-overs tri-series against the West Indies and New Zealand. Manoj Prabhakar and Nayan Mongia had been axed for 'taking it easy' while batting in a league game against the Windies, and Rahul and wicketkeeper-batsman Vijay Yadav were summoned to fill their places in the fourteen. The Indian limited-overs outfit was far too star-studded to allow any debutant to break in, especially a batsman, but Rahul made the most of his apprenticeship and partook of the delirious victory celebrations after the hosts beat the West Indies in the final at Kolkata.

After scoring 191 against Andhra in the Ranji Trophy, Rahul toured Bangladesh for the SAARC Cup as a member of the Praveen Amre-led India 'A' side. He was one of the chief architects of India's triumph, with knocks of 44, 16, 33 and 37. Coach Sandeep Patil was impressed with the 'transformation' in him: 'He had changed completely from the time I first saw him. He was displaying maturity in whatever he did, whether it was walking, talking, dress sense and of course, batting. He seemed to be in control of every situation. His mind was uncluttered. There are many youngsters who have ten shots in mind for a particular delivery, and by the time they decide which one to play, it is too late. This was never the case with Rahul.'

Back in India, Rahul was one of the few India 'A players to emerge with any credit against the visiting England 'A' side. The tourists swept the three 'Tests' and won the one-dayers 2-1. Rahul warmed up with 84 and 49 for the Board President's XI, and scored a 50 in each of the three 'Tests' and a 57 in the second one-dayer. He was one of five Indian batsmen who ended the 1994-95 season with over 1,000 first-class runs.

The next season witnessed the 'coming of age' of two cricket teams in South Asia. The much-maligned Sri Lankans stunned the world by pocketing the game's ultimate prize—the World Cup. Their aggressive tactics took other teams by surprise, and pundits the world over raved over the wisdom of Sri Lanka's administrators to blood a number of talented youngsters in the previous few years and persist with them despite some initial reverses. Under the watchful leadership of Arjuna Ranatunga and Aravinda De Silva, the players repaid the faith.

Something very similar happened in India at the same time. The young men who had debuted for Karnataka at the turn of the decade vindicated their backers with a splendid showing in the Ranji Trophy. Not only did Rahul contribute to the triumph, the fourth in Karnataka's history, as a batsman with three hundreds, including one each in the semi-final and final, but he also did a fine job as captain in the absence of Anil Kumble, who was busy on national duty. Kumble returned for the final against Tamil Nadu, in which Karnataka gained the crucial first-innings lead. Rahul starred in another team triumph in the season. He accompanied the India 'A' team for the Interface limited-overs tournament in Sharjah, where he was consistent enough to win the Man of the Series Award. Earlier in the season, he showed that he had the strokes and skill to succeed at the highest level with an innings of 145 for the Board President's XI against the touring New Zealanders. 'The hundred against the Kiwis attracted the attention of the think-tank and selectors. His deeds in the 1994-95 and 1995-96 seasons clearly suggested that he would be part of the national team very soon,' recalled Viswanath, who by then had become the Chairman of the National Selection Committee.

Rahul did his best in the Challenger Trophy, the BCCI's annual one-day series that divided the top 36 players in the country into three sides—India Seniors, India 'A' and India 'B'. The tournament, played in Hyderabad in the last week of 1995, was a 'selection trial' of sorts for the 1996 World Cup. The Seniors team was for all practical purposes the first-choice Indian XI save Tendulkar, who was leading India 'A'. Sachin's outfit stunned Azhar's at the league stage, but the Seniors recovered to make the final against the same team. In the final, the Seniors batted first and scored 213 on a slow wicket. India 'A' were 55-3 when Rahul, who had scored 78 against India 'B', found an enthusiastic partner in Sourav Ganguly. They were pitted against an attack that comprised frontline India bowlers Prabhakar, Srinath, Prasad, Kumble and Aashish Kapoor, all of whom made it to the World Cup squad. The young men batted superbly to raise the hundred of the innings and moved on towards the 150-mark. A shock result was a distinct possibility when, with the score at 148, Rahul drove Srinath to mid-off and called for a single. Ganguly advanced, then changed his mind and chose to stay put in his crease. Before Rahul, who had sprinted down the track could realize what had happened, he found himself at the same end as his partner, and was comfortably run out. His dismissal was the turning point and India 'A' collapsed for 180. Mohammed Azharuddin, the reigning captain of India, accepted the winner's cheque and the trophy, and he may well have thanked Ganguly. Had the left-hander not misjudged the run, Tendulkar might well have held the trophy, and it would have been pretty embarrassing for the India captain, a Hyderabadi, to lose on home turf to a team captained by his national deputy!

Viswanath and his fellow panellists did not pick Rahul for the 1996 World Cup. He was disappointed, but not unduly. He had already worked out that he did not have much of a chance to break into a line-up that comprised experienced heavyweights like Navjot Sidhu, Vinod Kambli, Ajay Jadeja, Sanjay Manjrekar, skipper Mohammed Azharuddin and the redoubtable Sachin Tendulkar. He was aware that the selectors would be reluctant to experiment in the World Cup of all tournaments.

'When you knock on the door and the selectors do not open it, then knock harder,' has been his idol Sunil Gavaskar's recurring advice to all youngsters, and Rahul set out to do just that. As had always been the case throughout his career, he made the most of his practice sessions, goading the quicker Karnataka bowlers to bowl at full tilt. In Javagal Srinath, Venkatesh Prasad, David Johnson and Dodda Ganesh, he had the right men to pepper him with bouncy, fiery stuff in the nets.

The deluge of runs in the Ranji Trophy knockout games ensured that the national selectors could not ignore him after the World Cup. Rahul did nothing of note in two limited-overs tournaments in Singapore and Sharjah, his highest score being a measly 11 in his fourth one-day international (ODI). There was the odd whisper about his 'unsuitability' to limited-overs cricket, and even he was worried that he had blown his chances for the tour of England. But to those who understood the nuances of the game, it was obvious that he was a big-match player, one who was ready for the big league after six seasons of first-class cricket. Viswanath and his fellow selectors certainly thought so.

The panelists—Sambaran Banerjee (East), M.P. Pandove (North), Anshuman Gaekwad (West), and Kishen Rungta (Central), had all seen Rahul excel at the state, zonal and India 'A' levels. Rahul's success on two private tours of England, besides his technique and temperament, tilted the scales in his favour. Viswanath was convinced that Rahul possessed the wherewithal to handle the bounce and movement in England.

Rahul was delighted with his inclusion, but far from happy with the cynics who were stuck up with his failures in the limited-overs tournaments and were referring to the 'Viswanath factor'. The derisive comments only made him determined to prove his detractors wrong and justify the Chairman's faith.

The Indian team chosen for its 13th Test tour of England comprised as many as five Karnataka players. Srinath and Kumble, both of whom had had successful stints in County Cricket with Gloucestershire and Northamptonshire respectively a year before, were the main bowlers. Venkatesh Prasad, a nippy bowler and canny 'mover' of the ball, had already appeared in 33 ODIs prior to the tour and hence could not be called inexperienced. Then there was the left-arm spinner Sunil Joshi, who in 1995-96 had become the first player to score 500 runs and take 50 wickets in a single Ranji Trophy season.

The job of an Indian cricket selector will be a frontrunner for the title of the 'most thankless' in the world. The selection of almost every Indian cricket team has traditionally sparked off a variety of reactions from the media and the fans. However, the reactions that followed the announcement of the team for the England tour in 1996 were unusually strong even by Indian standards.

Rahul with India and Karnataka teammate Javagal Srinath

The media was outraged at the omission of Vinod Kambli, who at that stage had a 50-plus average in Tests. Picked ahead of him was his fellow left-hander Sourav Ganguly, whose only game for India had been a solitary one-day international in 1991-92. Kambli's fellow 'Mumbaikars' were aghast and a group even went to the extent of burning an effigy of Viswanath. The selectors were hauled over the coals for playing the 'Bengal' card once again, and the names of cricketers who had shifted to Bengal in the recent past and promptly been 'rewarded' with places in the national team were splashed all over. Ganguly's 'proximity' to Sambaran Banerjee, under whose captaincy he had made his first-class debut in 1989-90, was written about, as was the close friendship between Ganguly's father and Jagmohan Dalmiya, then Secretary of the Board and Convener of the Selection

Committee. The man in the eye of the storm hit back, arguing that he had earned a place due to his consistent performances in the past few seasons.

> 'I find it hard to believe that Gundappa Viswanath has endorsed this team, and I find it even harder to digest that Azharuddin has approved of it.'
>
> —Kapil Dev, *The Indian Express*, 29 April 1996

The selectors were also criticized for picking only three quick bowlers and four spin bowlers for a tour to be undertaken in the first half of the English summer, when the conditions would be cold, wet and not at all conducive to bowling of the slower variety. Srinath, Prasad and the rookie Paras Mhambrey were to shoulder the new-ball burden on a hectic tour that comprised three Tests, the same number of ODIs and eleven first-class matches. The selectors defended Ganguly's inclusion by citing his ability as a right-handed seamer, in addition to his batting gifts. Their assertion that the Kolkatan had been picked as an 'all-rounder' was not taken seriously.

Like the quicks, the man expected to 'take' them behind the stumps was also expected to work overtime. Mongia was the only specialist keeper in the squad, with Sanjay Manjrekar and Rahul, both of whom had done a bit of keeping in their formative years, expected to fill in as his deputies. Rahul, who had not kept wickets for nearly eight years apart from a couple of Duleep Trophy games in an emergency situation, wasn't all that thrilled with the additional responsibility; but then, you don't say no to anything on your first tour.

It was a fairly inexperienced squad that coach Sandeep Patil had under his wings. Six members of the touring party made their Test debuts on the tour—Vikram Rathore, Venkatesh Prasad, Sunil Joshi, Paras Mhambrey, Sourav Ganguly and Rahul Dravid. Patil naturally stood by the selectors, contending that the best 16 players in the country had been selected. He stated he was 'extremely satisfied' with the composition of the team.

Nine years later, Patil told this author that the team was in a 'rebuilding process' on that tour. Azharuddin, the captain, had not been in the best of form on the field and on top of the popularity charts off it. The year 1996 had been a stormy one for him. He had formally announced his separation from his wife on the eve of the World Cup, by which time every living Indian was acquainted with his relationship with actor Sangeeta Bijlani. His indifferent form in the World Cup, and the semifinal disaster at Kolkata had only added fuel to the fire. The record books stated that he was India's most successful Test captain with eleven wins, but ten of those had been achieved at home, the eleventh in Sri Lanka. It was a decade since India had won a Test match or series outside the subcontinent. Coincidentally, the last victory had been achieved in England, but the team of 1996 lacked the experience and variety in the bowling department that Kapil Dev had at his disposal in 1986. Azhar's boys had also fared poorly in the tournaments in Singapore and Sharjah that followed the World Cup, and there was more than an iota of truth in the assumption that Azhar had kept his job for the England tour only because the selectors themselves had appointed him for one full year in September 1995. It was quite obvious that only an extraordinary performance on the tour would enable him to hang on to the captaincy. If that were not to happen, the inevitable would follow, and Sachin Tendulkar, his deputy for three years, would be entrusted the reins.

The Indian team in England, 1996. Rahul in standing fifth from left

The brilliant bowling of Anil Kumble on home pitches notwithstanding, every treatise and discussion on Indian cricket in the 1990s began and ended with Sachin Ramesh Tendulkar. By far the biggest draw in the game, cricket writers and fans in England could not wait to see him in action. As the baby of the team that toured England in 1990, he had scored his maiden Test hundred in the second Test at Manchester and received two bottles of champagne for his efforts. The bottles remained unopened. He was only seventeen years old at the time! Then, he was a boy on the threshold of greatness and superstardom, but in 1996, he was the Superstar of Superstars, a man poised to lead Indian cricket into the new millennium. Shortly after the England tour got underway, he received the ultimate accolade from Sir Donald Bradman, the greatest batsman of all time. 'I feel Tendulkar plays the same way as I played...his compactness, his stroke production and his technique,' the knight declared.

Everybody, English cricket-lovers included, was ecstatic when he began the tour with a match-winning 108 in the traditional tour-opener against the Duke of Norfolk's XI at Arundel. Rahul played in the first two games, one-dayers both, but missed the first three-day fixture against Worcestershire. He played in the next game against Gloucestershire and did very well, scoring an unbeaten 86 in the first innings. He concentrated on getting acclimatized to English conditions and playing himself in, rather than going for the big strokes. His part in the game was far from over, as he returned to the middle in a different set of pads. Mongia had been given the game off.

It was the first time Rahul was essaying the dual roles of batsman and wicketkeeper for the national team.

It wasn't the last.

# 2

## HERO AT HEADQUARTERS

> 'I had seen Rahul in the Ranji Trophy before the tour. He was a perfectionist, a sound builder of innings. Even in those early days, you could not miss the determination in his eyes. He was the same in England.'
>
> —Venkatapathy Raju

After the game against Gloucestershire, the Indians played Sussex, and Rahul once again stood behind the stumps and batted brightly in the second innings to score 44. Off the field, he was doing his best to convince Sunil Joshi, a strict vegetarian who was virtually starving, to eat at least omelettes, if not anything else. Joshi had been having a torrid time on the tour, and the biting cold wasn't exactly adding to his comfort. He was fielding at gully against Sussex with his hands in his pockets, when the batsman slashed hard. The ball flew towards him, but by the time he had brought his hands out of his pockets, it was too late and the catch was spilt! Rahul's coaxing worked. As it turned out, Joshi liked omelettes so much that he started eating them day in and day out!

Rahul was forced to take a break after the Sussex game as his teammates readied themselves for the limited-overs series, which was a catastrophe in more ways than one. England dominated the rain-affected first fixture that even a reserve day could not salvage, and dismissed India for a paltry 158 in the second to win by six wickets. The desperate situation demanded a change, and both Rahul and Sourav Ganguly were included in the XI for the third game, another encounter that spilled over to the reserve day. The Indians batted first and did well with Ganguly scoring 46 and Rahul an unbeaten 22. But a score of 236-4 from 50 overs was inadequate. England won the match and with it, the series, in the penultimate over. Back in the dressing room, the Indians were hit by a tornado.

Navjot Singh Sidhu, the senior-most member of the team, announced his retirement in protest at what he perceived as his 'humiliation.' It was claimed that he was told about his omission from the playing XI for the final ODI only after he had padded up to bat. That, apparently, was the 'final straw.' The team management rebutted this version and contended that both he and Manjrekar had been informed the day before the game that they were being left out for 'not pulling their weight.'

Patil, who had incidentally contemplated retirement during India's tour of England fourteen years previously, only to change his mind after encouraging words from his seniors and a rousing hundred in the second Test at Manchester, tried his best to placate Sidhu, but in vain. In a formal statement, Sidhu told a stunned media that he had promised his late father that he would lead his life with dignity. That dignity, he claimed, would be compromised if he carried on.

Sidhu's walkout divided followers of Indian cricket into two categories—those who supported Sidhu and those who didn't. The first group squarely blamed the captain and coach, while the second deemed it unbecoming of a senior player to desert his team in the middle of such an important tour. However, what both groups agreed on was that it was something that should never have happened. The selectors quickly summoned paceman Salil Ankola from the Northumberland league to replenish the fast-bowling department, in a bid to cover up their initial goof-up.

The first Test was preceded by a three-dayer against Leicestershire, in which Azharuddin scored a wristy 111 and added an unfinished 153 with Rahul, who contributed 58. Among the bowlers who suffered was the seamer Simon Hughes, who remarked that 'bowling to Azhar was like bowling into a revolving door' (*Sportstar,* 15 June 1996). Rahul's fine knock failed to win him a place in the team for the first Test, which turned out to be another disaster.

Rathore, who had looked unstoppable in the three-day games, fell cheaply to seamer Dominic Cork in both innings. He was cross with his second-innings dismissal, with the umpires not intervening even when it appeared that Graeme Hick at second slip had clasped the ball after it had hit the turf. Save a pugnacious 52 by Srinath, who batted as well as he had at Mumbai against the West Indies a year-and-a-half ago, no other batsman made a mark, and the visitors scored a mere 214. Srinath and Prasad, India's newest new-ball pair then brought their team back into the match with a superb display of bowling. But the Chennai-born Nasser Hussain, who was playing his first Test in three seasons, held firm and scored a fine 128. He took England to a lead of 99 on a difficult pitch, and when Chris

Lewis, Dominic Cork and Alan Mullally reduced India to 68-5 in the second innings, it looked all over. But that man Tendulkar would have none of it. He etched out an outstanding 122, but could not prevent defeat by eight wickets. Joshi, unfortunately for him, broke a finger and was ruled out for the rest of the series.

Tendulkar missed the next game, a three-dayer against Derbyshire that India lost in two-and-a-half days. The fiasco underscored India's total dependence on him. Geoffrey Boycott could not have put it better when he commented during the first Test that the Indians needed Tendulkar to bat at numbers one, two, three, four, five and six. The statement outraged many an Indian supporter, but it wasn't very far from the truth.

All that was to change.

India's saving grace against Derbyshire was Ganguly (64), who had been informed that he would make his Test debut in the next game at Lord's. As it turned out, he had company.

Manjrekar was nursing an ankle injury, and he was to undergo a fitness test on the morning of the Test. Rahul was told that he would play if Manjrekar failed the test. Ten minutes before the toss, Patil went up to Rahul.

> 'I told him that he will be playing. His face lit up. I cannot forget that moment.'
>
> —Sandeep Patil

When Venkatesh Prasad wished him luck, Rahul pointed towards the boards in the dressing room that bore the names of all the overseas cricketers who had scored a Test hundred or taken five wickets in a Test innings at Headquarters. 'You put your name on the bowlers' board, and I will put mine on the batsmen's board,' he quipped. A deal was struck.

Sourav and Rahul could not have asked for a grander setting in which to make their debut—the Home of Cricket. For the second time in a Lord's Test, Azhar won the toss and elected to field, although the pitch and conditions were a lot more bowler-friendly than they were in 1990 when England amassed 653-4 after he asked them to take first strike. The 'guard of honour' for Dickie Bird was English skipper Michael Atherton's idea, but the umpire was in no mood to express his gratitude. He declared Atherton out leg-before in the very first over! Atherton later remarked wryly on the irony of it all. When asked which stump the ball would have hit, pat came the sheepish response: 'Probably all three!'

England were pegged onto the back foot by another marvellous bowling performance by Srinath and Prasad. Unfortunately, as in the first Test, they had little support, and the hosts rallied around keeper-batsman-artist Jack Russell, who scored a fighting 124 in his unconventional and inimitable style. He came in to bat at 107-5, and helped take the score to a relatively healthy 344. The Indians needed a good start but did not get it, with Rathore being superbly caught by Nasser Hussain at second slip off Cork. This brought Sourav Ganguly to the crease. Mongia, promoted to open in place of Ajay Jadeja who had looked uncomfortable and susceptible to the new ball in the first Test, played some firm strokes, but was declared leg-before when he padded up to one from Chris Lewis that broke back. Tendulkar then took command of the proceedings with some cracking strokes. He looked imperious against all the bowlers save Chris Lewis, who was making the ball talk. An absorbing duel followed, which ended with Lewis delivering a beauty that pitched just short of a length on off-and-middle, forced Tendulkar onto the back foot, and then darted away to miss the bat and disturb the off-stump. There was not much even a batsman of Tendulkar's calibre could have done with a delivery like that.

Tendulkar's dismissal shifted the spotlight onto Ganguly, who had seemingly decided that every blade of grass on the offside was a detractor of his. Atherton kept plugging the gaps on the offside and Ganguly kept piercing them. It was stroke play at its most exquisite. Azharuddin fell cheaply when he poked at an away-going delivery by the left-handed Alan Mullally and was comfortably caught by Russell. The only plausible reason why Jadeja was sent in ahead of Rahul was because the 'number six' slot had been lucky for him. He had batted very well in the World Cup at that position, but then, this was a Test match, not a one-day game where a player could hope to get away with technical deficiencies. The score was 202-4 when he played all over a delivery by change bowler Ronnie Irani. Rahul's time had come.

'It's all right to be nervous. Even I was nervous when I started. Just stay there for 15 minutes and things will improve.' These words by Tendulkar kept ringing in Rahul's mind as he strode down the flight of stairs from the pavilion towards the wooden gate, through the MCC enclosure. As he swung open the gate at cricket's HQ, he experienced a tingle in his spine. He was living his childhood dream. He had been given an opportunity to fulfil his wildest cricketing ambitions. As he strode out onto the field, he said to himself: 'Whatever happens beyond this point, I am a Test cricketer, India's 207th, and nobody can take that away from me.'

Ronnie Irani bowled the first delivery Rahul faced in Test

cricket. It was pitched short, and Rahul essayed a back foot defensive stroke. The ball hit the middle of the bat, and he felt reassured. He fed off his co-debutant and partner's confidence, which by then had reached the stratosphere. The Indian supporters went berserk when Ganguly completed a century on debut with a cover drive, his 17th boundary. Never in the history of Indian cricket had an individual silenced his critics in such resounding fashion as Sourav Ganguly on 22 June 1996. Rahul at the other end followed his vice-captain's advice to the letter. The first 15 minutes went by and he got into the act, cover-driving Cork beautifully for four, his head, feet, hands and bat swooping down upon the ball in perfect harmony. He followed it up with a rasping square-cut off Irani that fetched him four more.

> 'After he got through the first 15-20 minutes, it, became just another Ranji Trophy game for him.'
>
> —VENKATAPATHY RAJU

When Ganguly was bowled by Mullally, the pair had put on 94 for the sixth wicket in a breathtaking display of batting, replete with emphatic, but orthodox strokes.

The battle was not yet over, as the Indians were 48 short of the English total when Ganguly fell for a magnificent 131. Rahul took charge and controlled the innings superbly. Bad light ended play 22 minutes before the scheduled close on the third day with India 324-6, 56 of those scored by Rahul. He returned to a sporting ovation by the English players. The performances of the two debutants had been powerful enough to elicit terms like 'fire in the belly' and 'determination' from the TV commentators, who had been at a loss for similar words after India's dismal showing in the first Test.

'Solidity' was the first word that sprung to legend Sunil Gavaskar's mind when asked to recall Rahul's first Test innings nine years later. 'He looked a well-organized player, sound and unruffled, when I saw him in the early stages of the tour. At Lord's, Sourav batted elegantly as all left-handers do, while Rahul at the other end was solid.'

Rahul kept going on the fourth day, even as all those watching looked forward to witnessing Test cricket's first instance of a pair of debutants scoring centuries in the same Test.* Rahul was given good support by Kumble and Srinath. But the English managed to stem the flow of runs, and there was a frustrating

---

*This feat was eventually performed by the Pakistani duo of Ali Naqvi and Azhar Mahmood against South Africa at Rawalpindi in 1997-98.

period when Rahul spent close to 50 minutes on 79. He got through this though, and entered the nineties with Mhambrey holding fort at the other end. Rahul had got within five runs of the magic figure when he got a nick to Lewis, and walked. The stadium rose to him, and he was passed on the way back by the new batsman Venkatesh Prasad, who was probably as disappointed as Rahul himself. By taking 5-76 in England's first innings, Prasad had fulfilled his part of the 'deal'. His colleague had come within five runs of fulfilling his, only to falter at the final hurdle. Rahul got as much cheers for his innings as for his 'walk' without waiting for the umpire's decision. When asked about it, he was quick to state that 'everybody at the ground had heard the nick'. He was deeply disappointed, but preferred to look at the cup as half-full rather than half-empty. He may have missed a hundred, but he had scored 95 priceless runs to cement his place in the team.

> 'You could sense that he had the talent and ability to be around for a long, long time at the international level.'
>
> —Sachin Tendulkar

'The Indian new-ball duo enjoyed far better support from their co-bowlers in the second innings. At 168-6, England were in a spot of bother, as they were only 83 ahead with four wickets in hand. But Alec Stewart bailed his team out with an obdurate 66. Irani scored 41 and Russell stonewalled for 38 in another difficult situation. The match was drawn, but the Indians had reason to feel satisfied.

Not surprisingly, Sourav Ganguly, the Man of the Match, hogged the headlines of the sports pages and covers of sports magazines in India. The reason one has to mention the country's name is because the Test series was comprehensively overshadowed in England by the ongoing Euro '96 Football Championships. In fact, when Sourav and Rahul were going great guns on the third day, play was interrupted by raucous cheering after the English soccer team beat Spain in the quarterfinal!

The Indian team's next first-class engagement was against a British Universities XI that included Chinmay, the son of Madhu Gupte who had represented Maharashtra with distinction in the 1970s. It was another of those glorified 'practice' matches that 'die' unless the two captains contrive a result with mutually decided 'sporting' declarations. Nothing of that sort happened in this game, but it was a significant one for Rahul. A fully recovered Manjrekar and Jadeja scored hundreds in the first innings. In the second, Rahul went in at number three, the first time he had batted at that number for India. He played his strokes from the word 'go' and scored an undefeated 101. Any elation that he may have felt evaporated in the next game against Hampshire, when Rathore, Tendulkar, he and Manjrekar were sent packing by Kevan James, a thirty-five-year-old seam bowler, off consecutive deliveries! Rahul had the dubious distinction of being the 'hattrick' victim. Ganguly and Kumble came to the rescue with a stand of 155, and the Indians declared at 362-7. James then came in to bat at number four and scored 103 to complete one of the greatest all-round performances in first-class cricket.

Azharuddin elected to bat after winning the toss in the third Test at Trent Bridge, Nottingham, in what was a do-or-die game for him and the team. His team needed a win to level the series, and he needed a win to retain the captaincy. On a flat track, the Indians prospered after the early dismissals of

Rathore and Mongia. Ganguly and Tendulkar continued their dream run, adding 255 for the third wicket. Sourav became only the third batsman after West Indians Lawrence Rowe and Alvin Kallicharran to score centuries in his first two innings in Test cricket. He scored 136, and his vice-captain made 177. It puzzled many to see both Manjrekar, who had returned to the XI at Jadeja's expense, and Azharuddin, batting ahead of Rahul. Manjrekar batted steadily but slowly. Azharuddin failed once again, superbly caught by Min Patel at short-leg off Lewis.

Lewis greeted Rahul with a bouncer, which the batsman ignored. Rahul quickly got into his stride and started playing his strokes. As at Lord's, his adherence to the basics could not be ignored—a still head, a backlift that like most of the greats, came down from second slip, and a straight bat. The manner in which Rahul took his stance was reminiscent of a certain diminutive opening batsman who hadn't done too badly in a career that stretched from 1971 to 1987. Like him, Rahul grounded his bat at the same time as he placed his front foot in position, and then placed his right (rear) leg alongside the left. Like him, Rahul moved 'back and across' before meeting the ball.

Rahul added 61 with Manjrekar before the latter fell for 53. For the second successive time in his Test career, Rahul found himself marshalling the lower order, and once again, he did the job with aplomb.

> 'As at Lord's, Dravid's bat had a mellow ring to it and even his defensive strokes had the hallmark of class.'
>
> —David Field, *Wisden Cricketers' Almanack*, 1997

Rahul scored 84 before falling to Mark Ealham in the same manner as at Lord's. The Indians finished with 521.

> 'I would value his 95 at Lord's more than the 84 at Nottingham. The Lord's wicket had something in it for the bowlers, but the Trent Bridge strip was so docile that even my great-grandmother would have scored on it.'
>
> —Salil Ankola

The visitors had little chance of squaring the series on that wicket once the hosts saw off the early threat posed by Srinath and Prasad. Atherton helped himself to 160 after being dropped by Rahul in the slips early on, and Hussain scored 107, his second hundred of the series. The game was already into the final day by the time England were all out with a lead of 43. With Rathore unable to bat due to injury, the think-tank promoted Manjrekar to open with Mongia, which meant that the team had two makeshift openers. Sidhu's 'retirement' had hit the team really hard. Manjrekar perished to a rising delivery on 11, but Mongia and Ganguly batted attractively, and Tendulkar came in, as it seemed, with the intention of providing a lovely parting gift to his fans in England. Much to their anguish, he mistimed a pull and was caught in the deep for a glorious 74, with his second century in the Test just round the corner. He finished that game with 251 runs, but the media didn't seem to be all that thrilled.

The reason for their ambivalence was his stint as stand-in captain for practically the whole of the England innings, after Azharuddin had left the field on the third day to tend to an injury. When England got off to a good start, it had become increasingly obvious that the game would be drawn, which in turn meant that Azhar could count his last few days as captain with the fingers of one hand. The captain-designate naturally became the cynosure of all eyes, and the tactics he adopted did not please many. To the watcher, it seemed quite out of character for Tendulkar to slow down the game and defend rather than attack. He later argued that India would have been in a spot of bother in their second innings had his bowlers dismissed England earlier than they did. He cited the poor form of his makeshift opening pair, the inexperience of Sourav and Rahul, and the injury to the captain to make his point. It was certainly a 'baptism by fire' for the heir apparent.

India had lost yet another series on foreign soil, but there were plenty of gains. The team seemed to have found its most, potent new-ball combination after Kapil Dev-Karsan Ghavri in the 1970s and Mohammed Nissar-Amar Singh in the 1930s. In fact, there were some striking similarities between the second Indian team to tour England for a Test series in 1936, of which Amar Singh and Nissar were an important part, and the side that toured six decades later. The 1936 tour was tainted by acrimony and intrigue, just like its 1996 counterpart. Lala Amarnath, a prominent member of the team, was 'sacked' from the 1936 tour on disciplinary grounds. Sixty years

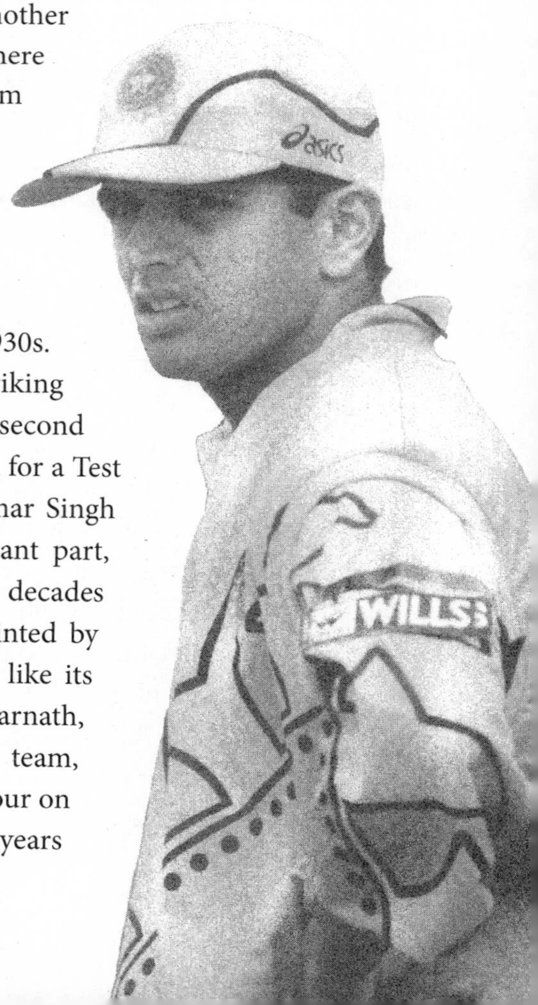

later, there was another premature return to India by a player from the Punjab, only this time it was self-inflicted. Mohammed Azharuddin was a far superior cricketer and a far inferior Machiavellian compared to the Maharajkumar of Vizianagaram who led the 1936 side, but he was probably as distracted. C.K. Nayudu, the premier batsman of the 1936 side, consolidated his reputation with a glorious 81 in the final Test at Manchester, just as Sachin Tendulkar consolidated his with masterly knocks of 122 and 177 at Birmingham and Nottingham respectively. The 1936 tour also saw the advent of two batsmen who did Indian cricket proud in the years to come—Vijay Merchant and Syed Mushtaq Ali.

> 'Had Sourav and Rahul not performed the way they did, god knows where Indian cricket would have been at the end of that tour.'
>
> —Sandeep Patil

Rahul finished the Test series with 187 runs and an average of 62.33 from two Tests, the third-highest tally and average after Ganguly (315 and 105) and Tendulkar (428 and 85.6) respectively. The first-class averages told the same story, with Rahul ranked third with 553 runs from nine games at an impressive average of 50.27.

Rahul's first tour had been an unqualified success. When he returned home, he told a close friend that he did not want to be remembered as just another Test cricketer. He wanted to acquire a stature similar to that of Gavaskar and Viswanath, his idols.

In Sachin Tendulkar, Sourav Ganguly and Rahul Dravid, India had finally gained an effective middle order, the backbone of a quality cricket team, for the first time since the mid-1980s. There was reason to believe that the Indian cricket team would no longer be condescendingly referred to as 'Sachin Tendulkar and ten others'.

3

# WASIM, WAQAR AND WHITE LIGHTNING

> 'Rahul's willingness to learn and expand his horizons has made him a highly successful cricketer.'
>
> —SUNIL GAVASKAR

Sachin Tendulkar scored a hundred in his very first game as India captain, a one-dayer in a quadrangular tournament in Sri Lanka against the home team. But predecessor Azharuddin apart, the other batsmen floundered, and a target of 227 was never going to worry the World Champions. India then beat Zimbabwe and took on Australia in what was effectively the semifinal. For this important clash, Jadeja, who had opened unsuccessfully in the earlier games, was relegated to the middle-order and Mongia moved up to open. Rahul was promoted to number three. The think-tank clearly felt that the Bengaluruan was a better bet to hold the innings together in the event of an early dismissal on wickets, which were not as batsman-friendly as most strips on the subcontinent generally were.

It was on 6 September 1996 that Rahul batted one-down for the first time in an international game. He made only 13 and India could score only 201, a total that Australia overhauled with three wickets in hand.

India's next engagement was at a new venue, the Toronto Cricket, Skating and Curling Club in faraway Canada, where the cricket boards of India and Pakistan had agreed to play an annual five-match series for five years. The first two days of the 1996 edition were washed out by rain. An extension to the tournament was impossible, as both countries had a packed schedule, and this meant that the first three matches had to be played on consecutive days. Tendulkar led from the front in the first game, a curtailed 33-overs-a-side affair, taking India to an eight-wicket win with a superlative 89. Pakistan won the toss the next morning and sent India in. Rahul, who had scored a fine 39 less than 24 hours previously, was in splendid nick.

It was a day on which all those hours facing Javagal Srinath, India's quickest, in the India and Karnataka nets, came in handy. Wasim Akram and Waqar Younis, two of the most dreaded fast bowlers in the world, were quite a handful on a moist track, but Rahul was equal to the challenge. He scored 90, adding 161 with Azharuddin for the third wicket. While the veteran was his usual wristy self, Rahul displayed the richness of his technique and thrilled aficionados with his cultured stroke-play. His innings included only six boundaries, which reflected the alacrity with which he and Azharuddin, one of the swiftest movers of all time, darted for the runs. The Indians finished with 264-6, but much to their discomfiture, their opponents snatched a win off the penultimate delivery.

The third game turned out to be a low-scoring affair in which India scored 191 and bowled out Pakistan for only 136. Prasad took three wickets and Kumble a sensational 4-12, but there never was any doubt in adjudicator Sir Garfield Sobers' mind about the Man of the Match. 'Any bowler can take wickets on a turning track, only a great batsman can get runs on it,' the greatest-ever cricketer proclaimed (rediff.com, 21 September 1996), while announcing Rahul as his choice for the individual award. Rahul had scored only 46, but for the second day running, he had held a quality attack comprising the two 'W's, seamer Azhar Mahmood and spinners Mushtaq Ahmed and Saqlain Mushtaq at bay on a strip that was aiding the bowlers. In 1996, one-day cricket's year of slam-bang batsmanship, Rahul's orthodoxy, even in the shorter form of the game, had been a revelation.

Sandeep Patil believes that the Toronto series marked Rahul's 'graduation' into international cricket. Harsha Bhogle, a member of the TV commentary team, remembered the graduate's 'urge to learn' on that tour: '... Ian Chappell was one of our commentators and he was never too far from an interesting conversation. There was a crowd around him and on the fringe, was young Rahul Dravid, his neck thrust forward like a little child... As the crowd thinned, he grew bold to ask a few questions himself... It was the first time I had seen him do it. It hasn't been the last.' (www.espnstar.com, 9 January 2005)

But the Pakistanis fought back, like they always did against India in the 1990s, and won the last two games to take the series 3-2. There was hardly any time for Tendulkar and his young team to introspect, as the Indian cricket season was upon them. It got off to a bad start with Patil being sacked as coach after only six months in the job. Those who criticized the move hoped that Madan Lal, his successor, would get some more time in the hot seat.

The 1996-97 season was one of the most hectic in Indian cricket history. After a one-off Test against Australia, the Indians were to play the same team and South Africa in a tri-series, to be followed by a three-Test series against the Proteas. Then came another three-Test tussle against the same opponent, this time in South Africa, and a tri-series against them and Zimbabwe. A week after their return to India, the players were to fly to the Caribbean for a five-Test series. Finally, there was a quadrangular tournament to celebrate the Golden Jubilee of India's Independence. Of course, players like Rahul and Sourav who had just begun their careers, were not complaining. The surfeit promised to provide ample opportunities for them to prove that they were indispensable to the team.

The one-off Test against Australia at Delhi was preceded by a whole new debate on the opening position. Sidhu was back in contention, but his 50-day suspension from international cricket for his 'walkout' was to end only after the game. The names being discussed for the opening slots included two middle-order batsmen who had little or no experience of opening. K.N. Prabhu, that doyen of Indian cricket writing, stated that the 'technically accomplished' duo of Sanjay Manjrekar and Rahul Dravid would make an ideal opening pair. It was the first time Rahul's name had been mentioned in connection with the opening slot. There was understandable confusion among his fans, who argued that he was a middle-order batsman and had proved himself as one. The selectors eventually decided to give the Rathore-Mongia combination another chance.

India won the Test, Tendulkar's first as captain, on a wearing wicket, thanks to a nine-wicket haul by Anil Kumble and a dour 152 by Mongia. Rahul batted at number six, a promotion of sorts as he had batted at number seven in his first two Tests. After all, he always preferred to look at the glass as half-full! Tendulkar was a proud first recipient of the Border-Gavaskar Trophy, which would henceforth be presented to the winners of all Test series between Australia and India. The two men who had lent their names to the trophy made the presentation.

Both Australia and India struggled against the meticulous and merciless South Africans in the tri-series that followed. India edged past Australia at the league stage and took on the favourites in the final at Mumbai. A walkover had been predicted, with the media hailing South African coach Bob Woolmer's 'revolutionary' use of a laptop to guide his team to success, as much as they highlighted the batting, bowling and fielding expertise of the Proteas. 'Don't you think you have peaked too early?'—a young Indian journalist had asked the South African think-tank after yet another comprehensive league-stage win and raised its hackles. Tendulkar spoke on the same lines on the eve of the final and declared that the opposition's weakest link was its batting, and it could collapse. What the media thought of his declaration is best illustrated by the fact that it was reported only after the Indian skipper and his team had walked the talk. Chasing a modest 221, the Proteas 'collapsed' for 185. Rahul played his part with a crucial 31 in the middle stages of the innings, as he had done in the final league encounter against Australia with a stroke-filled 56. Interestingly, Rahul began the competition in the number three position, but lost it after three games to none other than Srinath, who was promoted to 'get a move on'. Rahul's last game as 'number three', against South Africa at Jaipur, was a noteworthy one for India, for it was the first in which Tendulkar joined forces at the top of the order with Sourav Ganguly. The pair would go on to become India's most successful opening pair in one-day internationals.

A major gain for India from the tri-series was the Trinidad-born and Chennai-based Robin Singh, who had played two one-day internationals in 1989 before being consigned to domestic cricket. Seven years later, he was back, providing an all-round option the Indians had all but forgotten about, with his aggressive batting, restrictive bowling and brilliant fielding.

India won the first Test against South Africa, a low-scoring thriller at Ahmedabad, with Srinath exploiting a deteriorating wicket to take 6-21 in the second innings. The Test was Rahul's first in the number three position, but it was only a stop-gap arrangement as Ganguly was not playing due to a calf injury. It turned out to be the last Test played by Sanjay Manjrekar, a batsman who was first let down by form and then fate, after a brilliant start to his Test career in the late 1980s. It was also the first Test of a young man whose name was to be inextricably linked with Rahul's in the annals of Indian cricket.

> 'Rahul and I shared some good partnerships for South Zone in the Duleep and Deodhar trophies in 1995-96. He kept telling me that I had the potential to play for India. When I met him in Ahmedabad, he advised me to play my natural game.'
>
> —VVS Laxman

Rahul, the 'senior' player, scored 24 and 34, and the debutant contributed 51 in the second innings, a knock that enabled India to take a winning lead of 170.

The Proteas retaliated strongly and won the second Test at Kolkata by 329 runs, but not before Mohammed Azharuddin had excelled once again at his favourite ground with a belligerent 109. That effort apart, the Test was an ordeal by fire for the Indians. The return of Ganguly meant that Manjrekar, the most dispensable member of the team, had to be dropped. Rahul was 'pushed up', quite literally, to the opening slot. He did not do too badly, as scores of 31 and 23 suggest, but was not at all comfortable with the unfamiliar challenge of opening the innings in Test cricket.

'... Opening the innings is a specialist's job... I am basically a middle-order batsman and that's where I would like to stay.'

—Rahul Dravid, *Sportstar*, 1 February 1997

Rahul was relieved when the selectors recalled Tamil Nadu opener Woorkeri Raman for the final Test at Kanpur. Bob Woolmer's return to his birthplace turned out to be inauspicious for his team, as the visitors capsized on a slow and low pitch. As the Proteas searched for excuses for their 280-run loss, they conveniently forgot that the Indians had made 400-7, that too in the second innings, on the same wicket. Azharuddin, who had returned to his prolific ways, remained unbeaten with 163 and Rahul celebrated his return to the middle-order with 56. There was no time to celebrate, as the Indian players packed their bags to do battle on South African pitches, where retribution awaited them.

'I wouldn't say the team was bustling with confidence. The boys knew that the conditions in South Africa would be diametrically opposite to those in India. They expected quick wickets and hostile fast bowling,' recalls Charu Sharma, who was part of the TV commentary team in South Africa.

The Kanpur Test had ended on 12 December 1996. A mere 12 days later, the Indians took on the same opponents on a

Durban pitch that was to the Kanpur wicket what black was to white. The visitors' woes were compounded by the fact that that they got to play only one warm-up game before the Test series began.

There were scenes of great jubilation all over India when Srinath and Prasad bowled out the hosts for 235 after Tendulkar won the toss and elected to bowl. Giving them support was their state-mate David Johnson, who had made his Test debut in the one-off Test against Australia, and had been rated as quite a prospect.

Those were heady days for the reigning Ranji champions and deservedly so. The touring Indian side comprised six Karnataka players—pacemen Javagal Srinath, Venkatesh Prasad, David Johnson and Dodda Ganesh, middle-order batsman Rahul Dravid and leg-spinner Anil Kumble, who was also the vice-captain. A seventh—Sunil Joshi—would join the team for the tri-series.

The smiles on the faces of Indian supporters vanished when Messrs Shaun Pollock, Brian McMillan, Lance Klusener and 'White Lightning' Allan Donald, who bowled the delivery of his career to clean-bowl Tendulkar, annihilated their team on a lightning-quick wicket. India made only 100. The Proteas batted purposefully in the second essay and set India an unattainable target of 395. Before the visitors realized what had hit them, they were bowled out for a paltry 66, to lose by 328 runs. There was only one consolation—Rahul Dravid, who delayed the inevitable with a resolute, unbeaten 27. The batting practice against 'short-pitched' wet tennis balls on the steps of the pavilion at Bengaluru's Chinnaswamy stadium had paid off.

At the end of the Test, Tendulkar took Rahul aside and

made an offer the Bengaluruan could not refuse.

> 'We wanted somebody to hang in there and see off the first spell, so that the stroke-players could then go out and play their natural game. At that stage, we felt that Rahul was better suited to the number three position.'
>
> —SACHIN TENDULKAR

Rahul, a voracious reader of cricket books and keen student of the game since his formative years, was well informed about the significance of the number three position, which was synonymous in cricket history with names like Sir Donald Bradman, Ian Chappell, and for a substantial part of his career, Sir Vivian Richards.

> 'I do feel that his elevation to number three did wonders to his confidence out there in South Africa.'
>
> —CHARU SHARMA

It therefore was an anti-climax when Rahul had to open with Raman in the first innings of the second Test after Mongia was hit by a bail in the eye while keeping wicket. The South Africans had amassed 529-7 in their first innings, and the early losses of Raman, Rahul and night-watchman Prasad before stumps on day two did not augur well for the tourists. The third morning was no different. The score was 58-5 when Tendulkar and Azharuddin got together to add a breathtaking 222 runs from only 40 overs. But even this wasn't enough, and India came apart in the second innings to lose by 282 runs. Rahul batted one-down in the second innings but did not impress, scoring only 12 before being caught behind off the unorthodox left-arm spinner Paul Adams.

The series was lost, but the Indians went into the third Test at the 'Bull-Ring' in Johannesburg with a positive mindset. It was a relief to see Rathore, who had made more comebacks in a period of six months than most players in an entire career, survive the initial overs along with Mongia. Adams was brought on, and Rathore was caught behind first ball! It was the first time in the series that he had batted long enough to confront a spinner, and he was probably no longer used to facing bowling of the slower type! Rahul came in and got off the mark with a tuck down to fine-leg for two. Cronje brought back Donald, but Rahul played him well on a strip on which the ball was coming onto the bat. The Indians lost their second wicket when Mongia was bowled by 'White Lightning'.

Rahul had looked assured from ball one. His timing was a joy to behold. He drove and pulled superbly, but the best shot of the innings was one that did not fetch him any runs. McMillan bowled a well-disguised slower ball that pitched just outside the line of the off-stump and moved away very late. Rahul, who had committed himself to playing it, loosened his grip on his bat at the moment of impact, and the outside-edge fell well short of second-slip as a result. Not even the dismissal of Tendulkar, who was caught by McMillan off Cronje, could dent Rahul's determination. He was severe on Cronje, off-driving him for four and then essaying a mighty pull to the boundary in the same over. When Donald gave him width outside the off-stump, Rahul rolled his wrists and essayed a stinging square-cut that would have done his idol G.R. Viswanath proud.

That Sunil Gavaskar and Mohinder Amarnath, two of India's best batsmen overseas, were commentating on Rahul's batsmanship on television, enhanced the enormity of the impending moment. It came after six hours of gritty batting. The spectators rose when Rahul completed his maiden Test hundred. He raised his bat and kissed the India crest on his helmet, a gesture that endeared him to the nation.

> 'It was a gutsy effort against a quality attack. A first Test hundred is always special. He completed it with a cut. The Johannesburg pavilion is located at backward point, and I can recall the ball beating Jonty Rhodes at point and coming towards us. He had come very close to scoring a century on earlier occasions, but had missed out. It was a richly deserved hundred and we were delighted.'
>
> —Sachin Tendulkar

Rahul carried on for 148 until he was caught by Pollock off Cronje.

It was heartening to see two youngsters take the fight to the enemy camp with a stand of 145. Ganguly batted beautifully to score 73. At the end of the second day's play, Sunil Gavaskar told Rahul that 'he would give him dark glasses if he were the captain, to keep away the "glare" of success' (*Sportstar,* 1 February 1997).

For the first time in the series, Srinath and Prasad had runs to bowl with, 410 of them. They responded well. Ganguly also took two wickets and the hosts were bowled out for 321 by stumps on the third day. The Indians expectedly went for quick runs on the fourth. Rahul came in after the openers had put on 90 and attacked from the start. Ganguly had his second productive outing of the game and fully justified Rahul's celebrated contention that 'On the off-side, first there was God and then there was Sourav'. The left-hander scored 60, and Rahul sacrificed his wicket for 81 when a selfish approach would have ensured another hundred. India came within two wickets of snatching a win on the last day, only to be thwarted by rain, poor light and Darryl Cullinan, strictly in that order.

The Indians were below par in the tri-series that followed. Rahul struggled in the first two games before being asked to open with Ganguly. He scored 50 and 83 in back-to-back games against South Africa, but neither was a match-winning effort. It wasn't as if the Indians were covering themselves with glory against the Zimbabweans either. A heroic innings by Robin Singh enabled them to tie the first of three matches against the 'minnows', but they lost the second. Zimbabwe batted first in the third and scored 240-8, leaving India with the onerous task of reaching the target in 40.5 overs to qualify for the final. It was a situation that demanded a Sachin special, and the skipper obliged. He returned to the opening slot and smashed 104 off only 97 balls. Rahul contributed 17 to a third-wicket stand that produced 85, and had the best view of the glory. India coasted to victory in 39.2 overs, and into the final.

Rain intervened in the final at Durban when South Africa were 42-1 in the 15th over, chasing a modest 192. The match was replayed the next day, and this time, the Proteas batted first and scored 278-8. The skies opened once again, but not for too long and India's target was revised to 251 from 40 overs. This meant that the Indians had to play their shots from the first ball. Ganguly fell in the third over. Rahul came in next, and essayed an emphatic pull off Pollock in the fifth over to show that he was in fine nick. Donald, introduced in the sixth over, nearly bowled Tendulkar with his first ball, an inswinger that sailed over the stumps. The Indian captain's response was a 'stroke' of genius. The bowler was left gaping as Tendulkar shuffled across to the off-side to tickle his next delivery, a short one, past short fine-leg for four. Rahul cover-drove Pollock's first ball of the next over for four, and then flicked a full-toss to the mid-wicket boundary. The over yielded 14 runs in all, and at 61-1 from seven, India were firmly on course.

Rahul completes his maiden Test hundred at Johannesburg, 1996-97

The score was 75-1 when Donald ran in to bowl the fourth ball of the tenth over. South Africa's ploy to bowl short to the Indians had backfired, and the bowler decided to bowl a slower one to try and befuddle the batsman. But Rahul picked it early, went onto the front foot, brought his bat down in a flash and deposited the ball over long-on. It was an incredible six, one that left Donald seething.

The next ball was shorter and quicker, and it rocketed over Rahul's head. It was followed by another rocket, this time a verbal one. Donald was clearly flustered. He had clearly not expected a young man in his first year of international cricket to be so disrespectful of his fast-bowling prowess. The paceman's fans, who sought to justify his verbal assault after that short ball by arguing that it was nothing but a fast bowler's typical rejoinder to a counterattack, were also left speechless by what he did after bowling the next delivery, another short delivery that pegged Rahul onto the back foot. A livid Donald strode towards the batsman and let the curses fly. It was disgraceful and inexcusable behaviour by a senior cricketer. Rahul responded with a deadpan look. He was clearly in no mood to take a backward step. Tendulkar had a word with Cyril Mitchley, the umpire, and exhorted Rahul to keep going. An entire nation was dismayed when Barry Jarman, the ICC Referee, allowed Donald to get away with murder.

Cronje then bagged the prized scalp of his counterpart, who glanced a slower ball to Rudi Bryson at short fine-leg. Tendulkar needn't have worried, for Rahul was on a roll. Amarnath noted during his commentary stint that Rahul was not committing himself to the front foot like he had in the earlier matches and had reverted to the 'back and across' technique, which was giving him more time to play the ball. Rahul nonchalantly flicked Donald to the mid-wicket boundary off the very first ball of the next over, and this time, the bowler had nothing to say. He reached his fifty off only 44 balls in the 19th over. India needed only 108 from the final 20 overs.

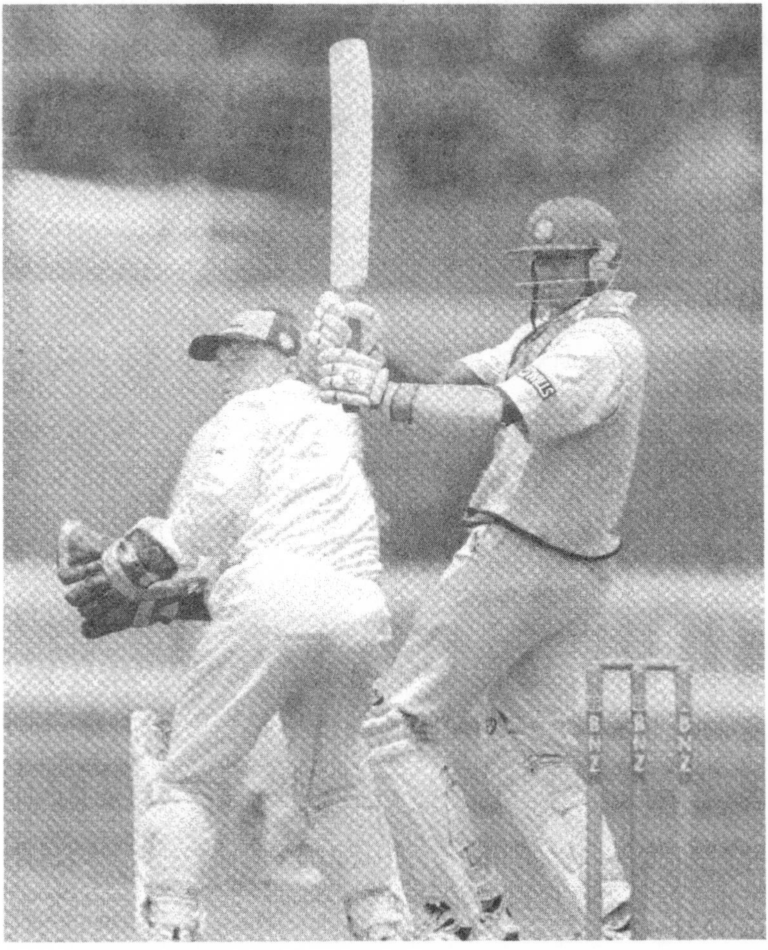

Jonty Rhodes gave his team a breakthrough in the 25th over when he dived to his left to catch Azharuddin off Pollock. Nevertheless, India needed only 86 more from 90 balls at the end of that over with seven wickets in hand, but that wicket had an inspirational effect on the Proteas. They came in hard at the batsmen and bottled up the runs. Jadeja fell cheaply, and Rahul was on 84 when he hit Klusener into Kirsten's waiting hands at deep mid-wicket. The score at that stage was 210-5. His dismissal opened the floodgates and the Indians wilted to 234 all out. There were two factors that made Rahul's innings poignant. His innings would have won India the match and series had he received more support. Then, there was the news of his father's ill-health. To have batted so well despite the obvious mental strain, was simply outstanding.

There were no dissenting voices when Rahul was named Man of the Match. The presentation marked the end of the most successful tour of his short career. There was nothing more the selectors and his supporters could have asked for.

'More than what he said, it was what he did not say that made him special,' states Charu Sharma, who interacted with Rahul on and off camera on numerous occasions during the tour. 'There was, and still is a calm self-assurance about him. He was a real "sweater" in the nets and took the game very seriously. He attended the odd party, but it was always a case of "Let's get this over with. I have got to get back and sleep, as I have work to do tomorrow." He was a complete professional.'

# 4

# BRANDED

> 'I never had to tell him anything. He always seemed to be in control of what he wanted to do.'
>
> —Anshuman Gaekwad, coach, Indian cricket team, 1997-99, 2000

The West Indies of 1996-97 were not the force they had once been, and Tendulkar fancied his battle-hardened team's chances against them. He knew that his new-ball bowlers held the key.

> 'If any one of them (Srinath or Prasad) breaks down in the Caribbean, it's going to be very tough.'
>
> —Sachin Tendulkar, *Sportstar*, 1 March 1997

These words, uttered days before the tour began, were prophetic, as Srinath was diagnosed with a rotator-cuff injury to his bowling shoulder and rendered unfit for six months.

The selectors attempted to resolve the 'opening' dilemma by recalling Navjot Sidhu, and 'creating' an opener out of VVS Laxman, who had returned home early from South Africa after breaking a finger in the Johannesburg Test.

The Test series was a tedious affair with one notable exception. Intermittent rain and slow scoring marred the first encounter at Kingston. The West Indies set India a target of 323 on the last day, but play was reduced to 58 overs and Rahul made the most of some friendly bowling to complete an unbeaten fifty. The second Test followed more or less the same pattern. West Indies showed little enterprise, and the Indians were no different, although Sidhu batted doggedly to score his first double hundred in Test cricket. Rahul retained his consistency with a knock of 57.

The teams then moved to Bridgetown, historically a happy hunting ground for the hosts. A hamstring injury to Courtney Walsh had given Brian Lara the chance to lead the West Indies for the first time, and there was tremendous excitement at the prospect of the two premier batsmen of the 1990s pitting not only their talent, but also their brains against each other. Tendulkar made a good start by winning the toss. He opted to bowl, the idea obviously being to let Prasad and the three-Test old Abey Kuruvilla have first use of a spiteful strip. The flip side was that his team would have to bat last on a wicket that was expected to deteriorate.

A superb bowling display by Prasad (5-87) helped restrict the West Indies to 298. The Indians lost their openers cheaply, but Tendulkar and Rahul batted well to add 170 for the third wicket. Rahul looked every inch the 'Rock' that Charu Sharma had christened him, but it seemed that he had taken the appellation a little too seriously. He took 243 balls to score 78, and while no one expected him to score at a run-a-ball in a Test, the general view was that he ought to have got at least fifty more. Admittedly, the West Indies bowled well with Franklyn

Rose (4-77) being the best of the lot. Tendulkar was unlucky to be given out caught in the gully off a no-ball for 92. The Indians took a slender lead of 21, which could have been greater had the batsmen who followed Tendulkar and Rahul shown a little more enterprise. Kuruvilla bowled his heart out in the second innings to dismiss five batsmen on a wicket that had turned spiteful. India needed only 120 to win with one full day to spare.

Streetlights in India were being switched on at around the time the teams arrived at Bridgetown's Kensington Oval for the fifth day's play. All over India, cricket-lovers were bracing themselves for the moment when they would run out of their homes and light crackers to celebrate India's first Test win outside the subcontinent since 1986. Thousands of miles away, the Indian batsmen were preparing to leave the dressing room, not to achieve a victory, but to look for devils—those that they were convinced, existed in the wicket.

> 'The pitch wasn't the best, and there was no way you could have survived by just defending. Some strategizing could have helped. Two or three batsmen should have been told to attack and the others instructed to be watchful. But there was no planning, and everyone just seemed to wait for the inevitable, unplayable ball.'
>
> —Charu Sharma

The final Indian wicket went down for 81 and the West Indians celebrated like there was no tomorrow. The 'captaincy round' of the Lara-Tendulkar duel had ended in a comprehensive win for the Trinidadian, whose handling of the bowlers on the final day was praised.

The last two Tests were ruined by rain, which meant that

West Indies took the series by virtue of their win at Bridgetown. As he had in South Africa, Rahul topped the batting table for India with 360 runs from five games at an average of 72. His only disappointment was not being able to convert at least two of his four fifties—the 78 at Bridgetown and the 92 in the final Test at Antigua—into hundreds. The media christened him 'Rahul "Well left" Dravid'. While the tag established Rahul's excellent 'judgement', it also implied that there was room for improvement.

> 'Dravid admits that he needs to play more shots and that should help him take a step closer to developing into a complete batsman.'
>
> —Vijay Lokapally, *Sportstar*, 31 May 1997

All those who believed that India couldn't get any worse at snatching defeat from the jaws of victory were at a loss for words after the third one-day international at St. Vincent. At that point, the series was level. The West Indies batted first and scored 249-9. Tendulkar fell early, but Ganguly and Rahul batted splendidly, adding 130 before Rahul was bowled by Otis Gibson for a fine 74. Sourav carried on in the company of Jadeja, and the Indians looked on course to go 2-1 up in the series. The score was 185 when Ganguly was caught by Curtly Ambrose off Rose for 76. Robin Singh and wicketkeeper-batsman Saba Karim, competent batsmen both, occupied the next two slots in the batting line-up. But the unthinkable happened.

The shots that the Indians played would have given the 'Kamikaze' pilots of the Second World War an inferiority complex. But while the Japanese pilots did what they did for a cause, the Indians looked listless and clueless. There were three run-outs and the innings ended at 231. Not one player had the courage to converse with an incensed Tendulkar at the dinner table that evening. The West Indies won the fourth and final game with ease to win the one-day series, and India ended yet another tour with tales of 'what might have been'.

The Independence Cup began back home in India precisely six days after the fourth one-dayer in the Caribbean. It was caustically suggested by some that the men behind the tournament ought to be made to stand in the middle of a cricket ground in a three-piece suit as a punishment for subjecting the cricketers to the heat and humidity of muggy May, after more than six months of relentless cricket. The decision to play all the matches under floodlights to 'avoid the heat' didn't make much of a difference.

It was the first time since 1984-85 that Mohammed Azharuddin had been left out of an Indian squad for a full series. The selectors felt that they had had enough of his 'carefree' hitting that in the Caribbean had bordered on the 'careless'. It turned out to be only a temporary 'break' and he was back when the new season began.

The Indians won their first game of the Independence Cup against New Zealand with Tendulkar scoring a hundred, and lost the second to the champion Sri Lankan side. Ganguly fell first ball, and the innings was in dire straits at 29-3 when Rahul and Jadeja launched a recovery. They added 95 before Rahul was bowled by Muralitharan for 61. The Indians scored 225-7, and Sri Lankan commentator Ranjit Fernando declared that his team would finish the match in 40 overs. Sanath Jayasuriya, a man who 'loved' the Indian bowling, bludgeoned an unbeaten 151 and let Fernando down by a mere five balls.

India's third and final league game was a 'semi-final', as both India and Pakistan had beaten New Zealand and lost to Sri Lanka. Pakistan won the toss and batted first on a Chennai belter, and for the second consecutive time, a left-handed opener enjoyed himself against the Indian bowling. Saeed Anwar did not stop at a hundred, and got within striking distance of the first double hundred in one-day internationals before falling for 194, the highest-ever individual score in the shorter version. His teammates batted around him, and for most of the innings, Shahid Afridi ran for him. With 328 to win, India were up against it.

The early dismissal of Tendulkar to a magnificent catch by Inzamam was a setback, but like he had at Durban, Rahul picked up the baton. He lost Ganguly when the Kolkatan was caught by Saqlain off Aaqib Javed for a rapid-fire 33. Comeback-man Vinod Kambli then gave Rahul spirited support. They braved the bowlers and the humidity to add 134 before Kambli fell for 65. Jadeja fell almost immediately, but the tiring and cramping Rahul found another ally in Robin Singh. Such was the quality of Rahul's strokes in front and square of the wicket that even his tough-as-nails opponents, who had earlier objected to his captain running for him, were impressed. When Rahul cramped and sprawled on the ground, Moin Khan, the Pakistani wicketkeeper, was the first to rush to his aid. By the time he completed his first limited-overs hundred, Rahul looked gutted. But his team needed him to carry on. However, that wasn't to be as he was caught by Afridi off Aaqib, who along with Saqlain had been held back for the slog overs. Rahul left for 107 and the Pakistanis won by 35 runs.

Thus ended Rahul's first year in international cricket, a

successful one. 'He has the right technique and temperament to become one of India's finest batsmen ever,' Clive Lloyd, the then manager of the West Indies team had remarked at the end of the Caribbean series.

The twenty-five-year-old had established himself in the national team, as Indian cricket's blue-eyed boy and India's latest pin-up boy. Cricket connoisseurs were captivated by his technical and mental skills and the fairer gender by his looks. Life couldn't have been rosier. However, quite a few thorns lay ahead.

Rahul and Sourav were expected to tide over the 'second-season blues', the bane of many a distinguished cricketer. Sourav did, with some big scores in Test cricket and a magnificent all-round performance in the annual Toronto series against Pakistan later in the year, but Rahul didn't. He had 'problems' in the shorter version of the game, in which he had done so well in his first year. Ironically, most of these 'problems' were imposed on him.

Century in the Chennai cauldron... Rahul completes his first limited-covers hundred against Pakistan in the Independence Cup 1996-97

He acquitted himself creditably in the one-dayers on India's tour of Sri Lanka in mid-1997, with scores of 69, 78 and

42 from six of the eight one-day internationals (he did not get to bat in two). In the Asia Cup that preceded the bilateral tussle against the Lankans, India beat Bangladesh, but the game against Pakistan was rained off.

Azharuddin was India's best batsman in the one-dayers with a century and three fifties, and all the other batsmen had at least one good performance to their credit, which placed them in the same boat as Rahul. But for some strange reason, some people had started questioning Rahul's presence in the one-day side, that too only two months after his innings at Chennai.

Two twenties in the second edition of the annual Toronto tournament further jeopardized Rahul's case. It did not matter that the series was a low-scoring one, played on lively pitches that assisted the bowlers. India won 4-1 largely due to Sourav Ganguly, who won the Man of the Series award (after winning four Man of the Match awards) for his 222 runs and 15 wickets. Even more special was the title bestowed on him by Geoffrey Boycott: The Prince of Kolkata. The elated Indian cricketers then went to Pakistan for a three-match one-day series, where they played the first game on a slow wicket at Hyderabad (Sind). The Indian batsmen struggled, with one exception. Rahul came in at 61-3 and controlled the innings brilliantly. It wasn't electrifying batting, but it was effective. He held one end up as Azharuddin and Jadeja played their 'natural game' at the other. Rahul was eighth out at 169 for a round half-ton, and the innings ended one run later. The Pakistanis did not have it easy, and the Indians made them sweat until the target was achieved in the 45th over. Once again, Rahul had delivered in a demanding situation.

Nobody has explained why Rahul played his next one-day international three months after this fine innings, and why he was left out of the one-day team subsequently.

Sunil Gavaskar reckoned that the move to drop Rahul from the one-dayers could well have been a part of an experiment. 'The one-day game is not an easy game. It is never easy to be able to be appreciated by everybody. This is why one-day teams are experimented with more than Test teams.'

Ironically, the very qualities that had contributed to Rahul's success were now being considered his weaknesses. His detractors actually blamed his rock-solid technique and ability to think about his game. *'Bahut sochta hain'* (He thinks too much), they complained, as if it were a crime.

> 'The selectors have always had their whims and fancies. But Rahul had by and large played well in the one-dayers and ought to have been persisted with.'
>
> —Robin Singh

Rahul's supporters were convinced that there was a 'conspiracy' to oust him from the squad. They claimed that his popularity and commercial endorsements had made others jealous. There were also claims that Rahul, along with some of his state-mates, had become a victim of vendetta. C. Nagaraj, the secretary of the KSCA, had apparently voted against the group that came to power in the September 1997 elections of the BCCI. Karnataka players were being made to pay for his 'impertinence'.

Even as the insinuations and allegations piled on, Rahul became increasingly concerned about his future in international cricket.

'It was in mid-1997 that I met him first,' recalled Sports Psychologist B.P. Bam, with whom Rahul has enjoyed a fruitful association since. Mr Bam passed away in May 2017. 'He voiced his fears about being dropped from the one-day side and later being edged out of the Test side as well. I told him, 'This is the last time you have uttered these words. Never talk with your tongue on this issue. Let your bat do the talking for you.' I encouraged him to focus on his strengths, his skills. I told him that a day would come when he would carry the team on his shoulders.'

Maybe Rahul was being overtly pessimistic as far as his place in the Test side was concerned, but he also had problems in the longer variety as well, albeit of a different kind. He scored one fifty in the two-Test series in Sri Lanka, which was obscured by hundreds from his teammates and a plethora of batting records by the Lankans. When the islanders toured India for a Test series at the end of the year, Rahul's sequence of scores read 34, 92, 93 and 85. He had missed three centuries for the taking.

B.P. Bam told this writer that it was perfectly normal for a batsman to think about a landmark when he nears it. 'But having done so, he should return to the immediate objective, which is to face the next delivery. The batsman should think about his hand movement, backlift, etc, anything that will help him focus on the next ball, and try and make these thoughts stronger than any other thought. The secret to breaking the jinx of getting out in the eighties and nineties is to continue playing each ball on merit. A bad ball has to be punished, irrespective of whether your score is zero or 99. A century should be treated as just an intermediate goal on the way to building up a huge total.'

Rahul, a quick learner, did not take long to absorb this. The big scores were around the corner.

He was included in the eleven for India's third and final league game of the quadrangular Champions Trophy at Sharjah in December 1997. The Indians, who had lost their first two games to England and Pakistan respectively, were shockingly undone on a turning track by three spinners from the Land of Pace. Carl Hooper, Shivnarine Chanderpaul and Rawl Lewis took eight wickets between them as India were bowled out for 188 to lose by 41 runs. Rahul was criticized for taking 45 balls to score 31, as was Azharuddin for running himself out in a manner that bordered on the irresponsible. The outcome—Rahul lost his place in the one-day squad and Azharuddin was reinstated as captain of India! It was a time in Indian cricket when the selectors were at their illogical best, and Rahul wasn't the only sufferer. They had justified the sacking of Tendulkar on the grounds that the captaincy was affecting his batting, conveniently overlooking the fact that he had accumulated four-figure aggregates in both forms of the game in the calendar year of 1997!

On the eve of the Challenger Trophy in 1997-98, Rahul accosted Sandeep Patil, coach of the India 'A' side of which he was a part, and asked him what he was doing wrong. 'That was the only time I saw him short of confidence,' Patil remembered. 'I told him that I would definitely let him know *if I felt he was doing something wrong*.' (author's italics)

The point was, there was precious little that Rahul was doing wrong. It was just that the pressure that had been 'imposed' on him was getting to him. The only solution, as B.P. Bam had advised him, was to 'let his bat do the talking'. Rahul's bat got an opportunity to 'talk' in the Tests against Australia in early 1998.

Rahul drives Shane Warne in the 1997-98 series. He scored three fifties in the three-test Series, but was still left out of the one-day squad

Tendulkar won his much-awaited bout with Shane Warne with a knockout. He seized the advantage with a double hundred in a three-day game prior to the first Test, and then scored a scintillating 155 in the first Test at Chennai, repeatedly hitting Warne into the gaps and over the top. His teammates, Rahul included, meted out the same treatment to the leg-spinner.

> 'We had decided to unsettle Warne by attacking him from the start and get him thinking. We were confident of handling the rest of the attack, which was rather weak.'
>
> —Navjot Sidhu

Rahul scored 52 and 56 at Chennai, and held three catches in the second innings in which India's resurrected spin trio of Kumble, Raju and Chauhan snared nine wickets to bowl their team to a 179-run victory. He missed out on another hundred in the second Test at Kolkata when he was dismissed for 86. In fact, three other Indian batsmen—Sidhu (97), Laxman (95) and Tendulkar (79)—narrowly missed a hundred in the game. The only centurion was Azharuddin, who scored his fifth Test hundred at the Eden.

Rahul had proved his versatility as a batsman with these performances. He had shown that he was as comfortable against quality spin on a turning track as he was against genuine pace on a green top. But the selectors chose to ignore him for the one-day series against Australia and a tournament at Sharjah that Tendulkar single-handedly won for India. Rahul utilized the 'break' most productively to lead Karnataka to victory in the Ranji Trophy. He scored 71 in a nail-biting semifinal against Hyderabad that Karnataka won by one wicket, and then 215 in the final against Uttar Pradesh. 'He was absolutely brilliant.

That innings silenced many who had dubbed him a 'slow' player,' Sunil Joshi recalled, several years later.

Rahul was recalled to the one-day side for a tri-series against Kenya and Bangladesh in May 1998, in which several 'fringe' players were being tried out. Anshuman Gaekwad, who had taken over as coach of the Indian team earlier that season, pleaded with the selectors to give Rahul at least three matches. They agreed, and Rahul produced scores of 5 and 49 in the first two. India's third match was played at Mumbai on 25 May 1998. No miracles were expected from the Bangladeshis, and they did not disappoint by being bowled out for 115. Tendulkar, who had been included for this game, much to the delight of his home crowd, got India off to a flying start. He was out when his team was only 42 short, with 40 overs still to be bowled.

Rahul came in next. He had been told by his coach to take it easy. The target wasn't a stiff one and there were plenty of overs left. It was an excellent opportunity to recover lost ground in one-day cricket. Or so he thought. He kept stroking the ball fluently, but the ball kept going to the fielders. As dot ball followed dot ball, the spectators turned restless. The Mumbai maestro had whetted their appetite with his clean hitting, and they couldn't quite understand the tactics of the new batsman. Their restlessness soon gave way to frustration, and then derision. Rahul could not believe his ears as the capacity crowd started abusing and willing him to get out. For probably the only time in his international career, he allowed the pressure to get to him, and was bowled by left-arm spinner Mohammed Rafique for one off 21 balls. It was almost as if the match was being played in Dhaka and not Mumbai, as the spectators roared like there was no tomorrow.

> 'I got a tremendous amount of grief from the selectors after that. They had this "we-told-you-so" expression on their faces.'
>
> —Anshuman Gaekwad

Exactly one year and four days since he had scored that 107 at Chennai, Rahul's reputation as a 'misfit' in limited-overs cricket had been sealed.

5

# BACK TO THE FOREFRONT

> 'Rahul has always found time to work on his mistakes, even in these days of non-stop international cricket. He is quick to spot mistakes and quicker in rectifying them. This has enabled him to get out of a bad patch quicker than others.'
>
> —G.R. Viswanath

Although the indifference of the selectors was unnerving, Rahul did not crumble. Rejection, he loathed, but he took it as a challenge.

> 'Not being in the side was obviously not a very comfortable situation to be in. I had the confidence, however, that I would return.'
>
> —Rahul Dravid, *The Outlook*, 18 January 1999

The 1998-99 season began with a coaching camp at Chennai for the thirty probables who were to be divided into two teams, one of which was to fly to Toronto for the third edition of the annual tournament against Pakistan, and the other to Kuala

Lumpur for the Commonwealth Games, where cricket had been included for the first time. A special feature of the camp was the presence of Bob Simpson, former Australian captain and coach, who had been signed on as a 'Consultant' to help the team prepare for the 1999 World Cup.

The Indian limited-overs side had won everything in sight in the first eight months of 1998, save a tri-series against Australia and Zimbabwe at home. A victory at Toronto would have been the proverbial icing on the cake. But it was not to be. The Indian Olympic Association demanded that the 'best' Indian team be sent for the Commonwealth Games. A jealous fraternity that has always treated cricket like a punching bag and regrettably not as a yardstick, accused the BCCI and the cricketers of lacking national pride and being 'obsessed with money'. The rabble-rousers kept quiet the moment it was announced that Sachin Tendulkar would go to Kuala Lumpur. Amidst all the talk of national pride, the fact that Pakistan, then very much a part of the Commonwealth, had decided to send a second-string squad to Kuala Lumpur and its 'best' team to Toronto, and England, the 'mother of the Commonwealth', had decided not to send a team at all to Malaysia, was overlooked.

Navjot Sidhu believes that no Indian player tried as hard to implement Simpson's tips as Rahul. Batting tips apart, Simpson imparted some secrets of the art of slip fielding, of which he was a master, to an enthusiastic pupil. Both did not know it then, but a day would come when the pupil would be considered the best 'slipper' in the world.

It was during the camp that Anshuman Gaekwad, who was to accompany the Toronto team, asked Rahul to 'be ready' for the series.

> 'He thought I was joking. But I was serious. I wanted him in the team. I argued with the selectors that it was far easier for a technically proficient batsman whose basics were right, to adapt himself to one-day cricket, and innovate and improvise… They finally agreed, probably because two teams were being picked.'
>
> —Anshuman Gaekwad

Rahul did not set the Toronto Cricket, Skating and Curling Club on fire, but neither did his teammates. In fact, he had a horrendous run with scores of four, 18, nine and one, and was dropped from the final game. He had a bit of ill luck as well. Mohammed Zahid bowled him in the third match with a superb yorker, and Shahid Afridi ran him out in the fourth with a brilliant throw from the deep. His failure demoralized even his die-hard fans.

> 'Fate presented him with one more chance, and Dravid abdicated. Two dismissals that owed to good cricket by the opposition, and two others that owed more to his own inner tensions, and there is an air now of finality about Dravid's one-day career.'
>
> — Ashish Shukla, rediff.com, 22 September 1998

But he had no time to ponder over the future as the team flew to Zimbabwe for a short tour. Rahul was included in the eleven for the first ODI, and he showed a welcome return to form with an innings of 64. In the same game, Tendulkar became the highest century-maker in one-day internationals by surpassing Desmond Haynes' tally of 17.

India won the one-day series 2-1, but played poorly in the

one-off Test to lose by 61 runs. Their failure to achieve a target of 235 on the last day underscored the fact that talent and flair can more often than not be upstaged by determination and application, both of which the hosts displayed in plenty. Unlike his teammates, Rahul applied himself well to score 118, his second Test hundred, in the first innings. He also top-scored in the second with 44.

These performances ensured his presence in the squad for the next two limited-overs tournaments—the first ICC 'Knockout' championship (renamed the Champions Trophy in 2002) in Dhaka, and a tri-series in Sharjah. Rahul figured in both games that India played in the Knockout, but was relegated to the reserve-benches in Sharjah for all the matches but one. It was a frustrating time, but he opted for the practical approach of accepting that there were others who had proved themselves in one-day cricket with consistent performances, and hence had the right to be picked ahead of him. He did not waste his time reflecting on the reality that those players had been given a much longer rope by the selectors.

The next assignment was a tour of New Zealand, where the conditions and wickets were not unlike those in England. With the Tests preceding the one-dayers, Rahul saw a potential springboard to bag a place in the one-day side. The first Test at Dunedin was abandoned without a ball being bowled, and the teams moved to Wellington, venue of the Boxing Day Test. There, India failed to deliver the knockout punch for the umpteenth time in their cricket history. New Zealand needed 213 to win a low-scoring game, and Srinath and Kumble reduced the hosts to 74-5 in the second innings. All they needed to do was break the McMillan-Cairns association and then attack the tail-enders, but they couldn't, and lost by four wickets. Brilliant hundreds by Azharuddin in the first and Tendulkar in the second innings went in vain.

The Indian team to Zimbabwe, 1998-99. Rahul, who scored his second Test hundred on the tour, is standing fourth from left.

New Zealand asked to bat first on a green Hamilton strip in the third Test, batted well to score 366. India were in trouble at 17-2 with the openers Jadeja and Sidhu (whose last Test it was), back in the pavilion. Rahul and Tendulkar, the two Indian batsmen best equipped to handle the conditions, added 109 before the gods smiled on seamer Dion Nash, who won a leg-before decision against Tendulkar that could well have gone the other way. Wickets then fell at regular intervals, but Rahul was steadfast.

'He succeeded overseas because he played the ball late.'

—Sunil Gavaskar

On a wicket where the ball was doing a fair bit and the bowlers were rampant, Rahul was assured and unruffled. When

Srinath walked in, the score a perilous 211-7, Rahul requested him to just stay in the middle while he would do the rest. The crowd rose to him as he scored a hundred, his third overall and second in consecutive Tests. He batted for 490 minutes until he was out for 190.

> 'He has a lovely style of batting. He has silken strokes and to me looks like a traditional player. I would go any length to watch him.'
>
> —MARTIN CROWE, *SPORTSTAR*, 23 JANUARY 1999

As the accolades poured in, Rahul reiterated his belief in 'playing each ball on merit'. What he did not say was that he had started looking at a century as just an intermediate goal'.

> 'Sports Psychology is useless unless the subject believes that it can help him. Rahul has always been a very serious and committed individual, and he had the courage to implement all that we discussed at the highest level of the sport, that too against quality opposition. The real challenge in cricket is to 'live' every ball. Every ball is a unique event in itself. No two consecutive deliveries are alike. A professional approach is one wherein the batsman concentrates on every ball and handles it on merit. He needs to start from scratch for every ball being bowled to him.'
>
> —B.P. BAM

This is a view that Sandeep Patil seconds: 'Those who treat every ball as a separate event are bound to succeed.'

In the second innings, with the match drifting towards a draw because of some poor Indian bowling in the second innings and a delayed declaration by the Kiwi skipper Stephen Fleming, Rahul and Sourav enjoyed themselves against some pedestrian bowling to score hundreds. Rahul's 103 made him only the third Indian batsman after Vijay Hazare and Sunil Gavaskar to score two centuries in a Test.

Rahul also completed 2,000 runs in Test cricket in the same game, which was his 25th Test. He had taken just 11 Tests to proceed from 1,000 to 2,000. His average of 57.45 was the highest among Indian batsmen who had played 20 or more Tests. His 'away' average of 65.90 from 15 Tests was also the highest among Indians.

> 'I relish the special challenge of coming good in alien conditions. It's also just the beginning. It's just these three years that have been good. I hope I can keep this record going.'
>
> —Rahul Dravid, *The Outlook*, 18 January 1999

Rahul could not be denied a place in the one-day side, and he went in at number three in the first game of the five-match one-day series, played at Taupo. He arrived at the wicket with only three runs on the board, Tendulkar having departed without troubling the scorers. The 'Class of 96' then added 116 before Ganguly fell for 60. It was the 26th over of the innings, and the Indians had been given a perfect platform from which to get a big score. But the latter batsmen floundered and Rahul was left to play a lone hand. He batted right through, striking the ball magnificently and running brilliantly to finish with an unbeaten 123, his second hundred in one-day internationals. But the lack of support meant that the Indians scored only 257-5, at least thirty runs less than what they should have got after that start. The Kiwis coasted to an easy win after their target was revised due to a floodlight failure. For the second time in his career, Rahul won the Man of the Match award in a one-day international despite being on the losing side.

His 38 in the next game helped India level the series with an exciting two-wicket win. He scored 68 in the rain-affected third game and a match-winning 51 in the fourth. These performances provided conclusive proof of his proficiency in the one-day game. In fact, he was a lot more attractive to watch than the boom-boom 'one-day specialists', with his penchant for playing aggressive, but orthodox strokes even in the 'instant' version of the game. Most significantly, he showed that he was capable of rotating the strike'.

During their search for chinks in Rahul's armour in 1997, his 'inability to rotate the strike' was an alleged weakness the selectors had latched onto. But Rahul retained the constructive approach even while working on this 'chink' in his armour.

> 'I explained to him that it was relatively easier to set a field to him since he was a classical, technically correct batsman. This was in the days when he was being accused of being unable to find the gaps in one-dayers. Middling every ball was his strong point, but trying to score only through strokes would get even a class batsman like him nowhere. Rahul then adopted a policy of modifying his strokes and placing the ball into the gaps instead.'
>
> —B.P. Bam

At the end of the series, an ecstatic Gaekwad confronted the selectors, who had so vociferously opposed Rahul's selection in the one-day squad. 'All they said to me was that Rahul had changed,' he recalls.

The only change was in the area between the ears.

> 'By early 1999, he had developed a very strong self-image. He no longer apprehended being dropped from the team. He had gained considerably in self-confidence and that showed in his performance.'
>
> —B.P. Bam

A man as delighted as Rahul himself was Sachin Tendulkar.

> 'Let us accept that there was a time when he struggled to rotate the strike in one-day internationals. His strike-rate was not upto the mark. Every player goes through such a phase, but the better ones come back hard, and Rahul did just that.'
>
> —Sachin Tendulkar

> 'I don't think he was bothered too much about what was being said about him when he was out of the one-day side. He did not make any major changes in his game. He worked on a few shots, worked on picking more ones and twos, and that was it. He carried his form from the Tests into the one-dayers in New Zealand in 1998-99.'
>
> —Robin Singh

> 'What did India gain from the tour of New Zealand? They lost the Test series, and drew the one-day series 2-2. But they did not return empty-handed. They unearthed a lost treasure. Rahul Dravid was always part of the team, but his talents were not being recognized. Not any more.'
>
> —*Cricket Today* (Hindi), February 1999

The Indian team had barely a week to recharge the batteries and regroup at the cauldron that was the M.A. Chidambaram stadium in Chennai, for the first Test of a historic series against Pakistan. It was the first time the two nations were meeting each other in Test cricket since 1989-90, and a lot was at stake. The series was supposed to begin in the capital, but the venues were switched after miscreants vandalized the pitch at Delhi's Ferozeshah Kotla.

Although the itinerary stated that the teams were to play a two-Test series, to be followed by another Test at Kolkata that would be a part of the inaugural Asian Test Championship, cricket-lovers in both countries were viewing it as a three-Test tussle. The tussle ended with Pakistan winning two Tests, both from losing positions, to India's one.

The outcome could well have been 3-0 in India's favour had Rahul not succumbed to two of the deadliest deliveries ever bowled in Test cricket. The first was in the second innings at Chennai. India, needing 271 to win, lost the openers with only six runs on the board, and Tendulkar joined Rahul, who had scored 53 in the first innings. The duo batted till the close on the third day. They had added ten on the fourth morning when Wasim 'Wizard' Akram propelled one at Rahul that pitched outside leg, and as the batsman watched in horror, darted across him to clip the off-stump. It was a delivery not too dissimilar, in impact and effect, to the two consecutive jaffas' delivered by the same bowler to devour Allan Lamb and Chris Lewis in the 1992 World Cup final. India, at one stage 17 short of victory with four wickets in hand, ended up losing by 12 runs. A disconsolate Tendulkar, who had battled incredible pressure and debilitating back spasms to score an epic 136, could not bring himself to collect the Man of the Match award.

India drew level at Delhi, where Anil Kumble produced the greatest individual performance in the history of Test cricket. His and Jim Laker's feat of bagging a 'ten-for' in an innings will remain the most outstanding until the rules are amended to allow a bowler to take eleven wickets in a Test innings! Rahul contributed to the feat by taking a simple catch at gully to dismiss Mushtaq Ahmed, Kumble's eighth victim of the innings.

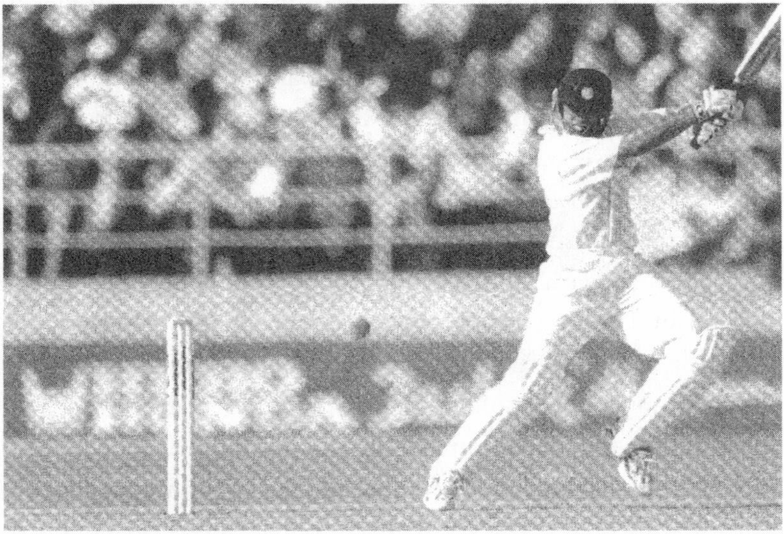

The action then shifted to Kolkata, venue of the first game of the Asian Championship. The Indian bowlers made a dream start, reducing Pakistan to 26-6 in the opening session. Moin Khan, a fighter to the core, scored 70 and took his team to 185. The Indians lost makeshift opener VVS Laxman early, but the Tamil Nadu opener Sadagoppan Ramesh, who had begun his Test career at Chennai two Tests ago, batted well along with night-watchman Anil Kumble. Rahul came in at 91-2. He had added 56 with Ramesh when Shoaib Akhtar, who had replaced Waqar Younis for this game, bowled him a lethal yorker that spreadeagled the stumps. In came Tendulkar to a tumultuous reception, only to meet with the same fate. The Indians were suddenly 147-4, and they collapsed to 223 all out.

What was galling for Rahul was that he had anticipated Akram's gem at Chennai as well as Shoaib's missile at Kolkata, keeping in mind the way both bowlers had operated until that stage, and yet had failed to do a thing. The fact that both deliveries penetrated his seemingly impregnable defence speaks volumes for Akram's wizardry in the first instance and Shoaib's raw pace in the second.

Pakistan's second innings was dominated by Saeed Anwar, who carried his bat for 188, and Javagal Srinath, who took eight wickets to make it 13 in the match. Ramesh and Laxman got their team off to a good start, adding 108 in pursuit of a target of 279, but the rest of the batsmen showed little resistance. The crowd reacted violently to Tendulkar's run-out, convinced that the bowler Shoaib Akhtar had impeded him deliberately. It took a while for the game to resume, but the damage had already been done. The break meant that Rahul, who was the other batsman when the controversy occurred, had to get his eye in all over again. Four runs later, he edged Shoaib to Moin Khan and departed for 13. The Kolkata crowd was as much to blame for his wicket as the Pakistani bowlers.

There was another fusillade of bottles and stones on the fifth morning when the second-last wicket fell with the target still 48 runs away. The police retaliated by driving the spectators out of the ground, and Pakistan completed the last rites in a virtually empty stadium.

India needed an outright win over Sri Lanka to stay in the running for a place in the final, but they were let down by a placid Colombo pitch and inept fielding. India scored 518-7, with Rahul (107) and Ramesh (143) scoring hundreds. The hosts replied with 485, and their first innings lasted till the final session on the fourth day, rendering a result impossible. It was obvious that Pakistan would prefer to play Sri Lanka in the final, and the latter duly made it to the summit clash by garnering enough bonus points from their game against Pakistan at Lahore, to shut the door on India. The Indians cried foul over Pakistan's alleged 'gifting' of bonus points to Sri Lanka. However, in letting Pakistan recover from 26-6 at Kolkata and giving double-centurion Mahela Jayawardene as many as five 'lives' at Colombo, they had only themselves to blame.

Pakistan thrashed Sri Lanka by an innings and 175 runs in the final at the Bangabandhu stadium in Dhaka, the first 'neutral' Test venue since Trent Bridge, Nottingham, which had staged the third Australia-South Africa Test of the 1912 Triangular Test Championship between England, Australia and South Africa.

The three Asian giants then met for a limited-overs tri-series on Indian soil. India made a bright start with Rahul and Sourav adding a record 230 against the Lankans at Nagpur. Rahul's 116 was among his better one-day innings, but he was overshadowed by Sourav, who followed his 130 with a four-wicket haul that sealed a win by eighty runs. Although the Indians had the better of Sri Lanka and later England in another tri-series at Sharjah, they were clearly inferior to Pakistan, who outclassed them in five games out of six, including the finals of both tournaments. Pakistan's margins of victory in both finals said it all—123 runs in Bengaluru, and eight wickets in Sharjah after dismissing India for 125.

Pakistan's dream run stretched right up to the final of the World Cup, which was played in the United Kingdom in May-June 1999. One of the most significant reasons for their transformation in the first half of 1999 after a disastrous home series against Australia in late 1998 was their three Tests and six one-day internationals against India. Several Pakistani cricketers of the 1980s and 1990s went on record to declare that matches against India 'brought the players together, induced them to forget their differences and helped them focus on the goal of victory'.

India were severely handicapped in both the tri-series by the absence of Tendulkar, who opted to tend to his back, and Azharuddin, who dropped out of the latter games of the first tri-series to rest a painful shoulder.

The tri-series in Sharjah witnessed a significant 'event' in Rahul's career, which had its origins in an epidemic of sorts.

The Indians arrived in Sharjah with half the side stricken by viral fever. There were only 14 players in the team, which meant that some of the sick boys had no option but to play the first game against Pakistan. One of them was wicketkeeper Nayan Mongia. Pakistan elected to bat, and Mongia battled on for an hour until it was too much for him. Rahul, with hardly any keeping practice since the 1996 England tour, then donned the gloves and pads and watched the Pakistanis amass a match-winning 279-8. India set England a target of 223 in the next game, and the match was interestingly poised when Mongia was struck in the face by a Kumble delivery and had to leave the field. That led to a rare instance of two 'substitutes' on the field, both of whom were actually part of the playing eleven; Rahul as the wicketkeeper, and Jadeja as the acting captain in the absence of Azhar who had injured his foot while batting. Rahul did pretty well, stumping the dangerous Graeme Hick and later catching England's top-scorer Neil Fairbrother off Jadeja to seal the game in his side's favour.

Rahul struck form in the next two games with 63 against England and 81 against Pakistan, both of which turned out to be match-winning efforts. He also stood in for Mongia for the third time in the tournament after the latter collided with Shahid Afridi in the last league encounter and had to go off for repairs. India raised expectations with a victory in that game, but two strikes by Wasim Akram in the very first over of the final reduced India to 0-2. A fighting 50 by Ganguly apart, the Indians were never in the hunt. They made only 125 and Pakistan coasted to victory with 22 overs to spare. Rahul was the second of Akram's victims in that first over, out leg-before first ball after Ramesh had gone in identical fashion.

The morale of the team was low after these reverses, but the return of Sachin Tendulkar ushered in a tide of optimism on the eve of the World Cup.

> 'The presence of Sachin Tendulkar should be an inspiration to everyone. The likes of Rahul Dravid and Sourav Ganguly should take over the mantle, and reduce the pressure on him. Dravid and Ganguly had done well on our last tour to England in 1996 and they should be familiar with the conditions…'
>
> —Mohammed Azharuddin, *Sportstar,* 15 May 1999

6

# ON THE ROLLER-COASTER

> 'For a long time, a lot of people have thought of Rahul as their hero for his cricketing abilities and the fact that he conducts himself with grace on and off the field and takes nothing for granted.'
>
> —Charu Sharma

Two 'Operations' were the talk of all India in mid-1999. Regrettably, 'Operation Encore' made more headlines than 'Operation Vijay', in the initial stages at least. That India had won the World Cup the last time it was played in the United Kingdom was highlighted and emphasized repeatedly by the media, and lapped up by the public.

The men expected to be Tendulkar's sidekicks in 'Operation Encore' were quite happy to return where it had all begun for them three years previously. Rahul and Sourav made a good start with scores of 54 and 97 respectively in India's first game against the Proteas, but their colleagues failed to click and India could make only 253-5, a total that the strong South African batting line-up overhauled in the 48th over. It wasn't the best of starts to the quest for an 'encore.'

The wheels came apart in sensational fashion four days later, when India lost to Zimbabwe at Leicester by three runs. It was a nightmarish day; the players woke up to learn that Tendulkar's father had passed away and he had flown back to India. Then came the defeat, their second in two games. As shattered as the players were the sponsors, who had spent an astronomical amount of money in the lead-up to the tournament, inundating even the members of the 1983 team with endorsements!

India, quite simply, needed to win all its subsequent matches to stay afloat. Tendulkar returned in time for the next game against Kenya, and moved even the most hardened of cricket-watchers with a century. The innings was bound to overshadow everything else, and so it did, including a knock of 104 by Rahul, his fourth limited-overs hundred and first in the World Cup. India finished with 329-2 and registered their first win.

The next game was against Sri Lanka at Taunton, headquarters of the Somerset County Cricket Club, situated right next to the river Tone.

It was a knockout game for all practical purposes, for both teams had won one and lost two out of three. Arjuna Ranatunga won the toss and sent India in, obviously fancying his bowlers' chances of exploiting whatever moisture there was in the pitch. S. Ramesh struck a boundary in the very first over, but Chaminda Vaas disturbed the timber with his fifth ball. In came Rahul, India's best bet to steer the team out of choppy waters. It was a day when the oarsman was at his most outstanding.

It was a day when Rahul Dravid was 'in the zone'. From his stance, as always a cricket coach's delight, the twitching of his head backwards to try and keep it as still as possible as he focussed on the approaching ball, the backlift that came down from second slip, the initial 'back and across' movement, precise footwork, and fluent stroke-play—everything he did was picture-perfect. It turned out to be a day when his bat only had a 'middle'. He warmed up with an effortless on-drive off Eric Upashanta in the fourth over.

Ranatunga replaced Upashanta with Pramodya Wickremasinghe in the sixth over. Wickremasinghe's first ball was a long-hop outside the off-stump that begged to be punished. Rahul obliged with a searing square-cut to the fence. The next delivery was overpitched, and Rahul essayed a gorgeous on-drive for four. The fourth ball was another offering, pitched on the feet, and Rahul flicked it delectably to the mid-wicket boundary. The over yielded 15 in all and India were rocking at 40-1 from six overs. The tempo was maintained and Rahul reached his fifty in the 15th over with a sizzling cover-drive off Wickremasinghe. India were 94-1 at the end of the 15th over.

Rahul's timing had been immaculate in all senses. He could not have chosen a better game or arena to showcase the skills that made him a special batsman. He was driving his side to an imposing score in a win-at-all-costs game with a display fit to be ranked alongside the best innings played by batsmen like Greg Chappell, Sir Vivian Richards, Sunil Gavaskar, Martin Crowe and Ian Botham, all of whom had represented Somerset in the English County Championship and for whom Taunton had been a home ground. Rahul's on-drives were as elegant as Chappell's, his straight-drives as graceful as Gavaskar's, his cuts as flawless as Crowe's, his cover-drives as stunning as those played by Richards and the lofted drives he essayed later in the innings as spectacular as Botham's.

Rahul raises his bat after completing his hundred at Taunton

Sourav, who was in no mean form himself, was quite content to let Rahul hog the limelight and the strike, and the Sri Lankans were at their wits' end against a left hand-right hand combination.

The introduction of Muralitharan into the attack pegged back the run-rate a bit, and led to the only alarm in Rahul's innings, when he played a ball on the leg-side and called for a run, only to be sent back by his partner. Rahul dived to make his ground and gave Sourav a glare. The duo would have remembered the 1995-96 Challenger Trophy final. But a lot of water had flowed down the Tone since!

Sourav completed his fifty in the 23rd over. What followed was an exhilarating duel between the two batsmen at the expense of the hapless bowlers. There was nothing the Sri Lankan bowlers could do, save go through the motions of completing the 50 overs and hoping that Jayasuriya, Kaluwitharana and Aravinda De Silva would bat as well later in the day. Rahul completed his hundred in the 36th over to become only the second batsman after Mark Waugh to score back-to-back hundreds in the World Cup. He then took on Murali with a brilliant inside-out stroke in the 38th over that cleared the cover boundary. Two sixes by Sourav immediately after completing his hundred in the 39th over, gave him a lead over Rahul for the first time in the match.

Rahul regained the lead with three boundaries off Vaas in the 44th over. The first, a lofted straight drive that hit the boundary-boards and rebounded half the distance, made their partnership the highest-ever in one-day internationals, surpassing the 275-run stand between teammates Azharuddin and Jadeja against Zimbabwe in 1997-98. An improvised square-drive and chipped shot later, Rahul had moved to 142, with Sourav seven runs behind. Sourav then took an unassailable lead in the very next over, with three boundaries and a six off consecutive deliveries by Upashanta, to complete his 150 in resounding fashion.

Rahul was run out in the 46th over for 145, scored off only 129 balls with 17 boundaries and that 'inside-out' six off Muralitharan. He and Sourav had added a record 318 for the second wicket. Sourav continued the massacre and surpassed Kapil Dev's 175 to become India's highest individual scorer in one-day internationals. He was two sixes away from overhauling Saeed Anwar's 194 when he fell in the last over. The last 15 overs had yielded an astonishing 170 runs, the last ten 128. India finished with 373-6, and Srinath rubbed salt on Sri Lanka's wounds by running out Jayasuriya in the third over. There was never any doubt about the result after that.

Rahul had been designated keeper for this match after Mongia hurt a finger in the previous game. This made him only the third 'keeper' after Zimbabweans Dave Houghton and Andy Flower to score a World Cup hundred.

> 'It was Rahul who initiated the onslaught. That was the clay he proved beyond doubt that he was as capable of overpowering a bowling attack in a one-day international as anybody else.'
>
> —Anshuman Gaekwad

Rahul top-scored with 53 in India's next encounter against England. Disciplined bowling by his teammates elevated it to the status of a match-winning innings, and the Indians were through to the 'Super Six' stage. Their fans started weaving fantasies all over again, only to see them go up in smoke in the very first game against Australia, who like India, needed to win all their matches to win the tournament. The Aussies scored 282-6 and then Glenn McGrath produced a devastating spell to send back Tendulkar, Rahul and Azharuddin, while Damien Fleming bowled Ganguly at the other end. India were 17-4 in the

When their bats talked… Rahul and Sourav Ganguly after yet another boundary, Taunton, 1999

seventh over. The Indians were never in with a chance after that early burst, although Jadeja and Robin Singh fought hard.

'Operation Encore' was all but over, but 'Operation Vijay' had added a whole new dimension to India's next encounter, against its traditional foe at Manchester on 8 June 1999.

The third Ind-Pak tussle in World Cup history began with Wasim Akram shocking Geoffrey Boycott and an entire subcontinent by calling it a 'practice' match. The Pakistani captain probably had his recent successes against India in his mind, as also his team's winning streak in the World Cup itself, but his proclamation still seemed way off the mark. Contrary to what players of both sides have claimed over the years, there has always been a needle in India-Pakistan matches. By the same analogy, there was a 'sword' in this particular game, because of all that was happening in Kargil.

For the third time in three World Cup games against Pakistan, India won the toss and elected to bat. Rahul, who was keen to atone for his failure against the Aussies, came in at 37-1 and got into a groove almost immediately. He scored 61, Azharuddin contributed 59 and the Indians finished with 227-5. Much to the delight of their fans and soldiers, India won by 47 runs with Venkatesh Prasad taking 5-27.

It was India's last moment of joy, and they ultimately finished sixth in the points table at the end of the 'Super Six' stage. But there was a silver lining. Rahul had accumulated 461 runs, the highest in the competition. Steve and Mark Waugh, who played two matches more, finished second and fourth in the run-getters' table with 398 and 375 runs respectively. With Tendulkar affected by a personal tragedy, the team needed someone to 'stand in' for him and assume the responsibility of taking the initiative with the bat. Rahul had done so admirably, that too in cricket's biggest event. At the end of the tournament, it was announced that he had topped the CEAT World Cup Rating with a tally of 22 points. He received the CEAT Cricketer of the World Cup award later in the year.

> 'Rahul's technique was ideally suited to English conditions, which provide some assistance to the bowlers. In England, bowlers look to take wickets and set attacking fields. But this creates quite a few gaps in the field. A batsman who has the ability to keep the good balls out, and a wide range of strokes for the bad balls, is bound to succeed.'
>
> —Robin Singh

Rahul capped a memorable tour by doing an impressive commentary stint during the final between Australia and Pakistan. Many viewers considered it a sign of things to come.

> 'I remember doing an interview with him before the tour of South Africa in 1996-97. One of the questions I asked him was what he would like to do after quitting the game. He was surprised. Remember, it was only his first year in international cricket! But he regained his composure and said that the job 'you guys are doing is what I want'. It seems easy enough, he said! I would say, 'Commentators, watch out!"
>
> —Charu Sharma

But the Board was not so impressed, and made him the second Indian cricketer after Bishan Singh Bedi (1974) to be reprimanded for appearing on TV in England without prior permission. They were apparently upset with his assertion during his commentary stint that the team had no knowledge of the rules of the 'Super Six' format. The fact was that the Boards of all the participating countries had received the playing conditions and rules of the tournament well in advance. This meant that there had obviously been a communication gap between the BCCI and players.

After the World Cup, Sachin Tendulkar was offered the captaincy when the selectors decided that they could no longer persist with Azhar. Ironically, the Chairman of the Selection Committee at the time was Ajit Wadekar, one of Azhar's staunchest supporters, who as Cricket Manager in 1992-93 had convinced the then selectors to extend Azharuddin's stint as captain of India. Tendulkar seemed to be reluctant initially and said as much, but he changed his mind after 48 hours of silence and introspection.

The biggest test for the 'new' captain and his team was the tour of Australia at the end of the year. The quality of the opposition and the Indians' unfamiliarity with the bouncy Australian wickets had several pundits recommending an intensive preparatory camp. The Board, on the other hand, had decided to 'prepare' the team by making it participate in four inconsequential limited-overs tournaments to be played in three different continents, followed by a Test series at home against New Zealand.

India's performances in the one-day competitions were average, save a three-match series against the West Indies at Toronto that was organized after India refused to play Pakistan post-Kargil. The West Indies consequently played the subcontinental giants in two separate three-match series and lost both. The India-West Indies leg in Toronto began just three days after the final of a tri-series in Singapore between the same teams, in which Rahul scored a magnificent 103, which looked a match-winning knock until Ricardo Powell arrived at the wicket with a mission to clear the ground as many times as possible.

With both Tendulkar and his deputy Ajay Jadeja nursing injuries, Sourav Ganguly was appointed captain for the Toronto series against the West Indies. Rahul, who was made vice-captain, scored a dazzling 77 in the third and final game and held four catches to take India to an 88-run win and a 2-1 triumph in the series. These catches he held as a fielder, as distinct from the five he had snapped as wicketkeeper from five matches a few days earlier. The think-tank had decided to bolster the batting during the tri-series in Sri Lanka by dropping specialist-stumper M.S.K. Prasad. Rahul accordingly kept wickets in two of India's four matches in Sri Lanka, and then in three more games in Singapore. Of course, he could not have been faulted had he refused to shoulder the additional responsibility. There was no way he could have been touched after his performances in the World Cup, after all.

> 'Rahul is a player who will walk on broken glass if his team tells him to.'
>
> —Navjot Sidhu

Rahul was effusive in thanking his teammates for their support when he received the Castrol Indian Cricketer of the Year Award for 1998-99 at a function in Delhi in November 1999. His performances in New Zealand and the World Cup had prompted a majority of former Indian Test cricketers to vote in his favour.

There were two new appointments in the Indian team on the eve of the series against New Zealand. Kapil Dev succeeded Gaekwad as coach, and Australian Andrew Leipus joined the team as physiotherapist.

> 'I knew Srinath from 1997, when he had come to the Centre for Sports Medicine in Johannesburg to tend to his rotator-cuff injury. I was a part of the centre then. Naturally, "Sri" was the first person I went to meet after joining the Indian team before the New Zealand series. Those were the days when the players shared rooms, and Rahul happened to be his roommate. That's where I met him first. In my initial days with the team, I would look to identify some enthusiastic guys and work hard on them, hoping that the improvements they would make would inspire the others who were not as enthusiastic about fitness or training. Rahul was one of the enthusiastic players I identified as a "leader".'
>
> —Andrew Leipus

So intense was the speculation over what Tendulkar and Kapil Dev would achieve in tandem that it outshone the criticism emanating from some quarters over the dropping of Azharuddin and Mongia from the Test side. Kapil Dev's first day as coach was not a happy one, with the New Zealand seamers bowling India out on a greenish and nippy first-day wicket at Mohali for a paltry 83. Although the Indians recovered in the second innings with centuries from Rahul and Tendulkar and drew the game fairly easily, their first-innings capitulation on a wicket that had something in it for the bowlers was not a good portent before a tour of Australia. Had Rahul and

Tendulkar fallen early in the second innings, anything could have happened. Rahul's 144, another fine innings wherein his technique was tested by some hostile bowling, was his fifth Test hundred and first on Indian soil.

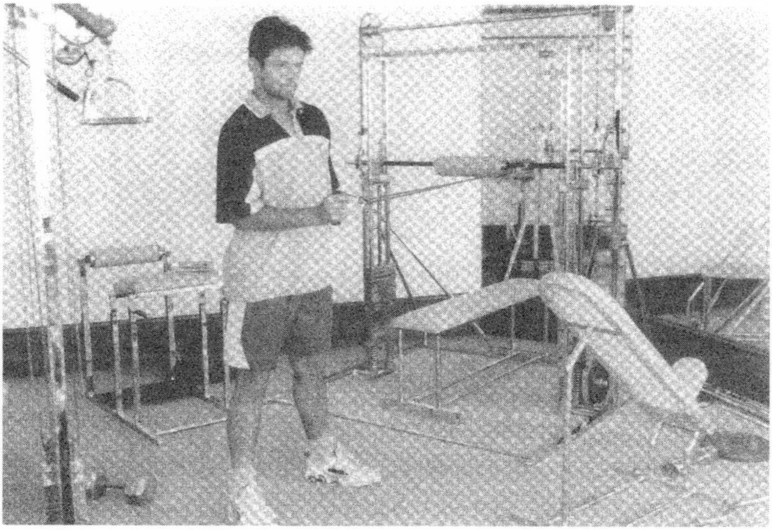

A stickler for fitness

The Test was followed by a three-day game between the visitors and Karnataka, the 1998-99 Ranji Champions, at Bengaluru. Leipus, who travelled to Bengaluru along with the Karnataka players in the Indian team, was touched when Rahul invited him home for dinner. The other guests were Kiwis Stephen Fleming, Dion Nash and Daniel Vettori, whom Rahul had played against in an Under-19 series in 1991-92. 'It was a wonderful gesture by someone I had just met,' Leipus told this writer.

The series returned to 'Indian' ways in the second Test at Kanpur, where the Indians prevailed by eight wickets on a dustbowl. The first double hundred of Tendulkar's career put them in another winning position in the third Test at Ahmedabad, but the think-tank strangely decided not to enforce the follow-on after bowling out the Kiwis for 308 and taking a first-innings lead of 275. The visitors batted well in the second innings to save the game, thus giving India the series 1-0.

The one-day series went right down to the wire with India winning 3-2. Rahul produced another Taunton-like display in the second game at Hyderabad, in which he and Tendulkar added 331 for the second wicket, and obliterated the record set by him and Sourav a few months earlier. Rahul scored 153, his highest in one-day internationals, and Tendulkar scored 186 to displace Sourav as India's highest individual scorer in one-day internationals.

> 'No successful cricketer's life is complete without a stellar performance in Australia.'
>
> —G.R. Viswanath

Not many teams in Test history have had three batsmen with a 50-plus average in Test cricket. The Indian trio of Tendulkar, Rahul and Ganguly belonged to this exclusive club, and expectations were huge when the Indian team boarded the plane for Australia. But the series was an anticlimax. They were drubbed in all three Tests by a rampant Australian team in the process of establishing a new record for the highest number of consecutive Test wins. India had lost 0-4 on their previous tour of Australia (in 1991-92), but they had run the hosts close in two of the five Tests that they had played. This time around, they were never in the picture. They lost at Adelaide by 285 runs, at

Melbourne by 180, and at Sydney by an innings and 141.

> 'The strategy of the West Indies in the 70s and 80s was to put the captain under pressure. If he starts worrying about his own form, the team was bound to suffer.'
>
> —Joel Garner, *Rookies, Rebels and Renaissance*, ABC Books, 2004

Australia, inheritors of the 'invincible' tag that belonged to the West Indies in the 1970s and 1980s, were following the same tactic. Tendulkar was put under enormous pressure on the field by the Australian players, and off the field by the media. He also ended up getting a couple of debatable umpiring decisions. However, he was at his tenacious best and excelled himself in an innings of 116 at Melbourne. VVS Laxman scored 167 in the second innings at Sydney, but the match still ended on the third day.

The biggest disappointment of the tour was Rahul, who scored 93 runs from six innings at 15.50. If viewed in the context of the law of averages, his slump could have been explained as a bad patch after a productive 12-month period. However, it wasn't quite so straightforward.

He was dismissed twice each by Brett Lee, who made his debut at Melbourne, and Glenn McGrath. They gave him hardly any margin for error, sticking to the corridor of uncertainty just outside the off-stump, forcing him to play at deliveries until he nicked one and was snapped up either by the keeper or the slips. And then, there was Shane Warne, whom Rahul had handled well in the previous series. But things were different this time. He dismissed Rahul twice at Adelaide and came away convinced that he had 'the wood' on him. Given the form the Australian bowlers were in, a batsman had to be assertive enough to exploit the rare bad ball and competent enough to make even good balls count. Rahul wasn't at his best, and paid the price.

> 'On that tour, Rahul was jabbing and pushing at deliveries.'
>
> —Sunil Gavaskar

An urge to succeed may have caused this. It was probably one of those rare instances when Rahul's perceptive nature actually backfired on him. He might well have got obsessed with the thought that all his achievements would amount to nothing if he did not pass the toughest examination in the cricketing world. This could have inadvertently made him apprehensive of failure. Then the law of averages struck, and the consequences were catastrophic.

> 'Rahul had a tough time in Australia, but he never gave up. He continued to work hard in the nets and pick up new points. The results were seen on the next tour.'
>
> —VVS Laxman

By the time Rahul pulled himself together to score three fifties in the triangular series against the hosts and Pakistan, it was too late. The Indians failed to qualify for the best-of-three finals and flew home licking their wounds.

Three weeks had elapsed since their last game of the tri-series when the Indians met the Proteas at Mumbai in the first Test of a two-match series. Spirits were still low, and Tendulkar's decision to quit as captain at the end of the series only added to the gloom. In what was another debacle for the Indians, they lost both Tests, and Tendulkar's second stint as captain ended with him becoming the first Indian skipper since Kapil Dev in 1986-

87 to lose a Test series at home. Ironically, the only centurion in the Test series was Tendulkar's two-time predecessor and one-time successor. It was even alleged that Tendulkar's decision to abdicate had a lot to do with Azharuddin's return to the squad. The stylist scored 102 at Bengaluru, the 99th Test of his career, which turned out to be his last.

The think-tank did a low-on-confidence Rahul no favours by asking him to open at Bengaluru after Laxman had been dropped. Once again, it wasn't a very pleasant experience. He scored 17 and 18, although he lasted for quite a while—75 balls in the first innings and 61 in the second.

> 'Dravid's problem today is not so much technique or talent, but a mental block that does not permit him to play his natural game. A defensive mindset is not the best antidote to failure. Sometimes it makes sense to take the bull by the horns and damn the consequences.'
>
> —Ravi Shastri, *Cricket Talk*, 30 March 2000

Rahul did take the bull by the horns in the one-day series. A 73 in the third game at Faridabad and 79 in the fifth at Nagpur boosted his confidence, although India did not win either game. But they did win the series 3-2. Sourav Ganguly, India's new skipper, led from the front with a succession of swashbuckling knocks at the top of the order, and Tendulkar, with scores of 122 and 93 in the last two games, appeared to be enjoying himself without the cares of captaincy.

The euphoria of Indian fans over the limited-overs triumph soon evaporated due to all the damning disclosures that made 2000 cricket's year of the 'Great Betrayal'.

# 7

## KENT AND THE COLISEUM

> 'The six months of county cricket in England came at the right time because I needed to get away to a new environment where I could just relax and be myself and just play cricket and enjoy it. I was on my own, and I learned things about myself and my game.'
>
> —Rahul Dravid, *Wisden Asia Cricket*, January 2004

'Hansiegate' and the can of worms it opened, tainted reputations and in some cases, ended careers. The charges levelled against the Indian coach were never substantiated, but the initial damage was done. He broke down during a TV interview and insisted that the Indian team was not in the right frame of mind for the Asia Cup, which was to be played in Dhaka in May 2000. His worst fears came true when India failed to qualify for the finals, losing to both Sri Lanka and Pakistan and winning a solitary game against Bangladesh.

The Indian squad in Dhaka comprised three players—Ganguly, Kumble and Rahul—who had flown in from England, where they were engaged in County cricket for Lancashire, Leicestershire and Kent respectively.

English cricket had undergone a steady decline in the 1980s and 1990s, but what had not changed was the fact that a cricketer's abilities were tested to the fullest on the varied pitches and fluctuating weather conditions in England. Rahul was keen to further his cricketing education by playing in the County Championship. The year 2000, when India had no major international commitment during the whole of the English season from April to September (the Asia Cup was scheduled subsequently), was the perfect year in which to do so. On India's tour of New Zealand in 1998-99, Rahul had discussed the possibility of his playing County cricket with John Wright, the former Kiwi opener and incumbent Kent coach, who had been particularly impressed with his two hundreds in the Hamilton Test. A formal offer to represent Kent in the 2000 season followed, which Rahul happily accepted. It turned out to be a memorable stint both for the club and the player.

> 'Rahul was a very quiet individual but fitted into the group very well and was well liked. He had a tremendous work ethic and set an example for others to follow.'
>
> —Simon Willis, Coaching Coordinator, Kent CCC

Rahul and Sourav, who had made their Test debuts together, made their County debuts in the same game, albeit on opposing sides. Ganguly scored a duck and Rahul scored an unbeaten two in a draw. In his next game, against the touring Zimbabweans, Rahul scored a sparkling 182, the best performance by an Indian within Kent borders since Kapil Dev's 175 at Tunbridge Wells in the 1983 World Cup against the same team.

The 182 marked the start of a purple patch. Rahul scored 90 against Somerset in his first game after returning from Dhaka.

In the next clash against the same team, he scored 88 and 95.

On 19 July 2000, Kent took on hosts Hampshire on a Portsmouth pitch prepared with Shane Warne, the home team's strike bowler, in mind. Rahul came in to bat late on the first day, his team reduced to a precarious 15-2 after the hosts had scored 320. Day two witnessed a clash of two masters—a leg-spinner out to deceive, against a batsman out to defend, disturb and destroy. The batsman triumphed. Not for the last time, Warne and his wares were subjugated by a pair of Indian wrists. Rahul's 137, scored over six hours of studied batsmanship, was his first hundred in the County Championship.

Warne took 4-81, but he would have willingly traded his four wickets for Rahul's. The innings inspired Min Patel, Kent's left-arm spinner and Rahul's close friend, to take 5-46 and send Hampshire hurtling to 136 all out. Kent needed 205 to win, a target they duly achieved for the loss of only four wickets. Rahul remained unbeaten with 73 and Warne went wicketless.

Later in the season, Kent needed one bonus point from their last game against Kumble's county Leicestershire to avoid relegation to the lower division of the County Championship. Rahul delivered when it mattered with a priceless 77 that enabled his team to score the 200 runs it needed to stay in the upper division.

He finished with 1,039 runs from 15 County matches, the highest by a Kent batsman that season. Counting the 182 against Zimbabwe, his tally was 1,221 from 16 first-class matches at a splendid average of 55.50. His best performances in the limited-overs variety were an unbeaten 60 off 43 balls against Lancashire and a 104 off only 98 deliveries against Worcestershire in the Union National League. Rahul elicited comparisons with Aravinda De Silva, the Sri Lankan maestro, who had plundered an astounding 1,661 runs from 15 games as Kent's professional in 1995.

> 'They (Rahul and De Silva) both preferred playing when the sun was out! Whenever they saw a good pitch, they knew when to make the most of their opportunities and made sure they got as big a score as possible. More importantly, they both played match-winning innings. They possessed "big match temperament".'
>
> —Simon Willis

The immediate challenge for Sourav Ganguly at the start of the new international season was to regain the faith of the fans. The team departed for Nairobi in Kenya for the second edition of the biennial ICC Knockout without the customary pre-season excitement. Cricket-lovers in the country were still disillusioned, although the inquiries and inquests had not thrown up any charges against the big five—Sourav, Rahul, Srinath, Kumble and Tendulkar. A piqued Kapil Dev had resigned as coach, having declared that he would 'never wear whites again'. Gaekwad was back in the hot seat.

India got off to a quiet start with a win over Kenya on 3 October 2000. Their next encounter was scheduled four days later against the world champions. It wasn't all that surprising that people in India were more involved in the 'Dassera' celebrations than the action on TV on 7 October.

Those who cared to watch were left gaping as Tendulkar took on McGrath with his bat and mouth. But the middle-order faltered. The score was 130-4 when Yuvraj Singh, whose batting and fielding had played a major part in the Indian Under-19 team's World Cup victory earlier that year, arrived at the wicket to score a magnificent 84. India totalled a handsome 265-9, with number eleven Venkatesh Prasad lashing a six off the last ball of the innings.

The events of the next three hours were a watershed. The Indians bowled superbly, fielded breathtakingly and caught sensationally to complete a 20-run win, which was invigorating enough for the fans to dig out the fireworks. The horrific memories of the Great Betrayal were consigned to the flames along with the effigies of the demon-king Ravana, and an entire nation renewed its relationship with cricket.

India outclassed the Proteas by 95 runs in the semi-final. Ganguly led from the front with 141, with Rahul (58) helping him add 145 for the second wicket. The Indian vice-captain delighted everybody with his batting except seamer Roger Telemachus, who barged into him as he completed a run, and incurred a one-match suspension for doing so.

The way the Indians were playing, only a performance of a lifetime could have thwarted them. Unfortunately for them, a semi-fit Christopher Lance Cairns delivered one in the final, first with a restrictive spell and then a splendid hundred, to seal New Zealand's first-ever title triumph. The Indians were dismayed, but they took heart from the advent of Yuvraj and the left-arm paceman Zaheer Khan.

It was during the next tournament, a tri-series at Sharjah, that Rahul sustained the first major injury of his international career, damaging a finger while going for a catch in a league encounter against Zimbabwe. Earlier, he had opened the batting and scored 85 after his captain strangely demoted himself despite scoring hundreds in the semifinal and final of the ICC Knockout. Rahul missed the rest of the series, and was thus spared the ignominy of being in the eleven that collapsed for 54 in the final, leaving Sri Lanka victors by 245 runs.

Bangladesh's inaugural Test, in which they played India, was also Sourav Ganguly's first Test as captain. The Indians won the game, played at Dhaka, quite comprehensively after conceding a first-innings lead, but their frontline batsmen missed out on runs. Rahul compensated by scoring tons of them against the Zimbabweans who toured India that winter.

The two-Test series against Zimbabwe marked the start of John Wright's tenure as coach of the Indian team. Rahul, one of his 'wards' at Kent, was among the senior players who had recommended him for the job. Wright's was not an auspicious start, with several former Indian cricketers slamming the appointment of a foreigner. They argued that there was no dearth of experts in the country. The men behind the decision to give Wright the job reacted only when it was time to have the last laugh.

Rahul 'welcomed' Wright with an innings of 200 in the first Test at Delhi, during the course of which he passed the 3,000-run mark in Test cricket. The game, which at one stage looked headed for a draw, was enlivened by a declaration immediately after Rahul completed the first double hundred of his Test career. India at that stage were only 36 runs ahead, but the new captain and coach were determined to be positive. A five-wicket haul by Srinath in the third innings laid the foundation of a seven-wicket win. India batted first in the second Test at Nagpur and scored a whopping 609-6. Rahul contributed a mammoth 162 to a 249-run stand with Tendulkar, their second double-century association after a partnership of 213 at Delhi. The visitors were bundled out for only 382, but led by Andy Flower, they batted pluckily in the second to force a draw. Sourav, who had timed the declaration perfectly at Delhi, was pilloried for delaying the declaration at Nagpur to enable Tendulkar to complete his double hundred. There was an interesting postscript to this incident, three years later!

India dominated the five-match one-day series that followed. The home team had already clinched the series with three wins from four games when Rahul exercised the captain's prerogative of delivering a team-talk on the eve of the final one-dayer at Rajkot. He was elevated to the helm when Sourav was asked to 'take a break' by the ICC Referee, after some petulant behaviour in the fourth game at Kanpur. The new recruits made Rahul's debut as captain of India memorable. Hemang Badani, a middle-order batsman from Chennai, top-scored with 77, and Reetinder Sodhi got 53. Ajit Agarkar clobbered a 21-ball fifty and took the total past 300. The Zimbabweans fell short by 39 runs.

Rahul's debut as captain of India. Tossing the coin at Rajkot, 2000-01

The Indians then had an intensive camp on the eve of their 'contest' against the Australians, who were seeing it more as an imminent 'conquest'. On the eve of the series, Australian skipper Steve Waugh, with 15 consecutive Test wins behind him, christened India the 'Final Frontier', a territory Australia hadn't 'conquered' since 1969-70. This statement made as much news as the shoulder injury to Anil Kumble that had forced him to withdraw from the series.

The man earmarked by Sourav to fill Kumble's shoes was a twenty-year-old off-spinner who had made his Test debut on Australia's last visit in 1997-98. Harbhajan Singh's brief cricketing career had been a rather turbulent one. First, the legality of his action was questioned, and he was asked to undergo remedial treatment. Then came the death of his inspiration, his father, and his 'rustication' from the newly-established National Cricket Academy in Bengaluru for alleged insubordination. The youngster and many others were convinced that his career was over. But the Indian captain thought otherwise. He badgered the selectors and won.

The first Test at Mumbai began on a tragic note with the demise of Sir Don Bradman forty-eight hours before the game. Steve Waugh won the toss and sent India in on what looked a 'sporting' wicket by Indian standards, meaning that there was something in it for the fast bowlers, but nothing that would deter batsmen who played to their potential. Rahul found himself in the middle with only seven on the board, after Adam Gilchrist snapped up a Ramesh mishook off McGrath.

Not a very common sight in 2001

> 'Dravid is fast becoming the new Ravi Shastri of Indian cricket, loved by female fans and hated by male fans (who want to see quick runs). And like Shastri, always there to score runs when the team needs them badly.'
>
> —B. Vijay Kumar, *Cricket Talk,* 2 December 2000

There was another reason the men 'hated' Rahul. They simply wanted him out of the way so that they could see Sachin Tendulkar, the next batsman, in action!

Rahul had provided enough ammunition to his 'haters' by taking 350 balls to score 201 against the Zimbabweans at Delhi, while Tendulkar had taken just 281 deliveries to score one run less at Nagpur. What the so-called 'cricket-lovers' who had dubbed him a 'slow' batsman were not appreciating was that he and Tendulkar were different types of batsmen, both equally important to the side. In an age of instant gratification where the 'moneybags' mobster was upstaging the cricket connoisseur, a cricketer like Rahul was trailing in the popularity stakes behind an extraordinary individual who possessed the ability to draw gasps from the aficionados as well as roars from the masses.

At Mumbai, Rahul obliged the mobsters by nicking the first delivery of Damien Fleming's second spell into Gilchrist's gloves, and the stage was set for the entry of the man who had reminded Bradman of himself. For the umpteenth time in his short international career, Rahul felt that his ears were going to explode moments after he was dismissed. The cheers welcoming the new batsman were deafening.

Tendulkar's incandescent 76 would have done the Don proud, but his was a solo effort and the Indians were bowled out for a pathetic 176. Australia too looked in some strife at 99-5 when Gilchrist and Matthew Hayden decided to have a wild party at the expense of the Indian bowlers. The Aussies amassed a lead of 173. India were in trouble at 57-2 in the second innings, when Tendulkar and Rahul staged a revival of sorts. The score was 103 when Rahul essayed a full-blooded pull off Gillespie, only to see Michael Slater at short mid-wicket dive in front and claim a catch. Rahul stood his ground and the TV replays confirmed that the catch was doubtful. What followed was deplorable. A livid Slater strode towards the batsman and virtually demanded that Rahul 'believe' him. Rahul was not amused, nor was S. Venkataraghvan, the umpire. Cammie Smith, the Match Referee, strangely took no action, springing to life only when Slater continued his tirade in a radio interview. He fined Slater half his match-fee and handed him a 'suspended' sentence for six months.

Disaster struck after Tendulkar completed his second fifty of the game. The score was 154-2 when he struck a full-blooded pull off Mark Waugh, who was bowling off-breaks. The ball ricocheted off forward short-leg fielder Justin Langer's left shoulder into the short mid-wicket region, where Ricky Ponting flung himself to clasp it inches from the ground. In keeping with the then prevalent tradition of Indian cricket, Tendulkar's fall triggered a collapse. The Indian captain ran himself out just two runs later. Laxman, who had made it clear before the start of the new season that he would not open, fell at 174, as did Rahul. He was bowled by Warne, the sixth time he had been dismissed by the leg-spinner in seven Tests.

India were all out for 219 and the Australians completed a ten-wicket triumph on the third day. It was their 16th Test win on the trot and Waugh's warriors were just one step away from crossing 'The Final Frontier'. Sourav, a captain beset by a lean patch on the field and alleged turmoil on the personal front, insisted during the presentation ceremony that his team would 'come back'.

But the hopes of even the most optimistic Indian supporter had sunk by the end of day two of the second Test at the Kolkata coliseum, a hattrick by Harbhajan Singh on day one notwithstanding. India were 128-8 in response to Australia's 445, and cricket-writers all over India were engaged in an unofficial contest for the most creative adaptation of the 'Obituary' of English cricket that appeared in the 'In Memoriam' section of *The Sporting Times* on 30 August 1882, after they famously lost a Test to Australia by seven runs. Among the eight Indian batsmen to come and go was Rahul, who was, once again, bowled by Warne, playing all over a well tossed-up delivery. Laxman, who had batted entertainingly on the second evening, was last out on the third morning for 59, and Steve Waugh, his team 274 runs ahead, walked across to the Indian dressing room and asked his counterpart to bat again.

Ramesh and Shiv Sunder Das gave India a much better start in the second innings with a stand of 52. Ramesh's exit brought Laxman back to the middle. The think-tank had asked him not to take off his pads at the end of the first innings, and promoted him to number three. It was a little hard on Rahul, who had manned that spot with distinction for years, but Wright and Sourav were two men who believed in living in the present. Laxman had batted better than any other Indian batsman in the game, and the team needed him to spend a lot more time in the middle, if they were to delay the inevitable, if not save the game.

Das broke his own wicket at 97, and Tendulkar failed to get past ten for the second time in the game. Enter Sourav, who displayed great character in a knock of 48. He stayed while 117 runs were added, with Laxman personifying elegance and ebullience at the other end.

It used to be said of Ken Barrington, England's great technician of the 1950s and 1960s, that his opponents could see the Union Jack waving behind him as he came in to bat. Rahul's opponents of the late 1990s had had similar visions of the Indian tricolour whenever he came in to bat, but on that late afternoon in Kolkata, the Aussies would have seen the tricolour flying at half-mast, an indicator of the state the Indian team and Rahul himself were in. As the outgoing batsman passed the incoming, Sourav paused and gave his deputy an encouraging tap on the back. As he made his way to the centre, Rahul would have heard the words 'slow', 'dull' and 'fair-weather', all epithets bestowed on him by his 'friends' in the media, ringing in his ears. He wanted to make them eat their words, and he had a wonderful opportunity to do so. The situation when he began his innings was as grim as grim could be. If he failed, his detractors would not be surprised; if he flourished, even they would not stop talking about his batsmanship for a long, long time.

Laxman and he saw India through to the close on the third day, at which point the score was 254-4 with Laxman having completed his second Test hundred. India were only twenty runs behind and the country was relieved that there would be no innings defeat.

Day four dawned bright and clear. Shortly after India took the lead, Laxman took four boundaries off a Jason Gillespie over. The first was a lucky inside-edge, but he compensated with a magnificent off-drive, an exquisite cut and a gorgeous cover drive. His 137 runs at that stage comprised 25 boundaries. The crowds at the coliseum roared in appreciation. But how long would this last?

Then Rahul on-drove Kasprowicz beautifully and stroked two fours off a Warne over. Not a single wicket fell in the first session, and the batsmen carried on in the same vein after lunch.

> 'We were constantly encouraging each other. There were times when I was tiring and not timing the ball well, and he would exhort me to keep going. I did the same when he started tiring. Our teammates, the crowd, everyone was so involved.'
>
> —VVS Laxman

The partnership passed 100, then 150, both men looking

more and more confident with every passing over. Rahul brought up the 200 of the stand with an imperious on-drive off Gillespie that beat two chasing fielders—the mid-on and the deep mid-wicket—to the fence. Laxman then completed his own 200 with a stunning drive off Mark Waugh. While there was no doubt that the Indians were batting brilliantly, they were helped greatly by the rigidity of the Australians, who persisted with an attacking field and left the boundaries largely unmanned. They were playing to the batsmen's strengths, and the latter weren't complaining!

Rahul's big moment came, quite appropriately in a Warne over. He came down the wicket and essayed an on-drive that brought up his first Test hundred against Australia. As Warne himself led the applause, Rahul stared hard at the press-box and commentary enclosures, where some of his 'friends' were seated, and brandished his 'mouthpiece' that had 'talked' splendidly to silence them—his bat.

His only worry at that stage was his old scourge—cramps.

> 'I remember John (Wright) yelling at me after Rahul's calf went. "Get him fit," John shouted. It was important for us that he stayed out there. I gave Rahul a bright red-coloured Vitamin B pill, which I told him was 'anti-cramping'. Now, there is nothing such as an anti-cramping pill. But Rahul believed me, and carried on. I am not saying that my lie worked. Rahul's fortitude enabled him to push himself.'
>
> —Andrew Leipus

Leipus swung into action again after the two batsmen 'swaggered' back to the pavilion at stumps on day four, and put both of them on saline drips. Laxman lay on the masseur's table and Rahul on the lunch-table after the cutlery and crockery had been cleared. Not a single wicket had fallen that day.

The cornered tiger who fought… Rahul completes his hundred against Australia at Kolkata, 2000-01

The stand ended on the fifth morning at 608, after Rahul and Laxman had put together 376, the second-highest association by an Indian pair in Test cricket. Laxman fell for a monumental 281, the highest individual score by an Indian in Test cricket. The lower-order was instructed to step up a gear and Rahul was run out for 180 in the ensuing scramble. He had taken 353 balls to score those runs, but nobody was complaining.

> 'India were down in the dumps when Rahul played that innings. In a situation like that, it takes strength of character, talent and temperament to play to your strengths

and not get overawed by the blazing strokes being played at the other end.'

—Sunil Gavaskar

Sourav declared 383 runs ahead, and out came a hungry Indian side. Not satisfied with all the records their teammates had set, they wanted more. The Australians were only three down at tea, but Tendulkar initiated an unbelievable collapse with three prized scalps, those of Gilchrist, Hayden and Warne, the last to an incredible googly. The wickets tumbled dramatically thereafter, and when Glenn McGrath padded up to a Harbhajan delivery and umpire S.K. Bansal raised his finger, there was bedlam. India had squared the series with their greatest-ever Test win.

The decider at Chennai was a humdinger. Rahul (81) was outstanding in a partnership of 169 with Tendulkar, who was determined not to finish the series without a hundred. Of the many fabulous shots Rahul essayed, the one that stood out was a straight six off Gillespie, which illustrated his new-found confidence in his aggressive capabilities. The Australians denied vehemently that they were clueless against Harbhajan, but the statistics told a different story. The off-spinner bagged 15 wickets at Chennai, in addition to the 13 he pocketed at Kolkata and four at Mumbai.

Indians needed only 155 to win, and with Tendulkar and Laxman in the middle at 101-2, the celebrations had already started. But the Australians would not give up. They played on the nerves of the Indians, bottling up the runs and luring the strokemakers to their doom. Six wickets fell in a heap, the highlights of the collapse being Steve Waugh's diving catch at mid-off to dismiss Rahul and his twin's blinder at short mid-wicket to dispatch Laxman. Debutant Sameer Dighe played some gritty strokes to take his team to the threshold, but all four results were possible when McGrath steamed in at number ten Harbhajan Singh, the target a mere two runs away. Harbhajan deftly dug out an intended yorker and placed it just wide of point. The batsmen completed a 'two' to spark off frenzied celebrations in the Indian dressing room and outside.

The ecstatic Indians ran a lap of honour around the M.A. Chidambaram stadium with the Border-Gavaskar Trophy. Harbhajan Singh, with a record 32 wickets from three Tests, was the toast of the nation, as was Laxman, who had followed up on his 'Kolkata Opus' with scores of 65 and 66 at Chennai. The fans heaped accolades on Tendulkar, who had scored 125 at Chennai and taken three vital wickets at Kolkata, and of course, Sourav Ganguly, who had inspired his team to outdo the Australians in every aspect—technical, mental and verbal. He had not allowed his poor form to affect his leadership skills.

Rahul had ended the series, a successful one for him, as an unsung hero. Of course, it wasn't as if he wasn't used to it.

# 8

## ONE FOR A CRISIS

> 'Rahul respects the game, which is why we cricketers respect him. He doesn't play "games" with the game.'
>
> —Ashok Mankad

Rahul's best performance in the one-day series against Australia that followed the epic Test series was a match-winning 80 in the first game at Bengaluru. He lost the race for the individual award to a newcomer who scored 58 and took three wickets in only the second ODI of his career. His name was Virender Sehwag.

Not one member of the Indian team that arrived in Zimbabwe in May 2001 knew what it felt like to win a Test, let alone a series, outside the subcontinent. It was a dubious distinction the players were determined to erase. They did everything right in the first Test at Bulawayo to win by eight wickets. Rahul, an awesome number seven (he batted below night-watchman Srinath), scored 44 in his only outing. However, complacency, the Indian team's old bane, came to the fore in the second Test at Harare. India were bowled out for 237 in the first innings.

Das impressed with a knock of 57 and Rahul scored a defiant, unbeaten 68. The visitors had managed to take a lead of 119 in the second innings when Rahul was caught behind off Andy Blignaut for 26. This triggered off a procession of sorts, and India slid from 197-3 to 234 all out. Zimbabwe won by four wickets and squared the two-Test series.

The team came back in the subsequent tri-series against the home team and the West Indies with a 100 per cent success record in the league games. However, the West Indies prevailed in the final, and Tendulkar sustained a toe injury that rendered him unfit for the subsequent tour of Sri Lanka. But his absence wasn't as demoralizing as it would have been before the series against Australia, as the team now comprised others who had delivered in crunch situations.

The tour of Sri Lanka commenced with a tri-series between India, the hosts and New Zealand. India began badly with three straight losses, two to New Zealand and one to Sri Lanka. Rahul's unbeaten 49 off 81 balls in the defeat against Sri Lanka was a throwback to the dark days of 1997-98, but he set the record straight with match-winning knocks of 43 and 47 in the next two games against the hosts. He led India in the first of those games following Sourav's suspension for one match. The captain of India had incurred the wrath of the ICC Referee once again, this time for expressing his displeasure at being given out leg-before.

Rahul's twin forties were complemented by fine knocks of 87 and 98 by VVS Laxman and Yuvraj Singh respectively. Both batsmen came in for praise; Laxman defied a knee injury that forced him to miss the rest of the tour and Yuvraj essayed his first noteworthy innings since his 84 against Australia in the ICC Knockout. Millions of Tendulkar fans had a sense of deja vu in the final league game against New Zealand, after the Indians were set a stiff target of 265. In came Virender Sehwag, the 'Tendulkar of Najafgarh', who took the Kiwis to the cleaners with a sizzling 69-ball hundred. Rahul (57) and Badani (35) completed what he had started by securing a comfortable win with 4.2 overs to spare.

The final against Sri Lanka sealed India's reputation as the 'chokers' of the cricketing world. They lost by 121 runs. It was their eighth straight defeat in the final of a limited-overs tournament involving three or more teams, starting with the loss to Pakistan at Bengaluru in March 1999.

There was another thrashing in the first Test at Galle by a quadrangular seam attack and Muttiah Muralitharan. India went down for only 187 in the first innings, and a joyous Jayasuriya banged a century. Muralitharan tied the Indian batsmen in knots after Sri Lanka had secured a lead of 175. The performance of the Indian batsmen in both innings was abysmal, with one exception.

> 'None of the batsmen except Dravid showed any application and most of them were out to injudicious shots. Dravid stood like a rock among the ruins, displaying a lot of character and determination to fight.'
>
> —*The Tribune*, Chandigarh, 17 August 2001

India were a hopeless 130-8 at stumps on the third day, still 45 runs in arrears. With Srinath not slated to bat due to a finger injury, the Lankans were only one wicket away from completing a 'hattrick' of innings wins at Galle after humiliating South Africa and England in similar fashion in previous series.

Rahul and Venkatesh Prasad salvaged some pride by wiping out the deficit, although the final lead was only five.

The defeat delighted the detractors of the out-of-form Indian captain. The onus was on him to rally his despondent team and silence his critics. He started the second Test at Kandy on a positive note by winning the toss and electing to field on a juicy' pitch, topped by an overcast sky. Most captains who were down 0-1 in an overseas series would have opted for the conventional 'bat-first' approach, more to protect their side from the menace of Murali on a deteriorating pitch in the fourth innings than anything else. But then, Sourav Ganguly was different.

India scored 232 in response to Sri Lanka's 274, and the hosts were 52 for the loss of Jayasuriya in their second innings at the end of day three. 'The only way the home team can lose is by getting complacent,' Ravi Shastri, former Indian captain-turned-commentator stated before the start on day four.

That was exactly what happened, much to the delight of the Indians. The batsmen played some loose strokes and came apart against the new-ball duo of Prasad and Zaheer Khan. At 157-9, a famous Indian win seemed on the cards, when Muralitharan played one of the most entertaining—and for the Indians, exasperating—knocks of all time. He got to 64 before Harbhajan had him caught in the deep. The 'chokers' needed 264 to win. Memories of their struggle at Chennai earlier in the year were relatively fresh, and not many gave them a chance.

Das and Ramesh started well, adding 42 before the former played at Murali, missed and was bowled. The end of the day's play was only a few overs away and the light poor. It was a situation in which most teams with a defensive mindset would have sent out a night-watchman to 'protect' the mainstays. But

Rahul, by now restored to the number three slot, thanks to a series of exhilarating Laxman cameos that promised a lot but could not become classics, walked in. It was a bold move. He got off the blocks with a fluent on-driven boundary off Murali, and held on until the umpires offered the light.

Rahul and Ramesh took the score to 103 on the fourth morning when the opener fell, caught by Jayasuriya off Fernando. In came Sourav Ganguly, with much more than the match at stake.

It was a day when the seniors needed to summon all their reserves of concentration and resolve against a team already leading in the series, having in its ranks one of the greatest wicket-takers of all time. Rahul essayed a classic. He played Murali like a master, his eyes riveted on the bowler's wrist before the ball was released, trying to anticipate what lay in store for him, his eyes then following the cherry itself as it descended onto the pitch and hissed off it. Rahul defied deliveries pitched on middle-and-off with his bat well in front of his front (left) pad. He thrust out his front foot to turners that were pitched wide outside the off-stick, off which there was no possibility of the umpire upholding a leg-before shout. He utilized Murali's prodigious turn brilliantly, waiting till the very last moment to nudge incoming deliveries 'around the leg-side corner' for singles and twos. The rare bad ball that Murali bowled, he gave it the treatment. He got six of his first eight boundaries off Murali. Rahul's footwork was immaculate, his timing precise.

But Murali would not let him relax. In the 46th over, his 14th of the innings, he bowled two vicious deliveries that pitched outside off and skidded inwards, which Rahul just about managed to keep out. Rahul's grit inspired Sourav to take on the off-spinner. The Indian captain confounded Murali in his next over by using his feet. Murali, whose stock ball was the one that spun away from left-handers, had not expected an out-of-form southpaw to leave his crease against him. Perplexed, the bowler responded with a short delivery, expecting the left-hander to come down the wicket again. But Sourav leaned back to cut it to the boundary. It was Test match cricket at its glorious best. India went into lunch at 151-2. All they needed to do in the second session was to maintain the momentum of the first.

Rahul executed two scintillating boundaries after the break; an on-drive off Murali for four, and a cover-drive off Jayasuriya that was placed just wide of the man posted at short extra-cover, with no 'cover' behind him. An enthralling duel ended when Rahul committed his first major mistake of the innings, playing a straighter delivery by Murali with his bat alongside the pad and not in front as he had done all along. The ball hit his pad, then his bat, and the silly-point fielder did the rest. He had scored an impeccable 75.

Sourav batted splendidly in the company of Mohammed Kaif to knock off the remaining 70 runs. The skipper was unlucky to remain unbeaten on 98, but it had been a defining 'Test' of his aptitude as batsman and captain. It was the highest total chased by India to win a Test since the successful pursuit of 403 at Port of Spain in 1975-76. The enormity of the achievement, India's first Test win in Sri Lanka since 1993, could be gauged by the fact that the team was without four frontline players: Tendulkar, Laxman, Srinath and Kumble.

The smiles on Indian faces vanished in four days. India started superbly on a featherbed in the third Test at Colombo with the openers putting on 97, but Murali then put them through the shredder with a sensational bowling display. He took eight wickets in all at a cost of 87 runs. The Indians then bowled atrociously and fielded abysmally to allow four Sri Lankan batsmen to score hundreds and take a lead of 376. But all hope was not lost, as the track did not seem to have any demons in it. For the second time in the game, Ramesh and Das gave a good account of themselves with a century-stand. Das' dismissal at 107 set the stage for another back-to-the-wall performance by Rahul, who had got 36 in the first innings. He added 40 with Ramesh before Murali dislodged the latter's off-bail with what was described as the off-spinner's equivalent of Shane Warne's 'Ball of the Century'. The ball pitched on leg and spun past Ramesh's bat to take the off-bail. India needed the captain and vice-captain to repeat their Kandy duet, but Marvan Atapattu played spoilsport with a direct hit at the non-striker's end to run out Rahul. Once again, a Sourav-Rahul stand had ended with a run-out, and yet again, Rahul's dismissal was followed by a collapse. The score 186-3 became 211-6, and the innings ended at 299 on the fourth day after some enterprising hitting by Zaheer Khan. The Kandy win apart, a positive for the team was Rahul's completion of 4,000 Test runs in only his 48th Test.

The defeat in Sri Lanka notwithstanding, Sourav Ganguly was a happy man as the team boarded the plane for South Africa in October 2001, where India were to play a tri-series and three Tests. The return of Srinath, Kumble, Laxman (for the Tests) and Tendulkar meant that he was leading a full-strength Indian team for the first time since his appointment as Test captain. But a lower back injury to Sadagoppan Ramesh, who had forged a good opening combination with Das, upset the apple-cart, as did a mediocre showing in the tri-series that preceded the Tests, wherein the team's performances oscillated from the awesome to the awful.

During the tri-series, Rahul, who had been troubled by a pain in the right shoulder for four years, decided to consult a doctor.

> 'Cricketers tend to develop shoulder-niggles because of persistent throwing while fielding. Rahul had what is called a labrum tear in his right shoulder. The doctor whom we approached advised an operation, but Rahul and I decided to adopt the conservative approach of training and rehabilitation. We reasoned that he would not be doing much of throwing, as he fielded in the slips most of the time. Rahul started doing some special exercises. He then spent a month in South Africa for the rehab, due to which he missed the one-day series against England later in the season. The shoulder has been okay since then.'
>
> —ANDREW LEIPUS

Rahul did well in the tri-series with three fifties against South Africa, including an unbeaten 77 in the final in which his teammates made no attempt to shed their 'choker' tag. He had prepared assiduously for his second trip to South Africa, having requisitioned a new set of bats with a slightly higher 'sweet spot'. The objective obviously was to counter the extra bounce on South African wickets. But what he hadn't prepared for was a return to the opening slot. The management was reluctant to try out the rookie Connor Williams, which meant that the most malleable member of the team had to do the job in the first Test at Bloemfontein. A week previously, Rahul had chipped in as wicketkeeper in the last two games of the tri-series, after the team management decided to give the struggling Deep Dasgupta, India's fifth one-day gloveman of the new millennium, a break.

The 'opening' experiment failed, and so did India despite a sensational first day's cricket, on which Tendulkar and his 'disciple' Virender Sehwag scored marvellous hundreds, the latter becoming the eleventh Indian to score a hundred on Test debut.

> 'I was considered a one-day specialist until then. I remember Rahul telling me before that game to concentrate on Test cricket, as success in that format defined a true cricketer more than success in ODIs.'
>
> —Virender Sehwag

South Africa made 563 in response to India's 379, and Shaun Pollock then bowled a captain's spell to eliminate the Indians for only 237 in the second innings, setting up a nine-wicket win for his team. Rahul scored two and 11.

India went into the second Test at Port Elizabeth in a state of confusion, the cause of which was the 'top-order' conundrum. With none of the middle-order batsmen keen on opening, the team management promoted Dasgupta, who had made his Test debut at Bloemfontein after Sameer Dighe, the senior keeper, hurt his back minutes before the start.

Dasgupta's chance to accompany Das to the middle came late on the second day after South Africa had amassed 362. The Indian reply was a meagre 201. But the bowlers hit back, and the Proteas were in a spot of bother at 139-5 on the third day when Kallis and Pollock got together to bail them out. They held their nerve against accurate and aggressive bowling, supported by a testy cordon of close-in fielders who did what members of their tribe generally did—support the bowlers, indulge in a bit of gamesmanship, all within accepted parameters.

But Mike Denness, the Referee, had evidently seen something that the world had missed. He placed six Indian players in the dock; Das, Dasgupta, Harbhajan Singh and Sehwag for 'intimidating the umpires', Sourav for not 'controlling his players', and Tendulkar for 'ball-tampering'. While five of the players got 'suspended' sentences, Sehwag was actually suspended from the next Test. These announcements led to acrimony. Indian Parliamentarians cried foul, the Indian public burnt effigies of 'Denness the Menace' and Indian cricket administrators threatened to call off the tour. That a Test match was in progress was all but forgotten.

The Indians were 28-1 at stumps on the fourth day, and needed to bat out a whole day to save the game. The man best qualified for the job took the initiative. Aided by the dour Dasgupta, Rahul batted with poise against a South African outfit wanting to capitalize on the turmoil in the opposition camp. He displayed astute judgement on a track that had assisted the bowlers on all five days. The stand yielded 171 runs, a draw, and smiles. Rahul's 87 was not a match-winning innings like the 75 at Kandy, but it was certainly a morale-boosting one.

> 'We were determined to draw the Test. The entire team was out on the gallery, encouraging Rahul and Deep. This is something one rarely sees.'
>
> —VVS Laxman

The ICC withdrew the 'official' status of the third Test when the South African Cricket Board, under pressure from its own

Government that did not want its relations with India to get strained, took a unilateral decision to appoint Denis Lindsay as Referee in place of Denness. But the Indian team was told by the BCCI to treat it as an official game. Rahul cut a dapper figure in the India blazer and cap as he accompanied Pollock for the toss after Sourav pulled out due to a neck strain. Sehwag was 'benched' to ensure that he fulfilled his sentence in case the match gained 'official' status later. Indian cricket-lovers were glad that it didn't, for their team, the one that was instructed to take the match seriously, was soundly beaten by a team that had treated it as an unofficial encounter from ball one.

The Indian team followed an all too predictable script for the next seven months. They beat England at home in a three-Test series. After the victory came a spell of under-performing, and a grateful England levelled the six-match one-day series. Rahul, who averaged an impressive 40 in the Tests, gave the one-day series a miss to tend to his shoulder.

After the English came the Zimbabweans for their second India tour in a little over a year. India won both the Tests, but not before getting a massive scare in the second game at Delhi, where they lost six wickets en route to a target of 115. The first innings was dominated by Sourav, who promoted himself to number three and scored 136, his first Test hundred as captain. Rahul did not complain about losing the one-down spot once again, but he had reason to be miffed when he was run out yet again with his captain at the other end!

The Zimbabweans took the confidence they had gained at Delhi into the one-day series, where they gained a 2-1 lead. The fourth game, a 'day-nighter' at Hyderabad, looked to be going their way when Rahul fell for a subdued 32. India at that stage needed a further 109 from 112 balls. With Sourav and Laxman already in the pavilion and Tendulkar and Sehwag not playing due to injury, Rahul's dismissal was seen as the final nail in the Indian coffin, but the 'Young Turks' rose to the occasion. Yuvraj Singh, recalled for this series after being dropped post-South Africa, and Mohammed Kaif batted superbly to square the series. Their partnership of 94 was the precursor to another outstanding performance later in the year. A magnificent 159 by Dinesh Mongia, another new face, in the final game at Guwahati settled the series in India's favour.

Sourav retained the number three spot in India's first

Test on their tour of the Caribbean, which began a couple of weeks after the Zimbabwe series. West Indies batted first at Georgetown to score 501, with skipper Carl Hooper flaying 233. Although Tendulkar and Laxman scored fifties and there were frequent rain-interruptions as was always the case in Guyana, the Indians did not get out of jail until Sarandeep Singh joined Rahul at 275-7 and played the kind of innings that Shivlal Yadav, one of his esteemed off-spinning seniors, had patented during his playing days. Rahul was on 59 when he ducked into a short-pitched delivery by Mervyn Dillon and received a nasty crack on the visor of his helmet. He had the option of coming off for repairs, but he chose not to and fought on after some cursory on-field treatment. He reached his hundred, the tenth of his Test career, with a gorgeous on-drive off Adam Sanford. His undefeated 144, a gritty match-saving effort, made his return to the number three slot a foregone conclusion.

The first innings of the next Test, an unforgettable one for India, witnessed a century-stand between the two top batsmen of the previous trip. Both Rahul and Tendulkar had scored plenty of runs in 1996-97 without reaching triple figures. Rahul had broken the jinx in the first Test of the 2001-02 series, and now it was Tendulkar's turn with his 29th Test hundred, which brought him on par with the Don. The other batsmen did their bit—Laxman with 69 and 74, and Sourav with 75 in the second innings. Superb bowling on the final day took India to a historic win, their first in the Caribbean since 1976. Against a West Indies outfit past its best, the Indians fancied their chances of creating history by winning the series, but not for nothing were they considered masters of self-destruction. They lost the next Test at Bridgetown, the third time since Bulawayo that they had won a Test overseas, only to lose the next. They were never in the game after their dismissal for 102 on the first day. Sourav waged a lone battle with 48, a knock played with blood on his hands after being involved in yet another Rahul run-out!

Rahul's 91 in the fourth Test at Antigua was obscured by five hundreds and Anil Kumble, who broke a jaw while batting and returned to the middle in a valiant bid to keep India's hopes alive. He dismissed Lara, but had to come off after bowling 14 overs. The match ended farcically with Rahul, Laxman and opener Wasim Jaffer, who had scored a fine 86 in India's only innings, taking their first Test wickets.

The Indian batting flopped, technically and cerebrally, in both innings of the final Test at Kingston. India were 237-7 at stumps on day four, their hopes of achieving a target of 408 having long vanished. But the dark clouds that were hovering over the ground on the fifth morning had a silver lining. All the Indian tail-enders had to do was hang on for an hour or so, and the series would end in a 1-1 stalemate. But they folded up in just 51 deliveries. The downpour began around 20 minutes later, when Hooper was posing with the Winners' trophy, and did not relent for the next ten days.

Rahul finished the Test series with 404 runs at 57.71, the second-best for India after Laxman, who ended a year-long streak of sweet cameos with some decisive outings, including a century and four fifties.

The Indian vice-captain's performances had endorsed what he had demonstrated right through 2001 that he was one for the trenches, who excelled when the going got tough.

The going was to get even tougher. So was Rahul.

9

# THE GREAT QUARTET

'Everyone praises Sachin Tendulkar. He may be a genius in his own right but in my book, Rahul Dravid is the artist. Dravid's defence tactics, his strokes, his cuts, his grace are truly amazing. I'd like to meet the chap sometime and take my hat off to him.'

—PETER O'TOOLE, *MID-DAY*, 23 MAY 2004

It was quite appropriate that Rahul chose England, the land where he made his formal entry into Test cricket in 1996, where he did so well in the World Cup in 1999 and excelled as a professional in 2000, to complete his metamorphosis from 'good' to 'great'.

After outplaying the West Indies in the one-day series that followed the Tests, the Indians started their tour of England with some splendid performances in a tri-series against the hosts and Sri Lanka. The 'men in blue' beat England in a humdinger of a final.

England hit back with a comprehensive 170-run win in the first Test. Nasser Hussain, who scored a hundred on the first day, did not enforce the follow-on after bowling the Indians out for 221, 266 runs behind. England set India a Himalayan 568 to win, and the Indians batted like mountaineers trying to climb the Himalayas without ropes, protective gear and oxygen masks. Ajit Agarkar helped himself to a strokeful century, prompting many to speculate on the value he could add to the side if he were to consistently score even half as many runs in pressure-situations. Rahul scored 46 and 63, but Sourav had a poor game with 5 and 0, as did Tendulkar with 16 and 12.

Virender Sehwag, India's latest 'convert' to the opening position, scored 106 on the first day of the second Test at Nottingham, thus debunking the theory that he would struggle in the 'seaming and swinging' English conditions with his 'unorthodox' batting style. A 68 by Sourav and a thrill-a-minute 54 by Harbhajan helped India reach 357. Frequent interruptions for rain and bad light on the first two days, not to mention the efforts of Sehwag, Ganguly and Harbhajan, ensured that the hosts began their first innings only on the third day.

Michael Vaughan top-scored with 197 in a total of 617, and India, 260 behind, needed to bat out nearly four sessions to save the game.

The three seniors led the way, scoring heavily and crucially, staying in for a long time. Tendulkar scored 92 and Sourav the second 99 of his Test career, but Rahul stood out. Nothing the bowlers hurled at him on that fifth-day wicket, nothing they moved away or into him, had an adverse effect on his resolve to battle it out. He scored a magnificent 115. Agarkar, clearly in the batting form of his life, scored 32 to add to his 34 in the first innings, and the seventeen-year-old debutant Parthiv Patel defended well in the last hour-and-a-half.

The draw lifted spirits in the Indian dressing room. The team had proved to its supporters and to itself that it possessed the perseverance to keep a rampaging opponent at bay. A positive and proactive attitude would take them to the next level.

Then came Headingley.

When a future historian sits down to pen the history of Indian cricket, he will mark the third Test of the 2002 series between India and England as a watershed, for a sensational performance that was set-up by two sensational 'un-Indian' decisions on the eve of the game.

Headingley, at Leeds in the county of Yorkshire, has always been a fast and swing bowler's paradise. The wicket traditionally is on the greener side and the conditions generally overcast, a dream setting for young men who like to bend their backs and run in to propel seaming and swinging thunderbolts at the batsmen. In such conditions, a batting side needs application and determination, along with some luck. A decent start amounts to winning half the battle.

The Indian think-tank had decided to drop Wasim Jaffer from the playing eleven despite his 53 at Lord's, leaving two contenders for the slot of Sehwag's opening partner—Shiv Sunder Das and Sanjay Bangar. The competitors were slated to have a joint selection trial in the form of the three-day game against Essex prior to the third Test. Much to the duo's delight, Sourav won the toss and elected to bat.

The score was 60 when Bangar was bowled for only 21. The Railways all-rounder, who had made it to the Indian team less than a year ago after doing the grind in the domestic circuit for years, trudged back to the pavilion after his dismissal, wondering whether he had blown it. On the other hand, his partner batted on, on and on. When Das fell after nine hours of solid batsmanship, he had scored 250, the second-highest individual first-class score by an Indian on English soil after Polly Umrigar's 252 against Cambridge University in 1959. Bangar opened with Parthiv Patel in the second innings and scored 74. Decent, yes, but was it as good as 250?

The Indian think-tank reckoned that it was! They took cognisance of Bangar's patience and technique, as also his ability as a medium-pacer who could move the ball around, a skill that could come in handy on that track, and picked him for the Test ahead of a batsman who had scored 250!

Then came decision number two. Standing on a green pitch under a 'loaded' sky, Sourav called correctly and told his counterpart that India would bat first. On that wicket, in those conditions, it seemed like the cricketing equivalent of biting a cyanide pill.

Any other Indian team would have picked the more prolific opener and opted to field first in those conditions. Not so Sourav's India.

Sehwag's dismissal with only 15 on the board set the tongues wagging. Sourav's decision was even likened to the disastrous call taken by Azharuddin at Lord's in 1990. At Headingley in 2002, in walked Rahul, at a stage in his career when his opponents would have undoubtedly seen the tricolour fluttering proudly behind him. A steely glance at Bangar and a quick reconnaissance of the field later, he got down to business. Deliveries pitched in the corridor of uncertainty were watched closely and either ignored or played cautiously. The priority was not to give the opposition another wicket. Deliveries that were off-line, he placed into the gaps for singles and twos. Those pitched short and which he could not make much of, he took on his body. At the other end, Bangar observed, imbibed and emulated. Of course, when the rank bad ball presented itself, both batsmen made sure that they dispatched it to the boundary. Not that there were too many of those in the first session.

Matthew Hoggard, Andrew Caddick, Alex Tudor and Andrew Flintoff were enjoying the conditions, and eager to exploit them to the fullest. However, their enjoyment declined as over followed wicketless over, with the first drinks interval giving way to lunch and later, the first drinks interval of the second session. They had aimed at testing the patience of the Indian batsmen with a tight line and hustling them with deliveries aimed at the ribcage. But here were two batsmen who were quite prepared to take a few knocks and battle on. The chagrin of the bowlers soon gave way to exasperation and consequently, a dip in their accuracy and efficiency. Exactly what Rahul and Bangar wanted to achieve.

The partnership lasted well into the third session, until Bangar nicked Flintoff to Alec Stewart for the best 68 in Indian cricket history. The score was 185-2.

> 'It was a nasty track with uneven bounce. Rahul and Sanjay Bangar batted brilliantly in the first two sessions and took many blows on their body. But they did not take a backward step. It was past tea, after more than four hours of play, when I went in, and the wicket was still damp. Bits of grass were still coming off and the ball was creating depressions when it hit the pitch. So you can imagine how the wicket must have been like in the morning. As

it started drying, it became even more uneven. That was certainly one of Rahul's best innings.'

—Sachin Tendulkar

Rahul, who by then was seeing the ball like a football, 'greeted' Tendulkar to the crease with two fours off a Tudor over. He had done the hard work, and the time had come to reap the rewards against a flagging attack. He clipped Hoggard to the square-leg boundary for four to complete his second Test hundred of the series and certainly one of his best, if not 'the' best. He was 110 not out at stumps. It had been a marvellous exhibition of application and character.

The press and pundits pilloried the English bowlers for bowling short and wide and not making the Indian batsmen play enough with a 'fuller' line of attack. But the bowling on the second morning was as uninspiring as it had been on the first afternoon. The first two balls of day two, bowled by Hoggard, went down the leg-side, and Caddick's first delivery of the next over was a juicy loosener on the leg-stump that Rahul directed to the mid-wicket boundary, the ball going past short mid-wicket. Ravi Shastri, watching from the commentary box, was quick to point out that most Indian batsmen would have rolled their wrists quickly at the point of impact to dispatch the ball just in front of square or even behind square (on either side of the square-leg umpire). But Rahul had been able to direct it well in front, in the mid-wicket area, simply because he had played it late with the full face of his bat. This was an indicator of the rich form he was in.

The bounce remained as uneven as ever, but Rahul stayed focussed. His technique was impeccable, his powers of concentration intense.

> 'Rahul loves to read biographies of sports personalities, not necessarily cricketers. He has always been very interested in finding out how different sports personalities prepare themselves 'mentally' before big events. I have never met anyone so focussed. It is extremely difficult to get through to him even when he is reading a book or watching television. I have to say, I pity his wife!'
>
> —Andrew Leipus

Connoisseurs at Headingley had a lump in their throats when Rahul, after being confounded by a short-pitched delivery from Caddick that kept low, took a fresh guard before facing the next ball. This when he was well past a hundred!

Tendulkar, who was looking ominous at the other end, completed his fifty with his ninth four, his own variation of Kapil Dev's 'Nataraja' pull. The stand had realized 150 when Rahul was beaten by Ashley Giles' flight and smartly stumped by Stewart for a classy 148. Sourav Ganguly and Tendulkar then demonstrated their appreciation of Rahul's batsmanship with a breathtaking attack that at one point yielded 90 runs from only ten overs. Sourav scored 128 and Tendulkar, who overhauled the Don's tally of 29 Test hundreds, fell short of a double hundred by only seven runs in the dash for a declaration. India finished with 628-8, and then the bowlers took over. England were bowled out for 273 and 309, leaving India victors by an innings and 46 runs.

Everything had gone according to plan—the early weathering of the storm, followed by a hell-for-leather stand, and then, a superb bowling and fielding performance, even by the spinners who were expected to come a cropper on that strip. Sanjay Bangar chipped in with two wickets to vindicate the management's faith in him.

Tendulkar did not receive the Man of the Match award although he had made the highest individual score in the match. A season or two ago, this would have been unthinkable. But such was the quality of Rahul's innings that it put everything else in the shade.

Coming as it did on the heels of Kolkata and Kandy, Rahul's 148 established him as India's greatest Test-winning batsman alongside Tendulkar; one of the most luminous stars in India's cricketing firmament. It was wonderfully appropriate that he produced the best innings of his career in what was India's biggest Test win overseas.

Two years later, he would make another monumental contribution to an even bigger overseas win, this time across the border.

The fact that the players had more on their mind than cricket made the Leeds victory even more memorable. The ICC's commitment to deny branding opportunities to competitors of its official sponsors during the forthcoming ICC Knockout (renamed the Champions Trophy) in Sri Lanka and the World Cup in Africa had led to a stand-off between the parent body, the BCCI and the superstars in the Indian line-up, some of whom were bound by contracts to the 'competitors', which had been signed long before the ICC entered into the agreement with its sponsors. There was even talk of the frontline Indian players pulling out of the tournament and the subsequent World Cup. A compromise was subsequently 'scratched' out.

The series, one that had featured some brilliant batting

performances by players from both sides, ended with another 'batathon' at the Oval in London, traditionally the venue of the last Test of the English summer. On a batsman's paradise, England amassed 515 with Michael Vaughan scoring 195, his third hundred of the series. India were 87-2 when Tendulkar, playing in his 100th Test, joined Rahul in the middle. The next three wickets produced stands of 91, 105, and 113, as the Indians also made certain that they would not lose and thus go home with honours even. These three partnerships had two things in common.

The first was Rahul, who for the third consecutive time in the English season, batted gracefully and gloriously to complete a hattrick of Test hundreds. His defence was immaculate, his strokes inspirational, his 'leaves' impeccable.

> 'If a Martian were to land on earth now and be told that the best batsman in the world was playing in this match, he would think it was Rahul Dravid and not Sachin Tendulkar.'
>
> —Christopher Martin-Jenkins, during the Oval Test

The second was the strange tactics of the English bowlers, who repeated their Headingley blunder and kept banging it in short. The worst offender was Dominic Cork, who had ostensibly been picked to bowl the length that Bangar had bowled so well at Headingley. But there was obviously a communication gap, and not many English supporters were amused to see Cork 'testing' Rahul with deliveries that were sailing harmlessly over the batsman's head, that too after the batsman was past 150! Rahul let the bowler spend himself physically and verbally, before taking him apart with two spectacular pulls in one over.

He then did an encore off Tudor, driving him on the up and cutting him magnificently in the same over. He moved to 199 with a straight-driven four off Hoggard.

The spectators rose when Rahul glanced Hoggard for a single and set off in celebratory style for his 200th run. It was the perfect finale to an unforgettable series. He was on 217, only four short of the then highest individual score by an Indian in a Test overseas (made by Sunil Gavaskar coincidentally on the same ground exactly 23 years ago), when he was run out in a mix-up with Ajay Ratra. As he ambled off to another standing ovation, there were no prizes for guessing the cliche that was uppermost in everybody's minds—that was the only way he looked like getting out!

The series ended in a stalemate, but Indian fans were not complaining after what they had witnessed at Nottingham, Leeds and London. Rahul's aggregate of 602 was the highest by an Indian in a Test series since Sunil Gavaskar's 732 runs from six Tests against the West Indies in 1978-79.

> 'The four consecutive Test hundreds were a monumental achievement, and a reflection of his determination to cash in on good form and not get easily satisfied. It was a living example of what it means to have a "hunger for runs."'
>
> —Sharda Ugra

Rahul had little time to savour his prodigious feats as the Indians travelled from cool and cosy England to hot and humid Sri Lanka for the ICC Champions Trophy. They were on course for the title when rain intervened and the trophy had to be shared with the hosts.

India's next assignment, a Test series against the West Indies at home, began with an unprecedented occurrence. For the first time since he made his debut in 1989-90, the spotlight was not on Tendulkar. Gavaskar had scored four hundreds in successive Tests twice in his career, but even he hadn't done so in four consecutive innings. Rahul was within striking distance of a special landmark, and nobody who met him on the eve of the first Test at Mumbai let him forget it.

The man who had batted for over 30 hours in England arrived at the wicket on the first day with India 201-1. Bangar had departed after playing another fine supporting hand, this time to Sehwag, who literally 'toyed' with the West Indian bowling. The swashbuckler scored 147.

India were 278-2 at stumps and looked headed for the moon. The West Indies had looked despondent on the first day, but they started day two on a positive note with two quick strikes, sending back Tendulkar and Sourav. The arrival of the strokeful Laxman induced Carl Hooper to go on the defensive. Leg-spinner Mahendra Nagamattoo kept pitching it into the bowler's rough outside the leg-stump from round-the-wicket, and the runs dried up. But Rahul, who was batting with the assurance of a man in form, and Laxman were quite content to play the waiting game, aware that the wicket was only likely to get worse for batting, and better for Kumble and Harbhajan.

As Rahul moved closer to the record-books, all those hours in the middle and Mumbai's October humidity started taking their toll. He had his heart in his mouth when he did not time a pull off Nagamattoo as well as he should have, only for it to fall short of Chanderpaul on the mid-wicket boundary. To add insult to injury, the ball ricocheted off the fielder's arm to the boundary.

Rahul regained his poise with a flicked boundary off Pedro Collins, and then essayed a cracking pull off Nagamattoo that had deep square-leg and deep mid-wicket almost colliding with each other in vain pursuit, to bring up the 400 of the innings. Laxman fell at the stroke of tea, but the crowd didn't notice.

Rahul was on 98, two short of becoming only the fourth batsman in Test history after Australian Jack Fingleton, South African Alan Melville and West Indian Everton Weekes to score a quartet of hundreds in consecutive innings, when he played Dillon on the leg-side for what looked like a boundary. He had advanced five steps when he clutched his left thigh with a horrific expression on his face. He somehow reached the other end, turned and stopped in what appeared to be uncontrollable agony. But so had the ball in the outfield. Parthiv Patel, who had dashed halfway down the wicket after completing the first run, turned to return to the striker's end after noticing Rahul's discomfiture. But he changed his mind when he saw his partner going for the second run. Rahul, who realized that there was no way he could continue his innings after that attack of cramps, hopped and hobbled along to make his ground and enter the record-books. He had to be helped off the field, but he and his team were satisfied with a job well done.

> 'I don't think anyone has contributed to the team as much as he has in varied roles, and that too consistently. Rahul's innate sense of discipline is reflected in his cricket. His achievements were never highlighted. It was only when the others were not as consistent, that he was written and spoken about. The fact is that he has been an achiever all along. He was always there when the team needed him,

> scoring 50s, 100s and 200s in crucial situations. I suppose it's a way of life, wherein the more flamboyant people are noticed more than those who do their job silently. Another reason he hasn't got what he deserves is that the number of people who understand the nuances of the game has declined. The media is partly to blame, for not explaining to the public that a ten in a do-or-die situation is often more valuable than a slam-bang hundred made when there is no pressure. Such has been the enormity of his achievements in recent times that the media and consequently the public have had to salute him.'
>
> —Anshuman Gaekwad

The spinners finished off the Mumbai Test in style on the fourth day, taking India to victory by an innings and 112 runs.

Fortunately, there was nothing seriously wrong with Rahul, and he was declared fit for the next Test at Chennai. On the eve of the game came another honour, to add to all the encomiums he had been bestowed with.

His 1302 runs from 16 Tests and 789 runs from 26 one-day internationals, not to mention his contribution behind the wickets in the 12 months from 1 October 2001 to 30 September 2002, made him the undisputed Castrol Indian Cricketer* of 2001-02, the second time he had won the Award after 1998-99. Rahul received the Award at a star-studded function in Chennai, in front of several former cricketers and his own teammates. An exchange between him and the MC Harsha Bhogle, shortly after he accepted the award, encapsulated the man and his mindset.

---

*The annual Castrol Awards for Cricketing Excellence were presented to Indian cricket's top performers, from 1997-98 to the late 2000s.

Harsha: *1302 runs from 16 Tests, Kandy, Port Elizabeth, Georgetown and Headingley. Was this the best cricket of your life?*

Rahul: *I hope not. I hope I can keep getting better.*

Harsha: *What's the secret of your patience? 31 hours in England and it seems it wasn't enough.*

Rahul (sheepishly): *The secret is that if I need to score runs, I need to bat that long! I am not Sehwag or Sachin who can do it quicker. I have figured out that this is the only way I can do it, so I better do it this way!*

# 10

## ALL-ROUNDER

> 'Rahul's commitment to Indian cricket is summed up by the fact that he has been keeping wickets in ODIs because the team needs it, and not because he likes it or is the best at it.'
>
> —Murali Kartik

'What should India do to win the 2003 World Cup?' was the subject of a Panel Discussion in Mumbai in March 2002. The panel comprised former international cricketers Ian Chappell, Sanjay Manjrekar and Yajurvindra Singh, and advertising guru Piyush Pandey. While the cricketers were at their diplomatic best, Pandey was blunt. *'India doesn't have a chance in hell!'* he chortled. Not many people in the audience were inclined to disagree with him.

Twelve months before the game's premier event, the Indian limited-overs outfit, was in a sorry state. The over-dependence on Tendulkar and Ganguly was sickening, the lack of consistency distressing. The think-tank was aware that for India to have any chance at all in the World Cup, the team needed to start preparing well in advance. Gone were the days in which one preparatory camp on the eve of the tournament, would serve the purpose. In any case, India's post-1983 record showed that it hadn't.

Both Sourav and Wright believed that tough decisions, if they had to be taken, ought to concern the senior players and not the juniors. They backed the seniors' ability to inspire the juniors by adapting to new roles and responsibilities. Batting was the team's strength. In seniors like Tendulkar, Sehwag, Rahul, Laxman, and Ganguly himself, and youngsters like Dinesh Mongia, Yuvraj and Kaif, India had batsmen capable of getting any total. It was imperative that as many of these had to play together.

Accordingly, two 'tough' decisions were taken before the one-day series in the Caribbean in May 2002, both of them involving senior players. Sachin Tendulkar's job-description was changed from 'opening aggressor' to 'mid-innings stabiliser', and Rahul was asked to keep wicket to enable India to play seven specialist batsmen.

He had not performed that role in competitive cricket for several years, save the odd game. His acceptance of an unfamiliar and potentially hazardous responsibility endeared him to his teammates and fans.

> 'He was not sure whether it would work but he was willing to try to see if it helped the team. When it did and the results began to show, he was convinced. At no stage, and I mean this completely honestly, at NO stage in any interaction with him did he complain about doing the extra physical work or complain or fear that keeping would cut his career

> short or that it would take too much of a toll.'
>
> —Sharda Ugra

Some former cricketers described the move as 'unfair'. What if he sustained an injury that could adversely affect his batting abilities, they asked. But then, didn't Rahul always see the glass as half-full?

> 'We had a discussion about-his being asked to keep wickets in one-dayers. We talked about the positives and decided that he had an opportunity to judge every ball from behind the stumps. When he would go in to bat, all he would have to do is change his response. He was tremendously focussed on the game as it is. I believe keeping helped him sharpen his batting skills.'
>
> —B.P. Bam

India's 'seven batsmen-four bowlers' experiment got off to a flying-start with a 2-1 win in the one-dayers against the West Indies in May 2002, and impressive performances in the league games of the tri-series in England in June-July. Rahul batted superbly to score three fifties, an unbeaten 82 in an abandoned game against the hosts being his best performance. His best knock was an undefeated 73 against the home team at Lord's, where he and Yuvraj Singh steered India to a six-wicket win with an undefeated stand of 131. Everything seemed hunky-dory until the Indians ran into rough weather, quite predictably, in the final. England amassed 325-5, and India were 146-5 in the 24th over, with all the senior players back on the Lord's balcony. A tenth consecutive loss in a one day final seemed imminent, but Yuvraj Singh and Mohammed Kaif didn't think so. They

SAHARA
INDIA
SAHA

brought their team back into the match with one of the most glorious rearguard actions in the history of the sport. Yuvraj departed after a 121-run partnership, but Kaif carried on, and the Indian contingent, players as well as spectators, went berserk when he and Zaheer Khan ran an overthrow off the third ball of the final over to complete an incredible win. The Indian players and supporters displayed their joy, their captain his torso!

The reactions to that one win vividly illustrated the Indian penchant for overreaction. The 'no-hopers' suddenly became the frontrunners for the World Cup. While it was true that the 'team' was looking and playing like one more consistently, Tendulkar was no longer expected to stage a 'one-man show', and the players were fitter than ever before and fielding like never before, one swallow did not make a summer. History was also not on India's side. Rarely had they played well when considered 'favourites'.

But September 2002 was an exception. The Indians played like champions in the third edition of the ICC Knockout (reformatted and renamed the Champions Trophy) in Sri Lanka, to prove that their win in the tri-series was not a fluke. There was a minor flutter in their opening game when they found themselves 87-5 against Zimbabwe, a suicidal state to be in on a batting belter. After the top order had succumbed to some cavalier strokes, it fell on the 'stayers' to steer their team out of trouble. Mohammed Kaif, in his first international outing after the 87 in the tri-series final at Lord's, scored an unbeaten 111 and Rahul lent able support with 71. They took India to 288-6, and not even a hundred by India's 'old friend' Andy Flower could win the match for Zimbabwe.

Sehwag annihilated England in the next league game with

126 from 104 balls, and Sourav helped himself to an unbeaten 117. This one-sided affair was followed by a 'Great Escape' in the semifinal against South Africa. The Proteas had virtually pocketed the game, needing only 68 more with nine wickets in hand and plenty of deliveries to spare, when centurion Herschelle Gibbs retired hurt with cramps. A remarkable turnaround ensued with the Indians, 'off-break' bowler Sehwag in particular, choking up the runs, aided by some incredible catching.

The tournament had a 'watery' climax, not once but twice. Sri Lanka batted first and scored an obtainable 244-5 in the final. India were 14 for no loss when rains dampened the proceedings. The match was 'replayed' the next day as per ICC rules. Unfortunately, the rain-gods entered the scheme of things once again, when the Indians were 38-1 in response to Sri Lanka's 222-7. The trophy was shared.

The 'all-rounder' essays an unusual role

Rahul was competent behind the stumps without being

Above: An emphatic hook during his match-saving 87 in the 'Denness' Test at Port Elizabeth 2001–02
Below: Rahul gives former South African skipper Shaun Pollock the treatment in the 2001–02 series

The complete batsman–equally proficient on both sides of the wicket
Opposite, Top: Up and about–On the attack
Below: Down, but certainly not out

FORD
FORD
FORD

PEPSI PEPSI PEPSI PEPSI
PEPSI PEPSI PEPSI PEPSI
PEPSI PEPSI PEPSI PEPSI

Above: India's premier all-rounder of the early 2000s.
Opposite: A tribute to G.R. Viswanath–a thumping square-cut in the 2003 World Cup
Below: Multan, April 2004–his first Test win as captain, Rahul (second from left) celebrates with his teammates

BRITANNIA
SAHARA

The transformation of a 'Test' specialist…
Top: Rahul in the 2003–04 tri-series in Australia
Below: Taking the aerial route in the ICC Cricket World Cup 2003
Opposite: Adelaide, 16 December 2003

Another typical 'one-day stroke'–a drive after 'making room' in the 2002 ICC Champions Trophy semi-final against South Africa

Above: 1999—Rahul is presented the Arjuna Award for Sporting Excellence by His Excellency Shri K.R. Narayanan, Honourable President of India
Opposite: Nairobi, 1999-2000–Rahul receives the CEAT Cricketer of the 1999 World Cup Award
Below: Rahul with Atal Behari Vajpayee, Prime Minister of India, on the eve of the tour of Pakistan, 2003-04

A role model for Generation Next ...
Top: With the future of Indian cricket
Below: MTV's Youth Icon, 2004

Above: The Indian team after winning the one-day series in Pakistan, 2003–04. Rahul (centre) holds the trophy
Below: India's memorable tour of Australia, 2003–04. The cheque says it all

INDIA

A cricketer and a gentleman

The Class of 1996

Unwinding on the beach, while on tour

Above: The Bangalore boy with the Big B
Below: The 2003–04 series between India and New Zealand ended in a 0-0 stalemate. Stand-in skipper Rahul shares the trophy with counterpart Stephen Fleming

The wedding, 4 May 2003

INDIA FIRST INNINGS
PARTNERSHIPS
SEHWAG DRAVID 8 (6)
LAXMAN DRAVID 5 (18)
TENDULKAR DRAVID 55 (86)
RAINA DRAVID 25 (63)
SHARMA DRAVID 2 (13)
DHONI DRAVID 42 (89)
MISHRA DRAVID 87 (143)
GAMBHIR DRAVID 40 (108)
RP SINGH DRAVID 36 (37)
SREESANTH DRAVID 0 (2)
EXTRAS 25
OVERS 94
TOTAL 300


The Oval, 2011—This TV screen-grab says it all

Bengaluru, 9 March 2012 - Rahul announces his retirement from international cricket. Seated next to him are N. Srinivasan, President, BCCI and Anil Kumble, President, KSCA.

27 March 2012—Rahul is presented a memento by Sanjay Jagdale, Hony. Secretary, BCCI, at the Farewell organized by the Board.

The Coach of the Indian team that won the ICC Under-19 World Cup 2018.

Rahul with the author.

The individual on the right made his IPL debut in 2008 under Rahul's captaincy.

spectacular, and his teammates weren't complaining. The support-staff was on the job as well:

> 'The responsibility of wicketkeeping meant that he had to do additional work on the lower back and hamstrings. But then, he was so fit in the first place that it was merely a case of conditioning himself to the demands of keeping. His fitness enabled him to adapt quickly.'
>
> —Andrew Leipus

Jermaine Lawson, the paceman from Jamaica, ensured that his fellow West Indian Everton Weekes remained the only batsman to score five consecutive Test hundreds, by dismissing Rahul for only 11 in the first innings of the second Test of the 2002-03 series at Chennai. But India won the Test by eight wickets to take the series. The West Indies then staged a comeback of sorts in the third Test at Kolkata by reducing India to 87-4 in the second essay, after taking a first-innings lead of 139. But Tendulkar (176) and Laxman (154) ensured a draw.

Invigorated by their performance at Kolkata, the West Indians came hard at the hosts in a ridiculous seven-match one-day series. Fortunately for the players, six of the games were scheduled in the adjacent states of Maharashtra, Gujarat and Rajasthan. This meant that the travelling time was relatively less. The visitors won the first two games, both of which were marred by the hurling of rubbish on the ground. The spectators at Rajkot, venue of the third game, embarrassed the nation further, and the game was abandoned when India were 200-1 in 27.1 overs, chasing a target of 301. It was later reported that the interruption was initiated by bookies who had taken bets on India losing, and were driven to their wits' end when Sourav and Sehwag started belting the bowling. Much to their consternation, the Duckworth-Lewis calculations were invoked and the game awarded to India!

India drew the series with a grand five-wicket win at Ahmedabad, in what was the first crowd incident-free (ironic in the light of what had happened in the city earlier that year) match of the series. The West Indies scored 324-4, but they came up against an opposition that had successfully chased a similar target a few months previously. India's heroes this time were Sanjay Bangar, who lashed a 41 ball 57, and Rahul, who combined old-fashioned grit with panache to remain unbeaten on 109. India won with 14 deliveries to spare.

The West Indies won the next game, another high-scoring affair in which the bowlers were battered on a belter. Retribution from the bowlers was long overdue, and it came in the sixth fixture at Jodhpur, where the West Indies were bowled out for 201, and the Indians crawled to a three-wicket win. Rahul led India in that game and the series-decider in Sourav's absence. It was the first time he was combining the roles of captain and wicketkeeper, and he coped pretty well. His 58 set up the successful chase that enabled India to square the series. The decider at Vijayawada was bathetic, with the Indians coming unstuck against Jermaine Lawson. His dismissals of Sehwag, Mongia, Laxman and Rahul derailed India's pursuit of an imposing 316, and not even a run-a-ball 68 by Yuvraj could salvage the situation. The defeat was hugely disappointing, but worse was to follow.

Two weeks after that calamitous one-dayer, the Indian Test openers Sehwag and Bangar found themselves standing on a damp wicket embellished with deep hues of green, in bitterly cold and windy Wellington. To the naked Indian eye, it did not look like the best wicket on which to play a five-day Test, the first of two that India were scheduled to play in Kiwiland. Of course, it was not that the Indian batsmen could not handle such wickets. The memories of Leeds were still fresh.

Sehwag had scored only two when Darryl Tuffey bowled him 'through the gate'. This meant that the first-day heroes of Leeds were back together in the trench.

Rahul began with a fluently driven two off the first ball he received from Kiwi spearhead Shane Bond, and then leaned into a half-volley by the same bowler to caress it through the covers for four. Bond, who like Tuffey had been miserly and menacing, then delivered one that reared from short of a length. Rahul countered by extending his hands to take his gloves as far away from the advancing ball as possible. He then allowed the ball to hit his upper left arm. A batsman who had copped a fair amount of such deliveries in his playing days was impressed. 'On a pitch like this, you have got to be prepared to take the blows and value your wicket. That's exactly what Rahul is doing,' Sunil Gavaskar observed from the commentary box.

Then came a major setback. Bangar was declared out caught when a rising, incoming delivery from Tuffey hit him on what looked like the arm-guard, and went to Scott Styris in the slips. India were 9-2, and in the soup.

Rahul's concentration, defence, judgement outside the off-stump and footwork were a joy to behold. He played two stunning strokes off Bond, the first a rasping square-drive and then a commanding square-cut. Tendulkar too hit two boundaries before offering no shot to debutant Jacob Oram and finding himself plumb in front. Sourav started tentatively, but gained in confidence with every delivery. Just when he looked to have gained the measure of the bowling, he nicked Bond and Lou Vincent snapped up a beauty at fourth slip. India were 51-4 at lunch and rapidly running out of wickets.

Rahul's post-lunch objective was to make the average balls count. The bowlers were having a field day, supported by an aggressive field, but as always, the flip-side of this was that there were many gaps. He lost Laxman almost immediately to a rising delivery from Bond to which the latter shouldered arms and got an edge. But Parthiv Patel stood firm at one end as Rahul kept watch at the other, his eyes, hands and feet in readiness to seize on any error the bowler might commit. When Tuffey gave him width outside the off-stick, he executed an imperious square-cut that rocketed past the two gullies for four. Tuffey was flustered enough to bowl one on Rahul's pads, one of the very few deliveries bowled that day on the leg-stump line, and Rahul flicked it for an easy two.

After thwarting Tuffey, Rahul set his sights on Bond and Oram. Both were hit for two fours each. Oram, taken aback by the counterattack, served a rare full-toss that was cover-driven to the boundary. It was becoming increasingly obvious that it wasn't as bad a pitch as was being made out to be. Application, determination and a big heart would enable a batsman to come through. Rahul possessed all three attributes.

He completed one of the most satisfying fifties of his career with an 'uppercut' off Tuffey, the ball going over the slips' heads for four. By then, he had lost Patel, who gave Vincent his second catch of the innings.

Agarkar came in at 92-6 and capitalized on Stephen

Fleming's decision to rest his main bowlers. He attacked change bowler Nathan Astle, but fell to Scott Styris, the other 'military-medium' pacer in the New Zealand side, when a ball rose higher than he expected, took the outside edge, and went to Astle in the slips. The score 118-7 turned to 118-8 one ball later, when Harbhajan Singh for reasons unexplained decided to 'hook' Styris, and Craig McMillan took a diving catch in the deep. Zaheer was clearly uncomfortable and very nearly caught by Vincent on the hattrick-ball, but he hung on till the tea-break, at which point Rahul was on 64 and India 126-8.

Rahul began the third session with a glorious pull off Bond for four. It was wonderful batsmanship; his bat coming clown onto the short ball and his body swivelling as he struck the ball, his eyes riveted on the cherry till the very end. He then took another boundary off Bond, this time with a cut shot that sent the ball flying past the cover-fielder's right. He was looking impregnable, when there was a rare lapse in concentration against Styris. A delivery jabbed back and somehow crept through the gate to castle him. Rahul was understandably cross with himself, but the way he had batted, it would be safe to say that had one of the frontline bowlers bowled that delivery, he would have negotiated it safely. He had lowered his guard a wee bit against a change bowler, and paid the price.

Rahul's 76 was a classic, one that he himself and those who watched it will remember for a long time. Unfortunately, like Tendulkar's 136 at Chennai, it was played in a losing cause.

Rahul's innings and two hundreds by Virender Sehwag in the seven-match one-day series were the batting highlights for India on what turned out to be one of its most disastrous tours of all time. India's scores in the Tests and one-dayers told a sorry tale—161, 121, 99, 154, 108, 219, 108, 122, 169-8, 200-9 and 122.

The Kiwis did not set the scorebooks alight either. They floundered against some incisive bowling, with Zaheer Khan bagging his first two five-wicket hauls in Test cricket. The hosts were marginally better and they passed with grace marks in comparison to the Indians, who failed miserably. The second Test at Auckland witnessed the first instance of both teams being bowled out for double-digit scores in the first innings: India made 99, and New Zealand 94. The home team, however, batted a lot better in the second innings to win by four wickets.

A 0-2 loss in the Tests and 2-5 in the one-dayers on terribly hostile wickets was not what the doctor had ordered on the eve of the World Cup. But expectations remained sky-high and the media once again went overboard with all the hype, overlooking the fact that the Indians did not have a particularly impressive record in South Africa.

As vice-captain, first-choice keeper and key member of the middle-order, Rahul was by now an integral component of the limited-overs side. But he was taking nothing for granted.

> 'He maintained his "first-to-arrive-last-to-leave" attitude towards practice in the lead-up to the World Cup. I remember watching him practise against a bowling machine at the indoor nets at the Chinnaswamy stadium in Bengaluru, with a bat just two-and-a-half inches wide. The machine had been programmed to deliver balls that landed short of a length just outside the off-stump, which is where bowlers aim to bowl in one-dayers to stifle the scoring. Rahul was rising and patting these deliveries

down in front of square on the off-side. The idea was to play them in an unmanned region of the field and steal a single. The thinking obviously was, "If I can middle the ball with this narrow bat, then I can middle anything". He practised this drop-shot for hours and hours.'

—Charu Sharma

Fans were stunned when the Indian team lost a practice match against a local side before the tournament got underway, and saddened when the team batted diffidently in the opening game against minnows Holland. When Australia trounced India in the second game of the competition, all hell broke loose. Effigies of the cricketers were burnt and the houses of some cricketers smeared with black paint, in what were bizarre and childish reactions. From South Africa, the captain, vice-captain and senior players appealed for understanding and patience.

While it would be unwise to attribute the subsequent turnaround to the outbursts back home, there was no doubt that they had a unifying effect on the team. India won its next eight matches on the trot. Barring one game against Namibia, the rest of the wins were achieved against top-quality opposition, first-time semi-finalists Kenya included. The co-hosts distinguished themselves by making it to the final four ahead of the West Indies, Pakistan, South Africa and England.

'India have always been a potentially dangerous force in world cricket, as they have had some wonderful players with bat and ball. It was just a matter of time before they were able to combine all those individual talents into a powerful team. I suppose when you are playing in the

World Cup, the team's objectives are first and foremost in your mind—this might not always be the case in a Test or ODI series.'

—Jonty Rhodes

Success, they say, has many fathers. In this case, all the fathers were legitimate. There was Sandy Gordon, the Sports Psychologist, who had sessions with the players and conceived the 'huddle' that became synonymous with the team. There were Wright, Leipus and Adrian Le Roux (appointed Trainer a year before), who maintained a tight vigil on fitness—technical as well as physical. The players themselves were passionate and obsessed with winning. Sourav batted excellently when the chips were down and captained splendidly, to lend credence to the steadily growing perception that he was India's finest captain ever. Yuvraj and Kaif fired with the bat and in the field. Rahul was assertive in front of the wickets, agile and audacious between them and assured behind. It also helped that Tendulkar was batting like a man on a mission. The decision of the team management to reinstate him as an opening batsman had evoked mixed reactions. All those who pointed to India's outstanding limited-overs record since his shift to the middle-order in mid-2002 were silenced by a succession of blistering knocks, the best of which was his 98 off 75 balls against Pakistan at Centurion. His blunting of Shoaib Akhtar made the headlines, but in all fairness to the bowler, he wasn't singled out. Every Pakistani who bowled that day—Abdul Razzaq, Shahid Afridi and the two 'W's—was brutalized by the 'Bombay bomber'.

The atmosphere was electric when Tendulkar fell to Shoaib with 97 still needed from 134 balls. Memories of Chennai 1999 loomed large. Could it end again in tears? Rahul, who was at the non-striker's end, saw Yuvraj Singh, the new batsman who was playing his first match against Pakistan, take guard against the Rawalpindi Express. The youngster negotiated the first ball. The second, he clipped to the mid-wicket boundary. That one shot settled Indian nerves. Waqar Younis, the Pakistani captain, then tested Rahul with his trademark yorker, only to see the batsman leg-glance it for four. The breathtaking start provided by Tendulkar had ensured that the middle-order did not need to do anything silly, and Rahul and Yuvraj were equal to the 'stroll'. The stroll ended in the 46th over, with Rahul pulling Waqar for four to complete the win.

Rahul's unbeaten 44 against Pakistan was one of his many plucky knocks in the tournament. His 62 against England was instrumental in India reaching a competitive and eventually match-winning 250-9 after struggling in the middle overs. An unbeaten 53 in the 'Super Six' game against New Zealand took India to a seven-wicket win and avenged the humiliating defeats against the same team not very long ago. He also emerged as the third-most successful wicketkeeper of the tournament with 16 dismissals, behind 'specialists' like Adam Gilchrist and Kumar Sangakkara. His champagne moment as keeper was a brilliant one-handed catch to dismiss the dangerous Razzaq in that crunch affair against Pakistan.

But it was the bowling that made the biggest difference to India's campaign. Indian batsmen had done well in the World Cup before (1999) and Tendulkar had scored over 500 runs in a World Cup before (1996), but the bowlers had lagged behind. 2003 was different. Zaheer Khan, Ashish Nehra and the veteran Javagal Srinath, who had come back from retirement for one last dash, were quick, accurate and hostile. Zaheer scalped 18 wickets, Srinath 16 and Nehra 15, which included a sensational 6-23 against England.

Rahul improvises in the 2003 World Cup encounter against England

Pre-match talk on the eve of the final between the two best teams of the competition revolved around one of the game's enduring cliches—the law of averages. All those who did not want Australia to retain the title claimed that the law was bound to catch up with them, for they had won ten matches on the trot after all. Unfortunately for the pundits, the law chose to strike the team that had won eight games on the trot. Put in to bat, Australia smashed 359-2 and then dismissed India for

234. Tendulkar, who fell in the first over to McGrath, would have gladly traded the 673 runs that won him the Player of the Tournament Award for a match-winning innings in the final. Sehwag, who had had an ordinary tournament by his standards, kept Indian fans interested with some blazing strokes before he was run out for 82 out of a total of 147. Rahul helped him add 88 for the fourth wicket. The score was 187 when Rahul inside-edged Andy Bichel onto the stumps for 47. The Indian innings died a frantic death thereafter.

With the World Cup ended an eventful and memorable year for Rahul and Indian cricket. Barriers had been broken and new heights scaled. They had all but scaled the summit of world cricket and faltered only at the final step. Stiffer challenges lurked on the horizon. But 'Team India' was ready for them.

11

# REDEMPTION AND IMMORTALITY

'Rahul has got better and better over the years. His record in Australia had not been that good, but in 2003-04, he dominated their bowlers at will. The last batsman to do that was Viv Richards.'

—MUDASSAR NAZAR

Rahul began the most important 'partnership' of his life after the World Cup when he tied the knot with family friend Dr Vijeeta Pendharkar. The couple spent the first few weeks of their marriage in the UK, where Rahul represented Scotland in the second division of the limited-overs National Cricket League and averaged an outstanding 66 from eleven matches, in what was an unusually long-off-season for the Indian team. He returned home on the

Rahul and Vijeeta on their wedding day, 4 May 2003

eve of Indian cricket's toughest season since 1999-2000. India were to host a competitive New Zealand outfit and then tour Australia for a four-Test series. The season was scheduled to end with a visit to Pakistan.

In a bid to provide much-needed match-practice to its frontline players, the BCCI scheduled the Challenger Trophy and Irani Trophy before the Kiwis arrived in late September. Rahul led India B in the Challenger and scored a match-winning 107 in the league game against the Seniors. He then took a match-winning 121 off the Mumbai bowlers for the Rest of India in the Irani Trophy fixture. VVS Laxman, who had a point or two to prove after being dropped from the World Cup squad, scored a scintillating 99 and helped Rahul add 168 for the fourth wicket. It was Sachin Tendulkar's first first-class defeat as Mumbai captain since 1993-94, *a first* in a season of many *firsts* for Indian cricket.

There was widespread speculation that the Kiwis would be made to play on slow, low and turning dust-bowls in the two-Test series, as revenge for the greentops they had prepared a year previously. Indeed, Stephen Fleming and his men had taken no chances and trained hard on such strips before flying to India. Sourav won the toss in the first Test at Ahmedabad, batted and declared at 500-5 immediately after completing a fine hundred. Fifth out was Rahul for a splendid 222, his third double hundred in Test cricket. On a surface that was inducing the ball to make the bat wait a little longer than usual for the inevitable collision, he was prepared to play the waiting game, and he did it quite well.

The second innings showcased another facet of Rahul's batsmanship. India's only hope of winning was to go for the runs and declare after the Kiwis had scored 340. Rahul scored an enterprising 73 from only 86 balls, propelling the ball all around the ground with aplomb. Sourav declared 369 ahead, but the Kiwis batted doggedly to save the game.

The visitors excelled themselves on a featherbed at Mohali by batting till the third morning of the second Test to score 630. Notwithstanding centuries by Sehwag and Laxman, the Indian batting was as toothless as the bowling. They were asked to follow-on 204 runs behind, and were a disastrous 18-3 when Laxman and Akash Chopra put down the shutters. Although Rahul made only 13 and 5, it was a significant game for him. Sourav had opted out due to an abscess in his left thigh and Rahul thus became India's 28th official Test skipper. While his debut as captain wasn't exactly memorable, Rahul made a huge impression on a player, India's newest 'opening' hope, who made his debut in the series.

> 'We were 30-3 at lunch on the final day. Rahul made me realize that there are times when a match-saving innings can be as crucial as a match-winning one. This was one such. He told me, "I know you are capable of batting the whole day. So go out and have a great day". That really pumped me up.'
>
> —Akash Chopra

The groundstaff at Ahmedabad and Mohali were criticized for not making pitches that assisted the Indian spinners enough, but the Indian players could have certainly performed better. They were no different in the tri-series, where they pipped New Zealand to the final, but let themselves down in the final against Australia, failing to achieve a modest target of 236. The defeat was hard to digest, particularly as the Indians had blitzed the Kiwis for 353 runs in the last league clash just three days previously. Sehwag and Tendulkar got hundreds in that game, but Rahul stole the show.

He drove, cut, glided and ran to a 50 off only 22 balls, an incredible exhibition of batsmanship in the so-called 'slog' overs. Eighteen years after India had displayed in the World Championship of Cricket in Australia that spinners were capable of winning one-day internationals, an Indian had proved that a batting traditionalist could be as lethal in one-day cricket as the 'rebels' who heaved and hoicked to glory.

> 'Rahul was a natural strokemaker with tremendous timing. Whenever he played his strokes, he succeeded and looked in control. I always believed he could be as destructive as Sachin or Sehwag.'
>
> —Sandeep Patil

During the tri-series, Rahul won the Castrol Indian Cricketer of the Year award for the second time in succession. He brought the house down in his acceptance speech at the function in Bengaluru by thanking the bowlers for 'understanding' that the keeper was not going to be able to 'collect' everything. The reference was to his prolonged stint as one-day keeper, necessitated by the fact that the think-tank still distrusted the batting capabilities of other specialist wicketkeepers. Consequently, they had opted to extend what was meant to be a stop-gap solution till the 2003 World Cup, well beyond that tournament.

But a greater challenge was around the corner. Rahul was determined not to repeat the mistakes, technical and mental, he had committed in Australia in 1999-2000.

> 'Rahul is a master at visualization and self-talk. Self-talk is an argument with yourself, wherein you are like two lawyers fighting a case in court, and the judge as well. The defence lawyer within you has to build a strong enough case that will prompt the judge within you to declare a "verdict" in your favour. Remembering past events, anticipating likely happenings in the future and imagining things are all part, of the process of visualization. This process you have to take charge of and control by regular practice. You should replenish your memory by remembering the correct action and build up a muscle memory. Your responses then become natural. The bat then starts meeting the ball in the desired manner. If you have made a certain mistake in the past, you should try to imagine how you would have fared had you not committed that mistake. If you do

this constructively, you will remember the one instance when you did not make that mistake and forget the several other instances when you made that mistake. Visualizing the future is not easy. It boils down to strengthening your commitment, focus and response to signals. A batsman playing at the international level may be under pressure due to a failure in the previous match or series. He knows his opponents and the venue of the next game. He should imagine and visualize the manner in which he wants to perform there. This will enable him to cultivate the right responses to the signals he will be facing at the venue.'

—B.P. Bam

Memories of 1999-2000 were still fresh, and Indian cynics were talking in terms of celebrating if their side managed to take the Tests into the fourth or fifth day against the world's premier team, which they knew would go flat out to give a victorious farewell to Steve Waugh, already the most successful captain in Test history. Those who predicted at least one Indian win were scoffed at, and that is putting it mildly.

A statement by Sourav Ganguly underscored the gravity of the tour: 'At the end of this series, we will know how good we really are'.

The captain led from the front with a rousing 144 that helped his team take a first-innings lead of 86 in the rain-hit first Test at Brisbane. Australia finished the first day at a commanding 262-2. The Indians, headed by Zaheer Khan, struck back on the second morning to terminate the innings for 323. The Aussies then reduced India to 62-3 with both Rahul and Tendulkar back in the pavilion, the latter to a doubtful leg-before decision.

Sourav then came to the rescue. Rahul had scored only one when he nicked a gem of a delivery by Gillespie that left him late, to Hayden at slip. It was not an auspicious beginning, but he was determined to be positive.

> 'The best thing about Rahul is his equanimity. Having played with him for a long time and having seen him prepare for every match the same way, be it a league match in Chennai or a Test, I don't think he was too worked up about his previous underperformance in Australia. He prepared the way he always did.'
>
> —Murali Kartik

Waugh declared in the final session of the last day and set India an unreachable 199 from 23 overs. Sehwag and Chopra fell with only four runs on the board, but Rahul and Laxman restored sanity. Laxman, sent in ahead of Tendulkar after his brilliant first-innings 75, remained unbeaten with 24, but the star of the innings was Rahul. He scored 43 off only 47 balls, replete with some sparkling strokes, before Waugh called a halt.

> 'Watching the match, and the manner in which it unfolded, I had the opinion that this was likely to be a turning point.'
>
> —Richie Benaud

Justin Langer and Simon Katich displayed their disregard for the Indian bowlers on the first day of the second Test at Adelaide. Towering over them was Ricky Ponting, who scored a pugnacious 242. The first day yielded an astonishing 400 runs. But the Indians refused to wilt. Anil Kumble's perseverance was rewarded with five wickets. The hosts ended with 556 runs.

Sehwag got going in characteristic style, and Chopra lent

him company in a stand of 66, five more than their first-innings association at Brisbane. But the Aussies bounced back with a bang. Bichel dealt a triple blow, sending back Chopra (caught-and-bowled), Sehwag (caught at slip) and Tendulkar (caught behind) in quick succession. There was another setback when Sourav was run out. He pushed Gillespie for a comfortable single to long-off, turned for a second, and was sent back by his partner. For a change, he and not Rahul had failed to make the crease when they were batting together! The score was 85-4 and Laxman made his way to the middle.

Rahul essayed an exquisite back-foot drive in Gillespie's next over, the ball rocketing to the fence. Ten runs later, he pulled Bichel hard and well, and then executed an elegant straight-drive to bring up the hundred of the innings. He was clearly sighting the ball well. At the other end, Laxman drove Gillespie through the covers in a manner that commentator Greg Chappell described as 'languid and imperious'. One word that came to the watchers' minds, but which Chappell did not use, was 'ominous'. The artiste completed his fifty, and India were 180-4 at stumps on day two. The two batsmen knew that it was important for them to bat as long as possible, for there was still a lot of time left in the game.

> 'There was not much to discuss. We were four down and the pressure was on us. We wanted to hang in there without thinking too much about other factors, and play each ball on merit.'
>
> —VVS Laxman

Early on the third day, Rahul took a single off a MacGill full-toss to complete his first Test fifty in Australia. This was shortly after he and Laxman had registered their sixth century stand in Test cricket.

Rahul carried on. A flowing cover-drive off Bichel disturbed a flock of seagulls that had gathered to watch. He followed it with a flick off the first delivery of Bichel's next over to enter the nineties. He had advanced to 98 when Gillespie tested him with a well-directed bouncer. Rahul saw it early, and went for the hook. The ball did not come off the middle, but it was hit well enough to clear the square-leg fence. It was a marvellous way in which to complete a hundred. Laxman completed his own hundred three overs later, and Steve Waugh found himself being subjected to a memory-test by Indian spectators from across the boundary: 'Remember Kolkata?'

Not that the spectators needed to ask. As at Kolkata, Rahul was a connoisseur's delight with his seemingly impregnable defence, aggressive but conventional stroke-play and nimble footwork, while Laxman was the elegant assassin.

> 'The Australians have the habit of forcing batsmen into making a mistake. But Rahul did not make a single mistake during that innings. They were trying to force him, but he was in no mood to oblige!'
>
> —Akash Chopra

Like Laxman, Rahul was severe on MacGill, demoralizing him with a series of emphatic cover-drives. The bowler tried changing his angle and bowling around the wicket, but in vain. Gillespie, Bichel and Brad Williams bowled their hearts out, but to no avail.

In a bizarre coincidence, Laxman cover-drove his *281st,* ball of the innings to the boundary to complete his second 300-plus partnership with Rahul in a Test. But the very next ball took the outside edge of his bat and finished in Gilchrist's gloves. He had scored 148. Rahul carried on, helped by a bright knock by Patel. He was unbeaten on 199 at stumps, and applauded all the way back to the pavilion by his opponents.

> 'This was my favourite Rahul innings.'
>
> —Virender Sehwag

Rahul was asked that evening what he thought about the knock. 'Ask me after the match,' he replied.

MacGill, who had done a Santa Claus on day three with several 'gifts' in the form of ordinary deliveries, began proceedings on the fourth day in the same vein, with a long-hop outside the off-stump. Rahul stroked it to the cover-boundary to complete a magnificent double hundred. The tail-enders helped him take the score to 523, 33 short of the Australian total, before he was last out, caught off a top-edged hook off Gillespie. The stroke was similar to the one that had got him his hundred the day before, only this one had gathered more height than distance.

Rahul returned to a standing ovation with 233 runs under his belt. He had batted for exactly ten hours. But the battle was far from over.

> 'Australians were amused to learn that Rahul is known as "Jammy". In the Australian vernacular, "Jammy" implies luck but, of course, there was nothing lucky or chancy about Rahul's wonderful redemption innings in Adelaide. It won him admirers galore and lifted a considerable burden from his shoulders.'
>
> —Mike Coward

The events that followed did every Indian proud. Inspired by the individual, the team took centrestage. Not that Rahul was a mere observer. Ajit Agarkar tormented Langer with a probing line and finally had him leg-before. Ponting cut Agarkar into Chopra's hands at gully, and Sehwag pulled off a sensational catch in the covers to dismiss Hayden off Nehra. At 44-3, Australia were on the edge of the precipice. Martyn and Waugh added 65 before both fell in quick succession to the Rahul-Tendulkar combination. Both nicked leg-breaks to Rahul at slip; his one-handed catch that dismissed Martyn was one of the best ever held by an Indian. Gilchrist survived a stumping opportunity and went for his strokes, but he was beaten and bowled by Kumble behind his legs. Agarkar then blew away Katich and the tail. India had eight overs and the whole of the last day in which to make 230 and achieve their first Test win in Australia since 1981.

The Indian bowling and fielding was praised, as was Sourav's captaincy, but some pundits interestingly attributed Australia's desperate state to the 'Boomerang Effect'. By scoring 556 runs in the first innings in less than five sessions, had they inadvertently given their opponents more time to get back into the game?

Rahul was back in the middle on the fifth morning after Chopra had fallen leg-before to Gillespie. The Australians, not used to being in a position like this, were expected to fire away on all cylinders. Indeed, many Indian supporters were still pessimistic.

A chart divided into 23 'blocks' adorned the Indian dressing room wall. With every ten runs, one block was torn off.

Rahul got off the mark with an on-drive off Gillespie that beat a diving MacGill and fetched him two. He looked in control as he caressed Williams through the tiniest of gaps between two men in the cover-region.

> 'He reacted to what the bowler bowled and trusted his ability to do the rest. It was this control that had enabled him to angle his bat and place the ball where he wanted it to go.'
>
> —Greg Chappell (on TV)

Williams retaliated in his next over with a delivery that pitched on a length and moved away, drawing Rahul out and taking the outside edge. But Gilchrist spilt a regulation catch. Fortune was on Rahul's and India's side.

Sehwag fell at 79 when he stepped out to MacGill to attempt another big shot after playing one in the same over, but missed, and Gilchrist completed an easy stumping. Tendulkar displayed his positive intent by 'back-driving' MacGill for four, and Rahul was solid at the other end. The duo displayed composure and a willingness to capitalize on the bad balls. They had added 64 when Rahul essayed the stroke of the innings, a spanking square-cut off a Williams delivery that to the layman seemed a little too close to be cut. He was on song, but the Aussies were not going to give up. They targeted the other end.

MacGill of all bowlers got the breakthrough, deceiving Tendulkar and trapping him leg-before. Sourav had scored only 12 when Katich brilliantly caught him in the slip-cordon off Bichel. India needed only 60 more with six wickets in hand, but even the most fanatical Indian supporter would have conceded that the match was delicately poised. But then, MacGill repeated his Santa Glaus act, and Laxman and Rahul had no hassles dispatching a delicious assortment of full-tosses and long-hops to the fence. Laxman fell with only nine needed. Patel helped Rahul take the team to the threshold, before perishing to an extravagant sweep. By this time, the scores were level, the Indian players ready with their handy-cams and Sourav down at the gate, waiting to greet his deputy.

The champagne moment came with another MacGill long-hop. Rahul smashed it past cover, roared and kissed the India crest on his cap. For three days, he had kept his emotions and words in check, aware that all his efforts in the first innings would amount to nothing if the ultimate goal—Victory—was not achieved. That he 'redeemed' himself on Australian soil in the process was incidental.

It was apt that Rahul's partner was Ajit Agarkar, the much-maligned 'Bombay Duck' of the previous tour, who had set up the triumph with 6-41 in the second innings. Among the first to congratulate Rahul was Steve Waugh, who handed him the ball as a souvenir. The Indian supporters celebrated wildly, and in the commentary box, the last Indian captain to win a Test in Australia struggled to tackle the lump in his throat. Sunil Gavaskar wasn't the only person who had got emotional. As delighted as the Indian cricketers and cricket-lovers was someone whose hometown was Adelaide—Andrew Leipus.

Only an extraordinary performance could have derailed the awesome Aussies in their backyard. Rahul's performance –233 and 72* –was one of the greatest. He could not have chosen a better venue to book his ticket to cricketing immortality—Adelaide, the Don's own territory. Ravi Shastri spoke for an entire nation when he declared that Rahul was India's 'fourth Indian batting great after Gavaskar, Viswanath and Tendulkar'.

> 'You are remembered for hitting the target, not for aiming at it. Rahul was never a finisher initially; he became one later. He harnessed his talent brilliantly and turned obstacles into stepping-stones. The credibility is always higher when you perform away from home. His performance at Adelaide was awesome.'
>
> —Navjot Sidhu

Rahul was his succinct self in a conversation with the TV commentators: 'We believed we could compete. There were phases when I got a little tired (in the second innings), but I reminded myself of how important this game was for us. I have been a part of teams that have failed to win by narrow margins, and I didn't want to experience that pain again'.

Rahul had passed cricket's most arduous test with flying colours. He refused to take off his whites during the celebrations that continued late into the evening. It was a unique tribute to the man whose swansong he had spoilt. Steve Waugh had done pretty much the same thing when Australia won the 1994-95 series in the West Indies.

An interesting sidelight of the win was the debut of a player rated by many as India's next Superstar. Irfan Pathan, a left-arm paceman from Baroda, found himself in the exalted company of Sunil Gavaskar, Dilip Vengsarkar, Syed Kirmani and Kiran More, all of whom had made their debuts in rare 'away' Tests won by India and had successful careers thereafter. Unfortunately, things did not go as per plan for Irfan. He did go on to complete the 'double' of 1,000 runs and 100 wickets in Tests, but he was let down by a combination of inconsistency and injury issues.

The winning boundary, Adelaide 2003-04

India lost the next Test at Melbourne, but came within four wickets of winning the final Test at Sydney. Anil Kumble bagged 12 wickets at Sydney, including 8-141 in the first innings, and said that it had taken him 14 years to learn how to bowl overseas. He was magnanimous enough not to mention the number of times his batting colleagues had let him down in those 14 years.

The batsmen reigned supreme. Sehwag plundered 195 in the third Test, Laxman 178 in the fourth, and Tendulkar a classy 241 in the same game to erase Rahul's two-Test old distinction as India's highest individual scorer overseas. Rahul himself batted beautifully to score 92 at Melbourne and an unbeaten 91 when the Indians went on the attack in the second innings at Sydney to press for a declaration. Sydney witnessed the *first* instance of India scoring 700 in a Test. The 'opening' conundrum also seemed to have been solved with Sehwag and Chopra putting together two century partnerships. Chopra was the only member of the top six who did not get a hundred, but his contributions were no less vital. Cricket historian David Frith paid him the ultimate compliment by christening him 'Boycott' Chopra *(Wisden Asia Cricket,* February 2004).

Rahul in the 2003-04 tri-series in Australia

'The big difference with the Indian team of 2003-04 and earlier sides was that this team went in with a splendid attitude. They had decided to carry the attack to the Australian team. In fact, they had copied the Australian tactic that Mark Taylor started and Steve Waugh continued that, if they were in trouble, attack was the best way to win. The drawn series was one of the finest that has been played in Australia.'

—Richie Benaud

India retained the Border-Gavaskar Trophy by virtue of a 1-1 stalemate. The rivalry between the two countries was touted as the game's biggest, and many a pundit opined that India would oust Australia as the premier cricket world power in the near future.

Their belief was not shaken by Australia's domination of the tri-series. Rahul scored three fifties, match-winning efforts all. However, he made more news for an alleged 'ball-tampering' episode in a game against the third team Zimbabwe in which he scored 84. The Match Referee fined him half his match-fee for applying 'cough lozenge' on the ball. His coach called it an 'innocent mistake', explaining that the lozenge had got mixed with the spit he was applying to the ball. He was spot-on. 'Rahul is everything the game needs,' Wright stated.

Everybody agreed with him. Except the Referee, that is.

# 12

## RUNS N' REINS

'We had absolutely no illusions about Rahul Dravid. We always knew that even in the presence of Sachin Tendulkar and the others, he would be the difference between the two teams because he had the ability to bat for hours and hours without feeling any pain in his back. We were aware that Sachin and the rest will play strokes and sometimes provide an opportunity. But Rahul was a batsman who would tire us and set the platform for the others to score. He was a brilliant batsman and in my book, deserved a permanent place as one of the top three batsmen in the world irrespective of his performance, because form is temporary and class permanent.'

—Moin Khan

'It's not a big wicket, it's huge!' commentator Michael Slater shrieked at a critical juncture in India's second innings of the second Test against Pakistan at Lahore, trying to make himself audible amidst the roars of the crowd. When the replay confirmed the dismissal, his compatriot and fellow-commentator Dean Jones screamed, 'HE IS GONE!'

Before April 2002, there was only one Indian player whose early dismissal in a tense situation would have elicited such a reaction. But things had changed. The player they were referring to was Rahul, whose run-out had made Pakistan's job of levelling the three-Test series that much easier.

The Indian cricketers were not terribly enthused at the prospect of crossing the Radcliffe Line for a full tour in March 2004. 'Security concerns' weighed on their minds.

> 'I was part of the Reconnaissance team that went to Pakistan. We submitted a report to the Board and told the senior players about the assurances made by the Pakistani Board and Government. The Board had made it clear that any player who wanted to drop out was free to do so. But all the players agreed to tour. It was nice to have a full-strength side.'
>
> —Prof Ratnakar Shetty, Administrative Manager, Indian team to Pakistan, 2003-04

The BCCI prevailed upon its relieved Pakistani counterpart to slot the one-day internationals before the Tests. This suited the Indian players, for they had just played the tri-series in Australia and were very much in a 'limited-overs' mood.

The 'Australia-hardened' Indian outfit was expected to dominate the one-dayers and Tests. But the players were wise enough not to take Pakistan lightly.

The one-day series commenced with a blockbuster in front of a vociferous Karachi crowd that seemed to encourage the Indians as much as they supported their countrymen. India's big guns boomed in the initial overs. The captain and vice-captain added 72 off only 75 balls in the middle overs, and after Yuvraj Singh's early fall, Kaif joined Rahul to add a run-a-ball 118. Rahul batted delightfully, finding the gaps with unerring precision, his orthodox stroke-play in sharp contrast to Sehwag's gung-ho tactics earlier in the innings. When Rahul played on to Shoaib in the 48th over, he had scored 99 out of a total of 338. The Indians finished with 349-7, in most circumstances a winning total.

Rahul in the thick of things in the one-day series against Pakistan, 2003-04

Inzamam-ul-Haq, the captain of Pakistan who had been slammed by one and all for putting India in on a featherbed, arrived at the crease in the eighth over with 316 needed from 254 balls. The assault that followed was staggering, his contempt for the bowlers drawing gasps of admiration even from Indian supporters. His countenance was almost apologetic. It was almost as if he was saying to the bowlers, 'Look, I am sorry to treat you like this, but I really can't help it'. Only 72 were needed from 48 balls when his attempted late-cut off Murali Kartik went straight into Rahul's gloves, a good take by the part-time keeper with hardly any reaction time. The Pakistanis fought right down to the wire, and it was only a stunner of a catch by Mohammed Kaif and a tight last over by Ashish Nehra that saved the day for India. Six were needed from the last ball when Nehra bowled a low full-toss to Moin Khan. But Moin was no Miandad and the Indians came through.

The day after the game, Rahul joined Murali Kartik on an excursion to the ancient Buddhist monastery in Taxila. The rigours of living out of a suitcase hadn't dampened his urge to explore new surroundings and learn.

A century by Sachin Tendulkar, the first by an Indian in a one-dayer on Pakistani soil, went in vain in the second game at Rawalpindi. Rahul scored 36 before being bowled by Mohammed Sami. At that stage, India were 260-5 and needed 70 from 49 balls. The lower-order made a good fist of it before falling short by 12 runs. India had their worst batting day of the series in the next game at Peshawar. Paceman Shabbir Ahmed did the early damage on a greenish track and the score was 37-3 when Rahul came in. The Crisis-man had scored 33 when he tried to sweep off-spinner Shoaib Malik, but got a top-edge that was gleefully accepted by Moin Khan. Yuvraj scored 65, but the maximum cheers went to Laxmipathy Balaji, who launched into Shoaib and Sami like a man possessed. Pakistan's pursuit of 245 was commandeered by opener Yasir Hameed, who was apparently upset with Rahul for 'mistaking him to be an off-spinner who had bowled to the Indians in the nets'. He scored a fine 98 before being induced to play a flashing drive wide outside the off-stump by Irfan Pathan, who had strangely been left out of the first two games. The opener was disappointed to miss a hundred with Yuvraj taking a good catch, but he had succeeded in his stated objective of ensuring that Rahul and the Indians did not 'forget' him. Abdul Razzaq then dealt some hefty blows and Pakistan romped home with four wickets in hand.

Inzamam scored another hundred in the fourth game at Lahore, a do-or-die affair for the visitors. Chasing 294, India lost their fifth wicket in only the 24th over, but they already had 162 on the board. The belligerence of the top-order despite the frequent fall of wickets had kept them in the game. The required rate of five an over was comfortably achievable, especially as India had the right 'brains' for the job.

> 'I was in my "blues" as I was slated to bat after Irfan, who was to go in next. Except for John (Wright), everybody was relaxed as we knew what both the guys in the middle were capable of. They were excellent runners between the wickets and had bailed the team out of tricky situations before.'
>
> —Murali Kartik

Rahul Dravid and Mohammed Kaif were unflustered. They conquered that Lahore evening with a cool and calculated display. The Pakistani supporters, who had welcomed their Indian counterparts with open arms and Indian flags stitched to their own, were briefly excited when Shoaib was brought on in the 34th over, but two deft placements by Kaif, one going to the fine-leg boundary and the other through the vacant slips, silenced them, as did four wides in the same over. The Pakistani predilection for 'extras'—they conceded 37 in the fourth game, and bowled 47 wides and 41 no-balls in the five matches—would cost them the series.

Rahul batted brilliantly, changing gears when he saw his partner opening out. He tapped the ball around with soft hands and ran superbly to give Kaif the strike. So determined was he to bat right till the end that he even took a fresh guard twice during his innings to retain his focus; shades of Leeds 2002. He square-cut off-spinner Shoaib Malik to level the scores and gave Kaif the honour of striking the winning single.

> 'The people back home deserve a fighting team.'
>
> —Rahul (on TV after the match)

Kaif scored 71 off only 79 balls compared to Rahul's 76 off 149, but the latter's contribution as guide could not be undermined. The manner in which they coasted despite losing half the side before the halfway mark put the Indian players in the right frame of mind on the eve of the series decider at Lahore. Both sides ridiculed allegations that the game had been 'fixed' to ensure a grand finale.

The finale was indeed a grand affair, and much to the home team's chagrin, their opponents did virtually everything right. Laxman scored one of one-day cricket's most incredible hundreds, his 107 runs coming off only 104 balls with little or no 'slogging'. It was his fourth limited-overs hundred of the season, a fitting reply to the men who were responsible for leaving him out of the 2003 World Cup squad. Rahul missed out, scoring only four before being castled by Mohammed Sami, but a final total of 293-7 was a strong platform from which to go for a historic win. Balaji and Irfan Pathan made the early strikes, but the Indians knew they had to get Inzamam. He fell to a marvellous catch on the long-on boundary by Tendulkar, who adroitly judged a bullet-like hit by the Pakistani skipper off Kartik inches from the rope, and retained his balance.

Razzaq fell almost immediately, and the match was as good as won. Moin Khan fought on in the company of Shoaib Malik and later Sami, but the run-rate kept climbing. Moin was the last to fall, bowled by Balaji, and Rahul's Bjorn Borg-like reaction, going down on his knees and looking skywards with arms raised high, emphasised what the win, India's first series triumph against Pakistan in their backyard, meant to the team.

> 'The difference between the Indian team of the 1990s and this team was "Self-belief." The 90s side was good, but the players didn't trust their instincts and prowess. This team was more confident. It was no more a one-man team.'
>
> —Moin Khan

Sourav, a delighted leader, had left the field after injuring his back in the tenth over. Rahul was entrusted the reins for the first Test between the two countries on Pakistani soil since 1989-90 when it was announced that Sourav would be flying back to India for treatment.

Rahul's stellar batting had helped Indian cricket smash several jinxes in the past. He now had the opportunity to break another, this time as captain. India's Test record in Pakistan was pathetic: 20 Tests, five defeats, and no wins. This was their best chance to succeed against an opposition that was already under the pump.

The Test series had been billed as a battle between the Indian batsmen and Pakistani bowlers. However, it became apparent on the first morning of the first Test at Multan that the hosts had serious reservations about the Indian bowling as well. This was a shock to all those who had chosen to take seriously Pakistani coach Javed Miandad's pre-series claim that bowlers like Irfan Pathan could be found on every street in Pakistan.

> 'There was some grass on the pitch, but most of it was removed at the insistence of the home team. In a way, they played into our hands.'
>
> —Prof Shetty

Rahul had no reservations electing to bat after calling correctly. He and his teammates then sat back to watch Virender Sehwag at his audacious best. He flayed the speedsters, flogged the spin of Saqlain Mushtaq and frustrated the fielders. They reprieved him twice, and like all great players, he made them pay. He took on an exasperated Shoaib, goading him to 'bowl and not beg' after the bowler had made some 'friendly' observations.

> 'Rahul's advice was to hold on to my wicket. "The rest would follow," he said. He kept repeating this throughout that knock. The confidence the captain had in me inspired me further.'
>
> —Virender Sehwag

Chopra was caught at short-leg after contributing 42 to an opening stand of 160. Rahul started well with a commanding square-cut off Saqlain, but then pulled Sami straight into Hameed's hands at square-leg. That was Pakistan's last moment of joy as Tendulkar joined his 'disciple' to pile on the agony. Sehwag scored 228 on the first day. He had reached 295 on the second when Inzamam did what any captain would in such a situation. He posted a deep mid-wicket and a long-on and asked Saqlain to toss it up. Sehwag responded as only he could. He stepped down the track and swung a six over the two fielders to become India's first triple centurion in Test cricket. He was eventually out for 309.

Laxman fell early, but Yuvraj and Tendulkar took the score past 600. With Tendulkar nearing his fourth double hundred in the last session of the second day, it looked like Rahul would call his batters in immediately after the landmark was achieved.

Yuvraj was fifth out for a splendid 59 when 18.1 overs were left for stumps. Tendulkar, then on 194, contemplated the situation. He would need a maximum of two overs to complete his double hundred, and with two more overs being consumed by the innings-changeover, it would still give India a substantial 14 overs in which to attack the weary Pakistani batsmen on the second evening. To his surprise, what he saw was not an incoming Patel, but the captain waving his arms. India had declared at 675-5.

There were several who called it a seminal moment in Indian cricket history, with the requirement of the team assuming greater significance than individual achievement. But there were others who disagreed.

> 'My initial reaction was that Rahul was kidding and will change signals. I firmly believe it was a big error of judgement. Sachin thoroughly deserved that double century as he had played beautifully. I don't think Rahul can ever succeed in convincing his critics.'
>
> —Moin Khan

'I feel Rahul could have afforded to wait for Sachin to complete his double century as there was no danger to his team. Centuries and double centuries are milestones in a batsman's career, and so such missed opportunities are always regrettable.'

—Hanif Mohammed

Another Pakistani legend thought otherwise and compared it to a similar incident that had taken place at Hyderabad in the 1982-83 series between the two countries, when Imran Khan declared with Javed Miandad on 280.

'I was brought up to win. A captain's first duty is to go all out to win the match. Personal milestones are fine, but memories you cherish the most are those of victories. India had a formidable batting line-up in 1982-83. You

> needed time to bowl them out twice in the match. Imran chose to declare and I thought it was a just decision.'
>
> —MUDASSAR NAZAR

In the Press Conference at the end of the third day's play, some media-men seized on what they construed as Tendulkar's 'unhappiness' at the declaration. Rahul was accused of being jealous' and 'conspiring with Sourav (who was to fly to India at the end of the game) to deny Tendulkar a 200'.

Even as the debate raged all over and outside India, the two men in the thick of the 'controversy' discussed the issue, sorted things out and threw themselves headlong into the job of winning the Test, which for both of them was paramount.

Subsequent events suggested that Rahul had erred in not giving Tendulkar at least one more over, for it would have made no difference to the outcome. But then, Rahul was no Nostradamus. He wanted to bowl a certain number of overs that evening. He was brave enough to admit later that he had made a mistake, even saying that it was something that might haunt him for the rest of his life.

> 'I was asked what I thought of the declaration. I said that whatever people thought was irrelevant. The fact that Rahul had the guts to declare when Sachin was only six short of a personal milestone and Sachin had the grace to accept the decision shows the spirit within the team. It proves that the team is on the right track.'
>
> —B.P. BAM

An injury to Zaheer Khan that forced him to pull out of the match and series, meant that Rahul had only three specialist bowlers at his disposal, in Kumble and pacemen Pathan and

Balaji. That the Pakistanis still lost twenty wickets in just over two days on what was still a good batting track, emphasized not only the ineptitude of the hosts, but also Rahul's astute handling of his resources. He crowded the batsmen with attacking fields and rotated his bowlers effectively. Kumble sealed the win with a phenomenal 6-71 in the second innings.

> 'We won at Multan because we had plenty of runs on the board and we kept the Pakistanis on the field for quite a while (it was very hot and humid). Another factor was the pressure built by the bowlers. Sachin and Yuvraj also chipped in with crucial wickets. Rahul used them when the situation demanded it. The bowlers knew what lines they were supposed to bowl and the fields they would get before they went out. Our plans worked.'
>
> —Murali Kartik

A historic win by an innings and 52 runs, India's biggest overseas, prompted the fickle-minded to advocate Rahul's appointment as full-time captain at the expense of Sourav, who they called the 'weakest link' in the team. It was an overreaction of the highest order. Rahul certainly had leadership qualities, but he had had just two Tests at the helm compared to Sourav's 37!

With the captain still unfit, Rahul stayed in charge for the second Test at Lahore and elected to bat on a greenish strip. Watchers described it as a 'bold' move, although it wasn't a new one for the Indians.

But the Indians were denied an encore of their Headingley heroics by a right-handed paceman named Umar Gul, who did what the Pakistani new-ball bowlers Shoaib Akhtar and Mohammed Sami did not. He bowled an impeccable length and maintained a consistent attack on the corridor of uncertainty, just outside the off-stump. India were 147-7 on the first day and lost the match there and then. The second innings was another disaster for India and Rahul, whose run-out without facing a ball induced frenzied reactions from the commentators.

Pakistan won by nine wickets, but had to encounter embarrassment even in their moment of triumph. Ironically, the cause was their bowling hero. When last-man Balaji fell leg-before to leg-spinner Danish Kaneria in the second innings, India were only 39 ahead. An ecstatic Gul came charging in and grabbed the stumps, only to be reminded by a bewildered Steve Bucknor that his team still needed 40 to win!

For the second time in the series, Rahul made the point that he would have done things differently with the benefit of hindsight. He displayed characteristic candour during the Presentation Ceremony, clarifying that the decision to bat first on a green track wasn't the only reason his team had lost.

Sourav returned to the fray for the series decider at Rawalpindi. Rahul, who had done nothing of note with the bat in the first two Tests, was eager to make a mark.

> 'We visited the Lahore University of Management Studies before the Rawalpindi Test. Rahul was the main speaker, and he thanked the Pakistanis for their warmth and hospitality. When a student asked him his plans for the forthcoming Test, Rahul said that he would like to score a double hundred. The crowd was stunned.'
>
> —Prof Ratnakar Shetty

Rahul got his chance to 'make a mark' fairly early. Sourav

called correctly and this time elected to bowl on another greenish pitch. The Indians bowled out their opponents for 224, and Sehwag fell to the first ball of the Indian response, getting a leading edge to Shoaib that a diving Hameed clung onto at gully.

Unbeaten on the first evening, Rahul skipped an official dinner, opting to sleep early as he had a job to do the next day. Clearly, nothing had changed since 1996-97!

He started day two with a flick off Shoaib that sped to the mid-wicket boundary. Patel, opening in place of Chopra, who had been dropped, reached his third half-century in four Tests. The keeper added 129 with Rahul before falling to the paceman Fazl-e-Akbar, who had replaced the unfit Umar Gul.

Only one run had been added to the score when Shoaib bowled a 'spitting cobra' to Tendulkar that took the edge of his bat. The score: 130-3. Enter Laxman to play a series of gorgeous strokes. Inspired by his sizzling straight-drive off Akbar, Rahul essayed an imperious square-cut off Sami. The bowler then served another short delivery outside off, which Rahul cut hard. The ball flew to Yasir Hameed at point, who failed to get his palms together, and spilt a regulation chance. Rahul was 71 at that stage. A shattered Inzamam might well have thought that the beneficiary would go on to score a hundred. This was a rather modest estimation, as it turned out.

Rahul completed his first hundred on Pakistani soil with a single off Kaneria. He had added 131 with Laxman when the latter missed a fast, swinging full-toss by Shoaib and heard the death-rattle. With Sourav lacking match-practice and the Indians only 37 ahead, the Pakistanis had another opportunity to come back into the game. But Shoaib left the field with a wrist injury, sustained after falling in his follow-through. He later complained of a back injury and did not bowl again in the match.

Sourav played himself into form with some magnificent off-side strokes, and Rahul's solidity and assurance gave the bowlers no hope. As over after over progressed, the Pakistanis wilted.

It is one of Indian cricket's greatest ironies that two individuals who started their Test careers together and went on to work together as captain and deputy, were rarely on the same wavelength while 'running' together. While batting with his deputy and co-debutant at Rawalpindi, Sourav had two close shaves before he was finally run out. It was his third run-out in Tests, and Rahul had been at the other end on all three occasions! But the fault this time was clearly Sourav's for not coming in the way of Imran Farhat's direct throw. For the record, Rahul at that stage had been run-out four times in Tests with Sourav as his partner.

Rahul kept the 'promise' he had made to the Management students and completed a double hundred, his fifth in Test cricket and an Indian record at the time, with a single off Kaneria. India had gained a monumental lead by then. 'The innings he played at Adelaide was a match-winning effort. But this one might well be a series-winning effort,' commentator Robin Jackman observed. It was.

Rahul went for his strokes soon after Yuvraj's dismissal. He passed his highest in Test cricket and then the 250 mark.

Rahul after his double century at Rawalpindi

> 'His performances in 2003-04 were incredible. His consistency was remarkable and his mental balance very good. He didn't start off all that well in Pakistan, but his patience enabled him to succeed eventually. He is a player who likes to take his time and build an innings, while there are others who like to score in boundaries. The way he prepares himself for a game is something all youngsters should keep an eye on.'
>
> —Sachin Tendulkar

The dash for runs saw him get away with a couple of edges, but those were well-earned. He was on 270 when he went for a reverse-sweep off part-time bowler Imran Farhat and missed.

He had batted for 12 hours and 20 minutes.

A deficit of 376 was expected to intimidate the hosts, and so it did. The Indian bowlers refused to get disheartened by some pedestrian catching by the fielders on the fourth morning, and kept firing away. Wickets fell steadily and the tail-enders dug their own graves with some cavalier batsmanship, when they ought to have supported Asim Kamal, who was batting well at the other end. The 'injured' Shoaib did not endear himself to his captain by swinging his bat merrily without any apparent pain or discomfort. The last wicket fell at 245 when Kaneria went for an almighty hit off Tendulkar and got a top-edge instead. The captain took the catch, and the party began. The job accomplished, John Wright treated himself to a cigarette to celebrate the culmination of a process that had begun way back in early 2001.

The team had finally learnt to win when and 'where' it mattered in Test cricket. It was India's first series win overseas since 1993. After the draw against the world's best side in its backyard, this triumph seemed like the next step towards greatness.

> 'It has taken us some time to build this team, so it really feels proud to see the way they played here and in Australia.'
>
> —Sourav Ganguly (at the presentation ceremony)

Rahul Dravid, with his third double hundred in a single season, two of which won India the match (one also won a series), was undisputedly the Player of the season. The whipping boy of 1998 had become the bulwark of the team.

13

# IN A CLASS OF HIS OWN

> 'Rahul Dravid is one of the premier batsmen in the world today. He has a classical style based around an extremely strong defence. When the situation arises, he can play all the shots, but he tends to play well within his limits, which is ideally suited to Test cricket.'
>
> —ALLAN BORDER

The ICC Player of the Year Award reaffirmed Rahul's stature in world cricket. A panel comprising contemporary captains, umpires and referees chose him as the Player of the Year (Overall) and Player of the Year (Tests), from a shortlist of nominees that was drawn on the basis of performances between 1 August 2003 and 31 July 2004. The presentations to Rahul and Irfan Pathan (Emerging Player of the Year) at the first-ever ICC Awards Ceremony in September 2004 were a consolation for Indian cricket-lovers unhappy with some lackadaisical cricket.

Sri Lanka and Pakistan had the better of India in the Asia Cup, India's first engagement of the new season. The team did not fare any better on a tour of Europe, which comprised a tri-series in the Netherlands, a bilateral ODI series against England and the ICC Champions Trophy. The fielding was

A double whammy at the inaugural ICC awards in september 2004. Winner of the ICC Player of the Year (Overall) and Player of the Year (Tests) Awards

poor, the bowling poorer and the batting poorest. The Indians, joint holders of the ICC Champions Trophy, went down to Pakistan at Birmingham in the quarterfinal of the 2004 edition. It was their third straight defeat against the traditional foe after the reverses in the Asia Cup and the Netherlands.

It seemed as if the law of averages had caught up with all the frontline Indian batsmen after two productive tours of Australia and Pakistan. A major blow was dealt by Tendulkar's tennis elbow, which forced him to pull out of the Netherlands and England tournaments.

Inevitably, Rahul delivered the best batting performance by an Indian in this dismal period. His 82 against Sri Lanka in the Asia Cup on a deteriorating wicket at Dambulla was a gem, featuring the by—now mandatory angling of the ball into the gaps, scoops over the infield and brilliant running between the wickets. Sadly, it ended up being a lone hand in a losing cause.

The reverses in the limited-overs format were followed by the biggest disaster of all—a Test series loss to Australia at home. Adam Gilchrist, who led Australia in the first three Tests in Ricky Ponting's absence due to a thumb injury, became the first Australian skipper since Bill Lawry in 1969-70 to conquer the 'Final Frontier'. The Indians came unstuck against a team that had done its homework. Gone was the 'attack-at-all-costs' policy; it was replaced by logical, and for the Australians, lateral thinking. Conscious of the Indians' love for hitting fours, they concentrated more on plugging the boundaries than the gaps. The densely populated slip-cordon was dispensed with after the first few overs. Different strategies were planned for different Indian batsmen, and their bowlers executed them to perfection with a resurgent Glenn McGrath leading the way. His break-back that squeezed through Rahul's defence to bowl him for a duck in the first innings of the first Test at Bengaluru was the ball of the series. Gilchrist could have enforced the follow-on at Bengaluru and in the third Test at Nagpur, but he didn't. Their objective was to pile on the agony for the Indians (needless to say, another was to avoid an encore of Kolkata 2001). It worked, with India losing both games. Incidentally, the second innings in Bengaluru provided the fourth instance of the Indian skipper being run out in Tests with Rahul at the other end!

The Indian camp did itself no favours by tinkering with the opening slot. The tried, tested and reasonably successful Akash Chopra was replaced by Yuvraj Singh in the second Test, only to be brought back for the third. Virender Sehwag, the common factor, produced a sizzling 155 in the second Test at Chennai, an enthralling game that was poised for a great finish. India needed 229 and Australia ten wickets on the last day. But rain had the final say.

Sourav's assertion that India had only a 50 percent chance of victory at Chennai was more realistic than pessimistic. Sehwag excepted, only four batsmen—Rahul, Irfan Pathan,

Mohammed Kaif and Parthiv Patel—had crossed the 50-mark in the first three innings of the series. Although Patel had batted well, he had been a complete disaster in his primary role behind the wickets. Laxman, the man identified by Australian veterans as their side's 'Enemy No. 1', was struggling. Tendulkar's tennis elbow kept him out of the first two Tests.

The maestro was back for the third Test at Nagpur, but his return was overshadowed by the events that preceded the game. There were reports that the Indians were shocked to see the wicket on which the Test was to be played. In the words of a former Australian captain, it was like being asked to play a Test at Brisbane in the middle of a series in India. Needless to say, the visitors were delighted and Glenn McGrath, among others, could not wait to bowl on the green and hard strip in what was his 100th Test. It was alleged that the pitch had been prepared the way it had by the Nagpur-based Vidarbha Cricket Association to spite the dispensation that was running the BCCI at the time. There was another setback for the home team, in the form of a thigh injury to Ganguly. The spirits of the players sank further when Harbhajan Singh, who had taken 16 wickets in the first two Tests, went down with food poisoning and joined the captain on the bench. Irfan Pathan was also declared unfit. As stand-in captain, Rahul had his task cut out.

Damien Martyn's second hundred of the series and a fabulous 91 by Michael Clarke, who had debuted with 151 at Bengaluru, ensured a total of 398. The Indian response was a poor 185. Nineties by Katich and Martyn in the second essay left the Indians with a modest 543 to win. They were bowled out 342 runs short.

Harbhajan returned to the squad for the final Test at

Mumbai. Sensing that the wicket was likely to take turn, the Indians also retained the left-arm spinner Murali Kartik, who had bowled well at Nagpur, in the playing eleven. Not many teams were known to go into a Test with a three-pronged spin attack, but the hosts had nothing to lose. That Rahul was still in charge was confirmed by a press release issued by the BCCI that 'enlightened' the cricket media on the 'exact' status of Sourav's injury: 'Medical investigations have revealed intraarticular pathology of the right hip joint noted by increased synovial fluid accumulation.'

Unseasonal rain delayed the start on the first day. Ricky Pouting, finally fit, accompanied Rahul for the toss. Even as he came in, Warne went out with a broken thumb. The leg-spinner had bagged 14 wickets in three Tests, a tremendous improvement on his previous visits in 1997-98 and 2000-01. But ironically, his team missed him the most in Mumbai.

India ended the first day at 22-2 with Sehwag and his debutant opening partner Gautam Gambhir back in the shed. Tendulkar fell early on the second morning, and the innings disintegrated rapidly. Rahul held fort at one end as the wickets tumbled at the other. He scored an unbeaten 31 out of a disastrous 104. A 0-3 loss seemed a foregone conclusion.

The Australians were wary of Harbhajan, who shared the new ball with Zaheer Khan. They played the off-spinner well, but floundered against the others. Kartik exploited the pitch superbly, as did Anil Kumble, who had already snared 21 wickets from the first three Tests, including his 400th in Test cricket. Martyn top-scored with 55 and the innings folded up for 203. Even as questions were being raised about a track on which the ball was turning at obtuse angles on the second day itself, Sehwag and Gambhir hung on until stumps, much to their team's relief.

Fervent brain-racking by the Indian captain had preceded the start of the second innings.

> 'Rahul thought that I should go in at number three to force the pace against the new ball and set the tempo.'
>
> —VVS Laxman

It was a courageous decision. The man for whom Rahul wanted to sacrifice his prized number three slot had had a nightmarish series with 53 runs from five innings and looked a pale shadow of the artist who had annihilated the Australians less than a year ago. Laxman made his way to the middle early on the third morning with the scoreboard reading 5-1. An individual who had joined the Indian team as 'Consultant' was impressed.

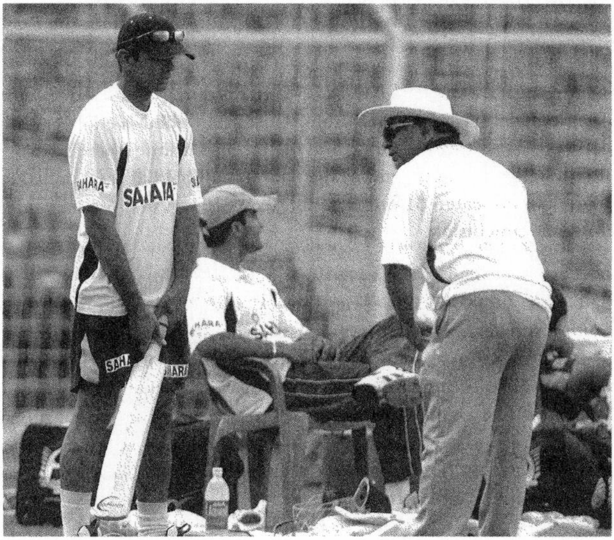

The quest for perfection continues...
Rahul discussing technique with Sunil Gavaskar, 2004-05

'It was Rahul's decision. The idea was to have someone who would attack at the start and take the initiative. It showed Rahul's dedication to his team's cause. He had no qualms dropping himself down the order.'

—SUNIL GAVASKAR

The score was 14-1 when Sehwag fell leg-before to McGrath. That brought in Tendulkar, and the turnaround.

'Laxman was to bat at number three only if a wicket did not fall on the second evening. In the morning, the ball would come onto the bat and he would get to play his natural game. He wasn't going through a good phase, and the idea was to bring some change in his number and allow him to bat freely. We knew that Australia would be under pressure if he initially scored in boundaries. When I joined him, we decided to try and get on top rather than defend. I thought that partnership changed the whole match.'

—SACHIN TENDULKAR

The pair batted cautiously for five overs and then took close to forty runs from the next four. Tendulkar started the counterattack with two fours in a Gillespie over and Laxman carried on. Nothing-seemed to bother them, not the bowling, and certainly not the pitch. Tendulkar fell when he top-edged the off-spinner Nathan Hauritz for 55. Laxman fell to the same bowler, but not before completing his first half-century of the series. His immaculate 69 turned out to be the highest individual score of the match. After his dismissal began the Michael Clarke show. A player who never bowled regularly at club level, let alone first-class level, he took six wickets at a cost of nine runs in an unbelievable spell. India were all out for 205 and Australia needed only 107 with around two hours and two whole days to spare. But it was a treacherous wicket they would have to bat on.

In the dressing-room, Rahul gave his team a pep talk.

> 'He told us that he wanted an honest effort that would satisfy every individual himself before the others. If our efforts were honest, we would walk with our heads held high.'
>
> —Murali Kartik

Zaheer Khan gave his side a 'bonus' with the wicket of Langer off the second ball of the innings, caught by debutant keeper Dinesh Karthik. But Hayden and Ponting were assertive. The innings was only four overs old when Rahul decided on a change. Strangely, he threw the ball to Murali Kartik and not Kumble, who had taken five wickets in the first innings.

> 'Murali's deliveries were drifting inwards like those of Anil's. But Murali was also getting vicious turn. That was more difficult to handle on that wicket.'
>
> —Sachin Tendulkar

Kartik struck twice in his very first over. Ponting edged the ball onto the keeper's thigh, from where it rebounded to Laxman at second slip. Then came the biggest blow of all, when he bowled one that 'drifted' in and trapped Martyn plumb in front.

> 'Rahul is an excellent reader of the game. I had taken four wickets in the first innings to Anil's five. What probably influenced Rahul to bowl me before Anil was the fact that Michael Clarke had taken six wickets with his left-arm

spin. So Rahul may have thought that a left-arm spinner would be effective at that point of time.'

—MURALI KARTIK

Kartik took those two wickets for Harbhajan as much as for his team and himself. The man nicknamed the 'Turbanator' after the 2001 series was inspired to step up a gear. He dispatched Katich and then Hayden. Kartik castled Clarke, and Gilchrist essayed a desperate lofted sweep after batting patiently to score nine from 50 balls. Tendulkar held the catch at mid-wicket and at 58-7, the chase had all but been derailed.

Gillespie, who had had a great series as bowler and lower-order batsman, batted positively with Hauritz before the latter was declared leg-before off Kumble. Kasprowicz became Harbhajan's fourth victim, caught in the slips by the captain. The score: 93-9. McGrath, the number eleven, then drove Harbhajan, only to get an outside edge and Laxman did the rest. India had snatched an improbable victory by 13 runs.

'Rahul has proven on many occasions that he has a great cricket brain. This was evident at Mumbai when he promoted the out-of-form Laxman up the order, which had an immediate effect. The only answer I can give for Kumble's late inclusion into the bowling in the second innings is that Rahul obviously felt that finger-spin would be much harder to face on that wicket than wrist-spin. I think it was a masterstroke.'

—ALLAN BORDER

Two masterstrokes by Rahul had enabled India to register a convincing, albeit consolation victory with two days to spare. The livid Australians slammed the track, whereas Rahul described it as 'interesting' in the presentation ceremony. Even as the debates raged on over the strip, one question remained unanswered: Was it so bad that the world's best team lost ten wickets in a little over two hours?

It was a happy end to what had been a poor series for Rahul and his team. The Australian bowlers had troubled him with a micldle-and-leg stump line, with two men patrolling the mid-wicket region and thus rendering his productive flick off the pads redundant. They did not want to give him width outside the off-stick, and such was the proficiency of Messrs McGrath, Gillespie and Kasprowicz that they were spot-on. Rahul's highest score of the series was a 60 in the second innings at Bengaluru.

At Mumbai, in his 82nd Test, Rahul became the second-fastest Indian after Sunil Gavaskar to break the 7,000-run barrier. It had taken him only nine Tests to reach that figure after completing 6,000 runs in the unforgettable Adelaide Test.

After Australia came a South African side for a two-Test series. Although the side comprised quality players like Jacques Kallis, Shaun Pollock and the new skipper Graeme Smith, it was still a far cry from Cronje's outfit of 1999-2000. The process of 'reconstruction' that had begun after the 'Hansiegate' fallout in 2000 was still going on. Rahul completed a hattrick of Castrol Indian Cricketer of the Year Awards (shared this time with Tendulkar) during the series. His 80 and 47 in the second Test at Kolkata set up an eight-wicket win and silenced Protean coach Ray Jennings, who had accused the Indian batsmen of 'sleeping' in the middle. Not to be outdone, the Indian team signed a pillow and sent it to the Protean dressing-room after the game!

India predictably 'walked over' the Bangladeshis in their next series, although they were subjected to an embarrassing loss in the second of three one-day internationals. But there were no surprises in the Tests. Rahul created history in the second Test at Chittagong. His innings of 160 made him the first batsman in Test history to score a hundred in each of the ten Test-playing entities of the time.

The arrival of a Pakistani side sans Shoaib Akhtar in February 2005 for a 'return' Test series provided Sourav and his team the opportunity of ending a season of mixed results on a happy note. In the first Test at Mohali, India did everything right until the fourth afternoon. Trailing by 204 in the first innings, Pakistan were 10-3 in the second and an early fifth-day finish was expected. Skipper Inzamam-ul-Haq and Yousuf Youhana put up a spirited fight, but the visitors were only 39 ahead when the sixth wicket fell. All-rounder Abdul Razzaq and wicketkeeper-batsman Kamran Akmal then joined forces in a spirited match-saving stand.

The Indians achieved at Kolkata what they could not at Mohali. Sourav won the toss and elected to bat, and Sehwag and Gambhir put on 80 before the latter was declared leg-before to the leg-spinner Danish Kaneria, who had come to India armed with a compliment from Richie Benaud: 'He has the best-disguised wrong'un I have seen'. Coming as it did from a wrist-spinner of high quality, a man who had played against and watched outstanding 'leggies' from Subhash Gupte to Shane Warne, this was no mean accolade. The 'wrong'un' or googly was one of the variations Kaneria had utilised to take six wickets at Mohali. In Shoaib's absence, he was his side's main strike bowler, and had been entrusted the task of denting the many daunting reputations in the Indian batting line-up, Rahul's included.

Kaneria's first delivery to Rahul was a flipper, a potentially lethal ball to receive at the start of an innings, but Rahul saw it early and brought his bat down in time. He got off the mark with an on-drive for two and then essayed his favourite cover-drive off Razzaq. He was on six when Kaneria and the close-in fielders went up in a hysterical leg-before appeal that was turned down. Commentator Ravi Shastri stated that the batsman had been fortunate, only to retract his statement after seeing the slow-motion replay, which showed that Rahul had inside-edged the ball onto his pad. Umpire Steve Bucknor, standing in his 100th Test, had seen what Shastri and millions of TV viewers had missed.

Rahul was intent on playing every delivery on merit, even in the last over before lunch bowled by Kaneria. Not for him the conservative approach of putting clown the shutters just because an interval was around the corner. He negotiated the first three deliveries and straight-drove the overpitched fourth to the boundary. The next ball was shorter in length, and he pulled it for two. His intentions were clear: If he would get a bad ball, he would give it the treatment, irrespective of the situation. Subsequent events would prove that his team was indifferent to this admirable trait.

After lunch, Rahul capitalised on the loose deliveries bowled by Shahid Afridi and the debutant Mohammed Khalil, and the occasional long-hop by Kaneria. The score was 156 when Sehwag was well caught by Inzamam off Afridi for 81. The disappointed spectators found their voice when Tendulkar completed 10,000 runs in Test cricket. Rahul had advanced to

83 when he subjected Arun Lal to the 'commentator's curse', driving Kaneria high and mightily for six, seconds after he had stated that 'Rahul was unlikely to go over the top'.

Tendulkar fell to Afridi immediately after completing a half-century. Twenty runs later, Ganguly and Laxman were consumed by Razzaq, who was making the old ball roar and 'reverse'. The score 278-2 had suddenly become 298-5 and India needed Rahul to bat right through the innings. Eight runs short of a hundred at that stage, he responded to the situation with two cracking strokes off consecutive deliveries by Mohammed Sami. The first one was a classical cover-drive to one pitched wide outside the off-stump, executed with a flowing bat, supervised by a still head and supported by the back foot resting on the ground and the front foot bent at a right angle. Sami's next delivery pitched on the line of off-stump and 'reversed' towards middle-and-leg. Rahul waited for it to come to him, and just as it seemed set to hit his front pad, offered the sweet spot of his bat and propelled it between mid-on and mid-wicket for the inevitable outcome. No sooner had he stroked it that he raised his arms in triumph, almost like a follow-through of the shot. As always, he turned in all directions with his bat raised to acknowledge the deafening cheers. He looked in command until he nicked a Kaneria leg-break in the very last over of the day.

The match ebbed and flowed for both sides for the next two days, and when the Indian openers began the second innings on the third afternoon only 14 runs ahead, the game was wide open. Sehwag showed what he thought of Inzamam's move to open the bowling with the inexperienced Khalil by doubling the lead in the very first over. But, Sami bowled Gambhir with a first-ball yorker. Rahul, back in the fray, ran a quick first-ball single and then pushed a rank bad ball by Khalil past mid-off for his first four of the innings. Sehwag's exit at 27 brought a determined-looking Tendulkar to the middle.

India's batting supremos bonded well. Tendulkar completed his second fifty of the match and was looking good for many more when Bucknor upheld a half-hearted appeal by Razzaq for a caught-behind. That the umpire had ignored the batsmen's appeal against the fading light moments ago, only intensified the fury of the nation. Nobody remembered Bucknor's outstanding reprieve of Rahul on the first day, as a result of which he had scored a hundred! Not for nothing is umpiring considered a thankless job!

Rahul completed his own fifty before stumps. Ganguly did not last long on day four, being caught-and-bowled by Sami off a horrid pull shot. Laxman was stunned by a Sami snorter that hit him above the left eye, and had to retire. India were only 170 ahead, and a couple of wickets at that stage would have put Pakistan in the driver's seat. Sami greeted Dinesh Karthik, the new batsman, with a fuller delivery first up, the aim being to catch the batsman on the back foot, literally and figuratively, but Karthik outsmarted him by anticipating correctly and going for the drive. He opened his account with a first-ball four and did not look back.

While Karthik asserted his batting capabilities, Rahul battled on, ignoring the strain of batting in intense heat and humidity for the second time in the match. He moved into the eighties with a back-foot punch off Kaneria that sped to the mid-wicket boundary.

A hattrick in November 2004…Rahul wins the Castrol Indian Cricketer of the Year Award for the third time in a row, Presenting him the award for 2003-04 is Naveen Kshatriya, MD, Castrol India Ltd.

He had inched to 99 when he cut Afridi to the left of the fielder at cover. Rahul hesitated, but took off when he realised that Karthik was responding. It spoke volumes for the vice-captain's commitment to taking his side to an unassailable position in the match that even as he was about to complete the single to give him his second hundred of the game, he turned to check if his partner had made it. Rahul completed the single running backwards, and became only the ninth batsman to score two centuries in a Test twice. Karthik, who had made his ground easily, ran towards his senior partner to congratulate him and also thank him for the inspiration he had provided.

This writer had the privilege of watching Rahul's second hundred of the match along with the only other Indian to achieve this feat more than once. Sunil Gavaskar led the applause of the entire PMG team when Rahul completed his second hundred.

Rahul had moved to 135 when, in trying to get a move on, he holed out. to Asif Kamal off Kaneria. Karthik, with whom Rahul added a crucial 167 for the fifth wicket, scored an enterprising 93 before Kaneria bowled him around his legs. Ganguly declared 421 runs ahead, and Anil Kumble bowled splendidly to take 7-63 and ensure a 195-run victory for the home team.

A mere eight days later, a billion people watched in horror as the victors of Kolkata surrendered the third Test at Bengaluru with six overs to spare and made Inzamam-ul-Haq's 100th Test a memorable one for the Pakistani skipper and his team. A target of 383 was admittedly a tough one to chase on a wearing wicket in the fourth innings. But what was certainly not difficult was playing each ball on merit, as Rahul himself had demonstrated in the last over before lunch on day one of the Kolkata Test. That would have certainly ensured a draw and a 1-0 win. It might even have given the hosts an outside chance of victory.

But first-innings double centurion Virender Sehwag apart, no Indian batsman made even the slightest attempt to disperse the cordon of close-in fielders with positive batting. They dug a huge pit, and jumped into it, giving their opponents the pleasure of burying them alive. Although Pakistan deserved every compliment they received for their 168-run win, even their most die-hard supporter will admit that India lost the match more than Pakistan won it.

The twin hundreds at Kolkata helped Rahul maintain his awesome Test average. At the end of the series against Pakistan, it stood at 57.86, at that stage, the best among contemporary batsmen.

# 14

# IN CHARGE

> 'Rahul has been an ideal vice-captain. He is very happy to have consolidated his position between Sourav and Sachin. If you see the equation, he fits in beautifully between the two. Had Sachin been captain, Rahul would have been a weak vice-captain, whereas, with Sourav as captain, he became a strong vice-captain. Sachin does not have to depend on anybody to dominate, while Sourav depends on people like Rahul to dominate.'
>
> —ASHOK MANKAD (2005)

At around 2215 hours (IST) on Monday, 28 November 2005, Mohammed Kaif drove Charles Langeveldt for four to take India to an ODI series-squaring win against South Africa at Mumbai's Wankhede Stadium.

The cheers of the capacity crowd reached a crescendo when Kaif's partner and captain, who had scored a match-winning 78, waded his way out of the cluster of players, placed his helmet on the turf and turned 360 degrees, holding his bat high in his right hand and tapping its face with the left. Rahul was acknowledging the support he and his team had received. Memories of the game against Bangladesh at the same venue in May 1998, in which the same crowd had jeered him for his 21-ball outing that had yielded just one run, were consigned to the scrap-heap.

No one doubted Rahul's credentials to lead India, just as no one had raised eyebrows when he was first picked in the Indian team as a 23-year-old. Ironically, an irreproachable character like him led his country during a volatile phase, in which the Indian team became the cricketing version of the 'girl with the curl;' it was either outstanding or appalling.

John Wright's swansong against Pakistan in 2004-05 was not a memorable one, with Pakistan squaring the Test series and then winning the ODI series. However, the losses did not take the gloss off his overall impact. Under his watch, the Indian team had started winning Tests overseas and finished second in the World Cup. The most consistent performer of the 'Wright Era' was Rahul himself. His average of 47.37 in the first 38 'pre-Wright' Tests of his career rose to 66.75 in the 51 that he played when Wright was coach. The purple patch coincided with his dual role in ODIs. B.P. Bam would have felt vindicated.

> 'Wicketkeeping was something he "grudgingly enjoyed." Sourav, Rahul and I were looking for an all-rounder who would be handy in the 2003 World Cup, which is why several wicketkeeper-batsmen were tried out in 2001 and early 2002. Incidentally, Sourav was keen from the very beginning that Rahul keep wicket in the shorter variety. But Rahul wasn't. However, we had convinced him to do the job if we failed to unearth a deserving candidate within

nine months of the World Cup. As it turned out, we didn't, and Rahul took the gloves in the one-day series against the West Indies in May 2002. His keeping certainly made our side more balanced. His footwork as a keeper wasn't all that brilliant, but he has excellent hands. I thought he struggled to take throws from the outfield more than the deliveries. Thanks to the emergence of Mahendra Singh Dhoni and Irfan Pathan, I don't think India and Rahul will have to face the same predicament again!'

– John Wright (India Today, The Rock, May 2006)

Mahendra Singh Dhoni, a wicketkeeper-batsman from the city of Ranchi in eastern India, made his ODI debut against Bangladesh in December 2004 on the strength of impressive performances for India 'A.' He cemented his place in the national team with an extraordinary 148 against Pakistan at Vishakhapatnam, in what was the second game of Wright's last series.

The new coach was appointed on 20 May 2005, a month after the end of the series against Pakistan. Greg Chappell, the former Australian captain and one of the all-time greats, was awarded a two-year contract. On the same wavelength as the BCCI's panelists who picked him was Sourav Ganguly. The Indian captain had sought Chappell's inputs to prepare himself for India's tour of Australia in 2003-04 and thought the world of him. There were reports that most of the Indian players were keener on having Tom Moody, Chappell's compatriot and a two-time World Cup winner, as coach, but Ganguly's view prevailed. Moody, who was also interviewed for the India job, took charge of the Sri Lankan team.

The Australians commenced their respective stints against each other, in a tri-series in Sri Lanka in July 2005. Rahul was assigned the captaincy, with Ganguly still serving the six-match ban that had been slapped on him for India's slow over-rates in two successive games against Pakistan, earlier in the year. He had accordingly missed the last two games of the Pakistan series and was slated to miss four more. As it turned out, Justice Albie Sachs of the ICC's Disputes Resolution Committee, to whom the BCCI appealed on Ganguly's behalf, reduced his ban to four games. This made him eligible to play in India's third league game of the tri-series and he was added to the squad as a 'player.'

> 'I have had people tell me that I must be aggressive and seek the captaincy... But captaincy is something that cannot be grabbed at or asked for. It is an honour that is accorded to you. I don't believe you need to be desperate, to go out of the way to pursue it. That definitely does not help the team dynamics.'
>
> – Rahul Dravid, The Outlook, 16 May 2005

India started shakily in their first league game against the hosts. 64-5 at one stage, Rahul's 54 helped them finish with 205-9. He then set attacking fields for his bowlers and gave them long spells, but in vain. India lost both their league games against Sri Lanka, but managed to beat the West Indies twice despite shoddy fielding and inconsistent batting. Rahul played five specialist bowlers in the final, in what was an attempt to plug the runs that had been leaked by the batsmen playing the fifth bowler's role at the league stage. However, the move backfired.

Needing 283 to win, India required 99 from 90 deliveries with eight wickets in hand at one stage, before throwing it away with daft cricket. A stand of 84 between Yuvraj Singh and Rahul ended when the southpaw was caught in the deep. Rahul's run-out in a mix-up with Kaif triggered a collapse. An extra batsman was missed and Sri Lanka won by 18 runs.

Much to the consternation of Rahul's fans, who had hoped that his appointment as captain would be permanent in the wake of the reverses suffered by the team in the previous season, Ganguly was reinstated for the tour of Zimbabwe. India swept the two-Test series against a team hit by defections and civil strife, but the captain and coach fell out. Simply put, Chappell believed that Ganguly was not at his best and therefore did not deserve to be in the team, let alone lead.

> 'It happened at a training session two days before the first Test (in Bulawayo). The skipper left training midway and returned to the empty dressing room. He came back and threw himself on to a chair, visibly disgusted. I asked him what happened. Pointing at Chappell, who was on the ground overseeing the net session, Ganguly said, "That guy's crazy."
>
> "I instantly understood what had just happened was explosive,"
>
> So after pacifying Ganguly, I had a chat with his deputy Rahul Dravid. Then we walked up to the coach to tell him that dropping the skipper was beyond his jurisdiction.'
>
> –Amitabh Choudhary, Manager, Indian team to Zimbabwe, 2005 (www.timesofindia.com, 8 August 2015)

The Ganguly-Chappell standoff carried on after the team's

return to India, with an email that the coach had sent to the then BCCI President somehow finding its way into the inboxes of journalists. The nation was divided; for every individual who supported Chappell, there was another who backed Ganguly. The BCCI sided with the coach. Rahul was named captain of India for back-to-back ODI series against Sri Lanka on 13 October 2005, just two days after the birth of Samit, his first-born.

So comprehensively did India dominate the first two games of the ODI series against Sri Lanka that the selectors decided not to tinker with a winning combination. Accordingly, Sourav Ganguly, who had been ruled out of the first two ODIs due to a tennis elbow, was not considered for the entire series, despite his returning to action with a century in the Duleep Trophy.

India got off to a rollicking start in the first ODI at Nagpur. Sachin Tendulkar, back after sorting his own tennis elbow out for good, scored 93 and Irfan Pathan, one of many youngsters to have impressed Chappell, got 83 after being promoted to no. 3. Nagpur's 'son-in-law'* then slammed 85 off only 63 deliveries and the innings closed at 350-6. India won the game by 152 runs and went on to take the series 6-1. The nation's celebration of its cricket team's 'resurgence' commenced after the victory in the second ODI at Mohali itself, when a group of 'Bhangra' dancers convinced Chappell to do a jig with them outside the dressing room. The stand-out performance of the series was Mahendra Singh Dhoni's 183 in the third game at Jaipur.

Another highlight of the series was India's intelligent use of two innovations that had been introduced by the ICC on a trial

*Vijeeta, Rahul's wife, was from Nagpur.

basis. The 'Powerplay' marked a departure from the mandatory fielding restrictions in the first 15 overs of ODIs, which had been in place for years. Under the new rule, the restrictions were mandatory for the first ten overs and in two blocks of five overs each later in the innings, at the discretion of the fielding side. The objective was to enliven proceedings between the 16th over and the 40th over, a period when batting sides would put the shutters down and consolidate before going for broke in the last ten overs. The other innovation took cricket closer to sports like football and hockey than ever before. Teams now had the option of nominating a 'Supersub' before the toss. The Supersub could replace a member of the playing XI at any stage of the game and he would be able to bat, bowl and even keep wicket if required.*

> 'When Rahul took over as captain, his primary objective was to win the 2007 World Cup. Another goal of his was to make India the number one Test side. I was vice-captain for most of his tenure and we shared a very good equation. He led by example and made the youngsters feel at home. He was an excellent man-manager and tactician and would encourage the active participation of every member of the team in meetings. He was an avid reader and would recommend books to us. We established a world record by chasing successfully in seventeen consecutive ODIs in his very first season as full-time captain.'
>
> –Virender Sehwag

*While the Powerplay continues to be in practice after undergoing further modifications, the Supersub was discontinued in 2006 as it was found to be unduly favouring the team that won the toss.

There was no room for Ganguly in the ODI series against South Africa that followed. India lost the first game at Hyderabad and won the second at Bengaluru. The third fixture at Chennai was washed out.

The fourth game in Kolkata was a bizarre affair. South Africa dismissed India for 188 and achieved the target without losing a wicket. The visitors were buoyed by the support they enjoyed at the Eden Gardens, with the home team being booed for the entire duration of the game; it was the city's way of expressing its disapproval of its favourite son's omission from the squad. Quite understandably, the Indian players were upset. India won the final ODI at Mumbai to square the series 2-2 and Rahul could not thank the spectators enough for their support.

> 'Most of the players had an equation with Rahul even before he became the captain. The captaincy did not change him. He was always impartial and upfront in his dealings with the players. He would always make it a point to distribute responsibilities. Rahul apart, the senior players like Kumble, Ganguly, Laxman and Sachin were in a class by themselves. They were disciplined and committed, and this rubbed off on the junior members of the side. It was a harmonious unit.'
>
> – Air Marshal M. Baladitya
> (Manager, Indian team, 2005-06)

Sourav Ganguly's five-year stint as 'Test' captain officially ended on 22 November 2005, when the selection committee handed Rahul the reins for a three-Test series against Sri Lanka. The former captain was picked as a 'batting all-rounder.'

The start of the Test series at Chennai was anti-climactic,

with Cyclone Baaz wiping out play on the first three days. India won the second Test at Delhi by 188 runs. Sachin Tendulkar scored a record-breaking 35th Test hundred and Anil Kumble returned match figures of 10-157. It was Rahul's third win as captain overall and first as incumbent skipper. A phenomenal run of 94 consecutive Tests since his debut at Lord's in 1996 then came to an end when he contracted gastroenteritis and pulled out of the third Test at Ahmedabad. Virender Sehwag took over and led India to victory by 259 runs.

Another absentee from the Ahmedabad Test was the former captain, who was dropped despite scores of 40 and 39 at Delhi. For Ganguly, it was a turbulent time; individuals who swore by him were at war with those who swore at him. This included fans, cricket administrators, the media and even the selectors!

His consistency in the Ranji Trophy won him a place in the Test squad for the tour of Pakistan. People were surprised when Wasim Jaffer and Gautam Gambhir, the two specialist openers in the squad, were left out of the XI for the first Test at Lahore. With Rahul, Tendulkar, Laxman and Yuvraj Singh in the side, there appeared to be no room in the middle order. The former captain had opened in a Test innings only once since his debut in 1996, but he was game to partner Sehwag. However, Rahul had other ideas.

The start of the Test was delayed due to inclement weather and the television cameras caught the Indian captain in an animated discussion with his predecessor and the coach. To say that the electronic media went berserk was an understatement. They had 'experts' pontificating on the facial expressions and 'body language' of the trio and one channel even invited a lip-reader to do his bit!

'A captain must be able to set an example of sacrifice. He did not want to expose Sourav Ganguly as an opener. He overruled the selection committee of which I was a part,'... We said "No, you can't open the innings". He (Dravid) said that let not somebody say that we made him (Ganguly) a sacrificial goat. So he opened the innings and got a hundred (128 not out)... 'He (Dravid) got up early on the morning of the match and went to (coach) Greg Chappell's room and said "I will open the innings".'

– Raj Singh Dungarpur, Manager of the Indian team on the tour of Pakistan (As quoted on www.hindustantimes.com, 21 February 2006)

Ironically for a sport that had seen some outstanding opening batsmen in the second half of the 20th century, a makeshift opening combination came the closest to breaking a world record set by the Indian duo of Vinoo Mankad and Pankaj Roy against New Zealand at Chennai in 1955-56.

Pakistan batted first on a featherbed and declared at 679-7. Rahul opened with Sehwag and was happy to play second fiddle to his deputy, who batted as disdainfully as only he could. The stand ended when the duo was only four runs short of surpassing the 413 put on by Mankad and Roy.* Those who criticized Sehwag for attempting an uppercut in that situation, only to get an edge, overlooked the fact that he could not have scored 254 off 247 balls with conventional methods alone.

'The best part about batting with Rahul was that he would

*The record was finally broken by South Africa's Graeme Smith and Neil McKenzie, who put on 415 for the first wicket against Bangladesh at Chittagong in 2007-08.

take on the bowlers who were posing problems and blunt them. I would then capitalize. Simply put, he would tire the bowlers out and I would then attack the tired bowlers. I have never seen Rahul as upset as he was when I was caught behind. Frankly, I was not aware that we were four runs short of breaking the existing world record for the highest-ever opening partnership. I would have been more cautious had I known. The way I saw it, the light was fading, and I wanted to score as many runs as I could before play was stopped.'

– Virender Sehwag

The second Test at Faisalabad was another 'batathon.' Pakistan scored 588 and 490-8 and India got 603. Rahul, who opened again, scored his second consecutive hundred of the series and became the sixth Indian to score 1,000 Test runs against Pakistan. There was a flutter in the Indian dressing room when Laxman (90) and he fell in the space of five runs and Tendulkar and Yuvraj did not last long, but Dhoni (148) and Pathan (90) came to the rescue. Refreshingly, the the Player of the Match award went to Rudra Pratap Singh, a left-arm paceman from Uttar Pradesh, who debuted in the game and took 4-89 in Pakistan's first innings.

The decider at Karachi exposed the traditional Indian proclivity to snatch defeat from the jaws of victory. Four minutes into the game, Pakistan were 0-3, with Irfan Pathan becoming the first bowler to perform the hattrick in the first over of a Test. Zaheer Khan and R.P. Singh, the other members of India's first-ever left-arm pace triumvirate, also chipped in and at 39-6, Pakistan were on the ropes. But then, they had history, Kamran Akmal and Abdul Razzaq on their side. The all-rounders bettered their match-saving display at Mohali in 2004-05 with a stand that turned out to be match-winning. Pakistan reached 245 in the first innings and then shut India out of the game, eventually winning the match by a mammoth 341 runs and with it, the series.

Rahul was censured for persisting with his pacemen and not bringing on the spinners 'to make the proceedings less predictable' when Akmal and Razzaq were going great guns in the first innings. His riposte was typical of the man.

Even the most ardent Indian supporters were surprised by their team's performance in the ODI series that followed. The visitors lost the first ODI at Peshawar, but levelled the series in the second encounter at Rawalpindi, losing only three wickets in pursuit of 266. Rahul's contribution to the chase was 56. Tendulkar set up a win in the third game at Lahore with a stupendous 95 and the Indians wrapped up the series in the fourth game at Multan. Rahul steadied the team's chase of 162 with a knock of 59. In the final ODI at Karachi, which was only of academic interest, India were set 287 to win. Rahul opened the innings and 'baked the cake' with a knock of 50. Yuvraj and Dhoni, both of whom had put the Pakistani bowling to the sword throughout the series, then applied the icing. India cruised to victory with eight wickets in hand and nearly four overs to spare.

> 'We took an unbeatable lead in the series with our win in the fourth game at Multan. The boys were delighted and wanted to celebrate. The catch was that we were in Multan, where "drinks" were not available! I had to contact the Indian Embassy at Islamabad for help. It was a memorable

evening. Sachin assumed the duties of the bartender and the likes of Yuvraj danced to popular film songs. Another memory of that tour is of experiencing India's "soft power" in Pakistan. People would accost us and talk about their favourite Indian actors, TV programmes and songs. The hospitality was overwhelming.'

– Air Marshal M. Baladitya
(Manager, Indian team to Pakistan, 2005-06).

Rahul's first full season as captain was far from over. The first Test against England at Nagpur was drawn and India won the second, played at Mohali, by nine wickets. The final Test at Mumbai was preceded by a ceremony at the Brabourne Stadium, where Rahul was felicitated for his imminent century of Test appearances. One of the speakers at the function was a legend who exhorted Rahul to 'do a Ricky Ponting' by scoring two hundreds in his 100th Test.

Andrew Flintoff, Rahul's England counterpart, was one of the thousands flummoxed by the Indian captain's decision to bowl after winning the toss.

'We'd taken five bowlers, and we had three seamers, and we thought there'd be a bit more bounce and seam movement early. We thought we could get a few wickets there, restrict them to a low score, and then bat big in the first innings to set the game up. It didn't do as much as we expected in the first session, they batted well, and once they'd got 270 for 3 on the first day we knew we were on the back foot.'

– Rahul Dravid, as quoted on www.cricinfo.com,
22 March 2006

India trailed by 121 runs in the first innings and England set them 313 to win on the final day. The score was 75-3 when Flintoff got one to angle away from his opposite number. The ball kissed the outside edge of Rahul's bat and Geraint Jones, the keeper, accepted the catch. That dismissal set the cat among the pigeons and India were skittled out for 100. Rahul let his disgust be known by picking up a chair and flinging it in the dressing room, an act he regretted later.

He got his side to pick itself up in the ODI series that followed. With Tendulkar unavailable due to shoulder trouble, Gambhir partnered Sehwag in the first two games, both of which India won. The four-wicket win in the second ODI at Faridabad was their 14th successful chase in a row, surpassing the record that South Africa had set earlier in the same season. The captain promoted himself to the opening spot for the remainder of the series and produced scores of 46, 65 and 69, all of them match-winning efforts. The fifth game at Guwahati was abandoned without a ball being bowled and Rahul missed the sixth at Jamshedpur. India took the series 5-1, which meant that they had won 17 of the 22 ODIs that they had played since the start of the Sri Lanka series in October 2005. The players got a breather after a two-match ODI series against Pakistan in Abu Dhabi, in which honours were shared. Rahul scored a match-winning 92 in the second game, once again as opener.

The Indians carried their limited-overs form into the first ODI of their tour of the Caribbean in mid-2006. Rahul set up India's seventeenth consecutive victory while chasing with an innings of 105. The delighted Indian coach then had a go at the opposing side. Chappell was quoted as saying that the 'West Indies had forgotten how to win.'

Not for the first or last time in sporting history, a dig triggered a turnaround. The hosts defended a score of 198 in the second game and the lights went out in the Indian camp. Brian Lara's side won the next three games to take the series 4-1. The 'girl-in-the-curl' syndrome showed no signs of letting up.

The Indians dominated the first two Tests, but failed to deliver the knockout punch. Virender Sehwag very nearly scored a century before lunch and Rahul scored 146 in the second Test at Gros Islet. Mohammed Kaif completed his maiden Test hundred later in the innings. India enforced the follow-on with a lead of 368, but they were thwarted by Lara, who scored 120. The Windies were the better side in the third Test at Basseterre, but India drew the game comfortably.

Rahul was lucky to win the toss in the last Test at Kingston and bat first on a wicket that seemed set to deteriorate rapidly as the match progressed. But thereafter, the Indian captain made his own luck.

He arrived at the wicket with the scoreboard reading 3-2. Jaffer and Sehwag, the openers, were already back in the pavilion. After negotiating some testing deliveries and surviving an appeal for caught-behind, he drove Dwayne Bravo for four and thereafter kept the scoreboard ticking with deft placements. Laxman was the third to fall, with the score at 34. With the ball keeping low and not coming on to the bat, a batsman's judgement and footwork had to be precise and decisive. It was imperative to capitalize on every scoring opportunity. When Collymore bowled into his pads, Rahul flicked him for four.

He brought the Indian supporters to their feet with a straight-drive off Collymore that sped to the boundary. A little later, he got a life when a delivery by Jerome Taylor reared awkwardly off a length and took him by surprise. The ball took the outside edge and flew over the outstretched fingertips of Runako Morton at third slip. While the West Indies players took their time to come to terms with what might have been, Rahul adhered to the 'one-ball' principle that he had followed throughout his career and forgot about the lapse. Taylor was bowling well, but when he gave Rahul the opportunity to free his arms, the Indian captain moved into position and thumped him to the mid-wicket boundary.

His team needed him to bat right through, but Rahul also needed someone to stay at the other end. Anil Kumble, who came in at 91-6, lent him the support he deserved. The Indian captain completed one of the most memorable fifties of his career and moved to 81 before Collymore had him caught behind. Kumble had fallen a few runs earlier for 45. India's total of 200 did not look imposing, but the Rahul-Kumble association of 93 had given the visitors a massive psychological boost. The hosts were dismissed for 103 in their first innings, with Harbhajan Singh bagging 5-13. The Indian openers then failed for the second time in the game and Rahul arrived at the wicket at 6-2.

He continued from where he had left off in the first innings. A square-cut off Pedro Collins was followed by a back-foot cover drive, which took his individual score to 20 and made him the sixth batsman to score 9,000 runs in Tests. The Sabina Park was undergoing renovation for the ICC Cricket World Cup 2007 and the teams had been accommodated in makeshift dressing rooms square of the wicket. This made it easier for the players to observe how every batsman in the middle was thinking on his feet, quite literally, on that strip; Rahul's footwork was a delight to behold for the junior members of both squads. His second batting 'masterclass' of the Test yielded him 68 runs before Collymore bowled him with one that kept low. The West Indies needed 269 to win.

A broken jaw had not deterred Anil Kumble from trying to bowl India to victory in the Antigua Test on India's previous tour of the Caribbean. Four years down the line, he was fully fit and in no mood to let anything get in the way. He took 6-78 and India won by 49 runs. It was their first Test series win in the West Indies since 1971.

The players failed to maintain the momentum. India did not qualify for the final of a tri-series in Malaysia and then crashed out of the ICC Champions Trophy, which they were hosting. A prominent member of the Indian team of the time told this writer that a 'divide' had been created between the senior and junior members of the side. This was the last thing the team needed on the eve of a tour of South Africa, one of the game's most daunting assignments.

The first of five ODIs against South Africa was washed out. The margins of the wins achieved by the hosts in the subsequent games—157 runs, 106 runs, 80 runs and nine wickets—spoke for themselves. Rahul broke a finger while compiling 68 in the third encounter and missed the remainder of the series. Virender Sehwag led the visitors to victory in the team's first-ever T20 International at Durban, in his absence. VVS Laxman, the vice-captain for the Tests, led the Indians to a 96-run win over a Rest of South Africa side at Potchefstroom. Irfan Pathan scored a century in the three-day game, but he was overshadowed by two of his seniors.

After being overlooked for the tour of the West Indies,

Zaheer Khan had flown to England, where he excelled for Worcestershire in the County Championship. He returned to India a better bowler and was rewarded with a recall, which he justified with five wickets in the three-dayer. A player in the same boat was Sourav Ganguly, who had been brought back for the Test series. The former captain scored 83 in the first innings.

While the victory at Potchefstroom raised the players' morale, it did not excite the media, with many journalists predicting an Indian surrender in the first Test at Johannesburg.

Rahul, who won the battle with his finger, won the toss and elected to bat on a green-top. The seniors then displayed their professionalism. Sachin Tendulkar, who had missed the Caribbean tour due to his shoulder surgery, scored 44 and Ganguly got an unbeaten 51. S. Sreesanth, the paceman from the south Indian state of Kerala, then took over. His 5-40 in the first innings ensured South Africa's capitulation for a mere 84. India's second innings featured a 'crisis classic' by VVS Laxman—need to be consistent. I think we should go with 'VVS Laxman' in the book, who went in at 41-3 with the South Africans a wicket away from coming back into the game, and defied them to score 73, enabling the visitors to set the opposition a target of 402. The bowlers did not let the advantage slip. India's 123-run triumph was their first in a Test on South African soil. At that stage, the series was theirs to lose.

Poor cricket cost them the second Test at Durban by 174 runs and the second innings of the decider at Cape Town witnessed some bizarre happenings.

India, leading by 41 at the end of the first innings, lost the openers with only six on the board and play was then held up for six long minutes. Tendulkar had been off the field during South

Africa's first innings for 18 minutes and he could not go in to bat till those many minutes had elapsed. The team management realized this late, and with Laxman in the shower when the second wicket fell, Ganguly had to hurriedly get ready and join Rahul in the middle. By then, the umpires had persuaded Graeme Smith, the South African captain, to not appeal for 'timed out' as the delay was unintentional.

Rahul and Ganguly added 84 before the latter fell for 46. This was followed by a bizarre passage of play in which it seemed as if two of the greatest batsmen of all time had forgotten how to rotate the strike. Rahul and Sachin Tendulkar managed a mere 24 runs in 15 overs. South Africa were too good a side to not capitalize on the diffidence of their opponents. Rahul was fourth out at 114 for a laborious 47, and Laxman and Tendulkar joined him in the dressing room in quick succession. India were dismissed for 169 and the hosts overhauled the target of 211 for the loss of five wickets.

The disharmony in the dressing room was not dispelled by victories in ODI series against the West Indies and Sri Lanka in the lead-up to the 2007 World Cup. Some members of the team met a senior BCCI official during the Sri Lanka series and suggested that Chappell be kept out of the World Cup squad altogether. As captain and the bridge between the warring camps, Rahul had his hands full.

He had a welcome, albeit temporary, reprieve of sorts during the third ODI against Sri Lanka at Goa, when he became the sixth batsman and third Indian after Tendulkar and Ganguly to score 10,000 runs in ODIs. It was a staggering achievement for someone who had been branded a 'Test specialist' at the start of his international career.

The 2007 World Cup turned out to be a disaster of colossal proportions, with the 2003 runners-up crashing out in the first round itself, with losses to Bangladesh and Sri Lanka. Back home, effigies of the players were incinerated and their houses put under armed guard. The BCCI convened a meeting of former India captains to prescribe remedies. Something had to give.

> 'The very tools that Chappell had used as a coach eventually nailed him. Leaks, e-mails berating players, tales about their misdemeanours, text messages to the press expressing his opinion came in such a flood that eventually they drowned him. When a TV channel said a "source close to Chappell" had called the seniors in the team a "mafia," nobody questioned the veracity of the source or the information. It was, sadly, just the kind of thing Chappell was expected to say and do.
>
> 'Dravid and Chappell, both selfstarters who had risen high in the game, vibed well intellectually. The men they were in charge of were not the same; it was in negotiating those differences that both the captain and the coach stumbled. In South Africa, a player admitted that most of the team had "switched off" from the coach. Dravid organized meetings without Chappell to draw the group closer together, older players were used to bring the younger men into the loop. The notion that seniors "hammered and abused" youngsters drew this terse response from a World Cupper; "Sack us, drop us, we deserve it, we played badly. But don't tell lies"... Pinning India's failures on one man would be dishonest; rather like Chappell's eager leaps to take credit whenever the players succeeded. "It starts with

me," Dravid had said after the Cup exit and every Indian cricketer would do well to accept the same.'

– Sharda Ugra (Indiatoday.intoday.in, 16 April 2007)

The man who had conquered many a challenge was not going to bail out in a crisis. Ironically for a team whose World Cup campaign was derailed by Bangladesh, the fact that its first assignment after the fiasco was a series against the same team, was a godsend. The players knew that they would get the room to regroup against a side that was talented but inexperienced.

India stuttered in the first ODI before Dhoni took them through. The remaining two games were won comfortably. The first Test was drawn and India won the second by an innings and 239 runs. Rahul was one of four Indian centurions in the game, with an innings of 129.

'The atmosphere in the dressing room was a lot more relaxed on the tours of Bangladesh, Ireland and England that followed the (2007) World Cup. There was greater communication, trust and transparency, and the camaraderie between the players was a lot more pronounced and obvious and this reflected in our performance on the field. Our victory over South Africa in an ODI series in Ireland, in conditions that suited them more than us, boosted our morale. The wickets were lively and conducive to pace and movement, but we outbowled them. Mr Chandu Borde, the Cricket Manager (in Ireland and England), was a great influence on the side, and Venkatesh Prasad and Robin Singh were brilliant as Bowling Coach and Fielding Coach respectively.'

—Sachin Tendulkar

The series win in Ireland ensured that the Indians were reasonably confident when they took on England at Lord's in the first of three Tests, but they played well below par. Set 380 to win, they were hanging on for dear life at 263-9 when stumps were drawn.

They went from awful to awesome in the second Test at Nottingham. Rahul elected to field after calling correctly, and unlike Karachi and Mumbai in 2006, his bowlers did not let him down. Zaheer Khan took 4-59 and the hosts were dismissed for 198. India then batted solidly, with every player from numbers one to six crossing fifty, the exception being the captain, who scored 37. The English did not do their cause any good by riling up India's pace spearhead when he came in to bat. Zaheer Khan cleared the jellybeans that were lying in the crease, only to discover a fresh lot a little later.

England needed to do a lot more than chucking jellybeans at an opponent, to avoid defeat after conceding a first-innings lead of 283. Michael Vaughan, their captain, led from the front in the second innings. Just when Indian shoulders were drooping, with the hosts 287-3 and their skipper batting on 124, Zaheer turned things around.

He served a delivery that was just short of a length. Vaughan went for the pull, but the ball came on to him a wee bit slower and lower than he expected. It flicked his pad and then dislodged the bails. When Zaheer trapped Ian Bell plumb in front at the same score, the result was a foregone conclusion. The paceman finished with figures of 5-40 in the second innings and India knocked off the target of 73 for the loss of three wickets. In the middle when the victory was achieved, were Ganguly and Rahul; while the former captain sported a grin, Rahul stayed expressionless and clenched his right fist. It was not as dramatic a gesture as his predecessor's jig on the Lord's balcony five years previously, but it was just as impactful.

India's 664 in the third Test at the Oval comprised a solitary century, that too by Anil Kumble. Much to the surprise of watchers, Rahul did not enforce the follow-on after England were dismissed for 345 early on the fourth day.

> 'Nobody understood the body language of my bowlers better than I did and I thought they were not in a position to bowl.'
>
> – Rahul Dravid (as quoted in Mumbai Mirror, 16 August 2007)

English supporters were ecstatic when Dinesh Kartik, Jaffer and Tendulkar fell with only 11 on the board. With a day-and-a-half left, anything was possible.

> 'Batting with Rahul at the Oval during the penultimate day's play of the Test series, I had noticed he was a shadow of his former self. On that particular day, he struggled. When I got out for 57 off 68 balls, he had barely made 10. At one stage, he had scored 2 off 52 balls.
>
> Having led the side for more than five years, I perfectly understood his problems. The burden of captaincy gets harder to bear over time.
>
> The biggest challenge of a leader is to stay in the present. I saw a different Dravid that day as he was thinking well ahead of the game. His mind was preoccupied with the result.'
>
> – Sourav Ganguly (A Century is Not Enough, Juggernaut Books, 2018)

The Indian captain may not have been his usual assured self, but the professional that he was, he did whatever he could to thwart the bowlers, who were on top after those early breakthroughs. In the final analysis, he was successful. He was fifth out at 89 before scoring 12 off 96 deliveries and his teammates added a further 91 before the declaration was made. The hosts, set an impossible 500 to win, were 369-6 at the close. It was India's first series win in England since 1986.

It was the first series to be played for the Pataudi Trophy, named for the father and son who had served the sport with distinction. Mansoor Ali Khan Pataudi, an individual known to be reticent in public, could not stop beaming as he presented the trophy to the Indian captain.

The euphoria in the Indian camp was somewhat dampened by reports that Zaheer Khan, who had taken 18 wickets in the series, had contradicted his captain by claiming to a news channel that he 'wasn't tired' on the fourth day of the last Test. The paceman later clarified that his comments had been taken out of context.

The batsman who had become stationary at the Oval went to the other extreme at Bristol, in the second game of the ODI series that followed. Rahul biffed and bashed his way to an unbeaten 92 off 63 balls. India finished with 329-7 and England retaliated strongly, but the visitors won by nine runs. Rahul followed the knock with 56 in a losing cause in the next game at Birmingham. The series went down to the wire, with honours even at the end of the sixth and penultimate game. The decider at Lord's was an anti-climax, with India being bowled out for a paltry 187 and England winning with seven wickets in hand.

The last game of the England tour was played on 8 September

2007, five days before the start of a competition that showcased the game's newest and shortest version. Four senior players—Sachin Tendulkar, Sourav Ganguly, Zaheer Khan and Rahul himself—had opted out of the inaugural 'ICC World Twenty20,' which was to be played in South Africa. The captaincy for the tournament was entrusted to Mahendra Singh Dhoni, who had impressed everybody with his poise and panache in his brief international career. India's first game against Scotland was only a few hours away when an unexpected piece of news came through.

> "I as not enjoying captaincy of the Indian team,' Dravid told PTI in his first public comment since his resignation. 'I began considering stepping down as Indian captain towards the end of the ODI series against England,' Dravid added. 'There is a shelf life to captaincy in India in which you can give it your best. Captaincy takes a lot out of you,' Dravid reasoned. 'May be the shelf life are (sic) becoming shorter as time goes by,' he commented. The thought of stepping down had crossed his mind after India's early exit from the World Cup in the West Indies for which he felt responsible, Dravid said, adding, 'but I still felt that I had the strength and energy to do it then' in the hope that things could be turned around. However, towards the end of the ODI series against England which ended this month, he had begun considering resigning. 'I did not want to take any decision there without first speaking to my family and wanted to give it a few days back home to see if I felt differently before taking a final call,' he said. The decision was 'personal and based on my observation of

> whether I would be able to give it my very best like I have always tried to', Dravid said. 'I haven't had much time to sit down and analyze the last two years and I think it will take a while being away from it to give me a better perspective of things,' Dravid said.'
>
> – WWW.NEWS18.COM, 17 September 2007

A parallel can be drawn between Rahul the captain and Shivaji, the Maratha warrior who took on the Mughals in the seventeenth century. Both individuals were unable to savour their many triumphs as each of them was followed by a setback. Not that this fazed them. Their resolute response to every challenge empowered them to eventually beat the cycle and break it. Shivaji laid the foundation of the Maratha Empire that was the dominant political force on the subcontinent for more than a century. Rahul resurrected Indian cricket after the World Cup catastrophe with the series win in England.

There were murmurs about Rahul 'having had enough of being taken for granted' by the selectors and Board officials. There was also talk of a 'Mumbai lobby' comprising Sharad Pawar and Dilip Vengsarkar, the then BCCI President and Chairman of Selectors respectively, trying to call the shots. It was even alleged that the Board's 'indifference' to Rahul had its roots in a plan to make Sachin Tendulkar captain.

Those who levelled these charges were in for a disappointment. A senior Board administrator of the time told this writer that Tendulkar, who had been vice-captain on the tour of England, was offered the captaincy after Rahul resigned. However, he declined and recommended a wicketkeeper-batsman from Ranchi instead. Rahul, who was consulted separately, felt the same way as Tendulkar.

India's 'T20' captain was accordingly assigned the job for ODI series against Australia and Pakistan. The Test captaincy was assigned to Anil Kumble later that year.

Something significant happened before the captaincy was split. India beat Pakistan by five runs in the final of the ICC World T20 and Dhoni and his young lieutenants became national heroes. A couple of weeks before the final, the BCCI announced the launch of an annual inter-franchise, inter-city league that would be played in the T20 format. Among those who attended the launch as prospective leaders of the proposed city sides, were Sachin Tendulkar and Rahul.

Indian cricket would never be the same again.

# 15

# LAST MAN STANDING

'We will have to take some tough calls if we want to win. I am taking a tough call today as captain and I want you selectors to take important call as selectors who want the betterment of Indian cricket. Three players are not fitting in the side. They are very slow as fielders and the format needs fitter players... Age is not the issue. Fitness is the issue. We are unable to choke the opposition because of their fielding...The strike is rotated and we can't build pressure...demoralizes teammates... I am a sportsman myself, I can understand that they don't want to give up, but the fact is that we just can't have them in the team...a good fielder will save runs in every game... I think we should also be looking at the World Cup. The sooner we form a core team, the better our chances will be. We have to let these three go, at least for this tour and then decide... We are all doing national duty... The media is going to burn us... People will feel bad... If we achieve results, then people will understand why we did what we did... More than players, we need characters. Characters who are desperate, who want to express themselves. We will get results only if we invest in youth today.'

– 'M.S. Dhoni,' as quoted in *M.S. Dhoni—The Untold Story* (Fox Star Studios, Inspired Entertainment, Friday Filmworks, 2016)

It was on 20 January 2008, just four days after he had scored a splendid 93 that set-up India's first-ever Test win at Perth, that Rahul learnt of his omission from the squad for the tri-series against Australia and Sri Lanka. Sourav Ganguly was also dropped.

With Zaheer Khan injured and Anil Kumble having retired from ODIs after the 2007 World Cup, Sachin Tendulkar was the only representative of the 'old guard' in the tri-series, in which India achieved their first limited-overs triumph on Australian soil since 1985. It did appear then that Rahul's ODI career was over, just six months after he had last led India.

Rahul did not do well in the ODIs against Australia at home that followed the ICC World T20. He scored 44 runs and got two ducks from six games. That cost him his place in the side for the next ODI series, against Pakistan.

India's top batsman of the Test series against Pakistan, which was played after the ODIs, was a certain S.C. Ganguly. He scored a century in the second Test in his hometown and followed it with 239 in the third at Bengaluru. The left-hander's cricketing rehabilitation was complete, or so it seemed. Rahul's performances on the other hand were average and his detractors went to the extent of questioning his selection for the tour of Australia.

What he meant to the team was underscored in the first two Tests, played at Melbourne and Sydney respectively. The team management, keen on accommodating Yuvraj Singh in the XI, requested its most adaptable player to open with Wasim Jaffer. However, the new combination failed, as did Yuvraj. India were outplayed at Melbourne and the Sydney Test was an acrimonious affair.

Rahul's 53 in the first innings at Sydney provided the foundation for the likes of Laxman and Tendulkar to capitalize on. Both scored centuries and India totalled 532 in response to Australia's 463. The hosts batted aggressively in the second innings and set India a target of 333, with a little over two sessions left. It was a situation reminiscent of the one that had confronted the Australians at Kolkata in 2000-01, in that the Indians did not have enough time to get the runs and a draw seemed the only option. But then, adopting a defensive mindset was always going to be fraught with risk, especially against a bowling attack like Australia's. The hosts snared three wickets, including those of the first-innings centurions, with only 54 on the board. Not for the first or last time, Rahul held the key to his team's fortunes.

India were 115-3 and he was on 38 when a delivery by Symonds grazed the knee-roll of his front pad on its way into Adam Gilchrist's gauntlets. The bowler and keeper appealed for a catch and Steve Bucknor, the umpire, raised his index finger. That decision proved to be the turning point of the game, with the Indians being undone by a combination of dreadful umpiring and the gamesmanship of their opponents. The last three wickets fell with a handful of minutes left for the close and Kumble stated at the post-match media conference that only one team had played in the spirit of the game. Insult was added to injury when Harbhajan Singh was formally charged for racial abuse. The BCCI took up the matter with the ICC and the Indian media went into overdrive. There was a question mark over the remainder of the tour, but sanity eventually prevailed.

The Indians channelized their hurt positively in the next Test at Perth. Back in the scheme of things was Virender Sehwag, who was playing his first Test in twelve months. He was not picked in the probables for the Australia tour, but Kumble insisted on his inclusion in the final squad. The six boundaries that he struck in his knock of 29 in the first innings gave his team momentum and its first 50-plus opening stand of the series. Rahul, back at no. 3, added 139 for the third wicket with Tendulkar. The senior statesmen batted splendidly, rekindling memories of their heroics on the previous tour. Tendulkar fell for an immaculate 71 and Rahul was only seven short of a century when he played his first false stroke of the innings, mistiming a lofted drive to be caught in the infield. India finished with 330 and its bowlers then dismissed the Australians for 212.

The visitors were in a bit of strife at 125-5 in the second innings, but VVS Laxman then did what he did best. His 79 ensured that the hosts had over 400 to chase.

They had runs to bowl with, but the Indians were aware that they needed to get the Australian captain early. Ponting was given a torrid time by Ishant Sharma, a teenager from Delhi, in a seven-over spell before Kumble asked him to take a breather. However, Sehwag, Sharma's Delhi captain, insisted that the bowler be given one more over. It was off the first ball of this additional over, which could well have been Sharma's last for a while, that Ponting got an outside-edge that was pouched by Rahul at first slip. The Indians then tightened the screws and won by 73 runs, thus ending Australia's second run of 16 consecutive Test wins for the second time in less than a decade.

Sehwag vindicated Kumble's faith in him with 63 and 151 in the drawn fourth Test at Adelaide. The Test series was lost, but the Indians carried the confidence they had gained at Perth, into the tri-series against the 2007 World Cup winners and runners-up. Rahul was among the many Indians who watched the tri-series win on television.

He had the best view of Sehwag's pyrotechnics in the first Test of India's next series. The Delhi opener put a formidable South African attack to the sword at Chennai, on his way to his second triple hundred in Tests. Rahul scored 111, but his 25th Test hundred was overshadowed by his 80th run. A single off Morne Morkel to mid-wicket made him the sixth batsman of all time, and third Indian after Sunil Gavaskar and Sachin Tendulkar, to complete 10,000 runs in Tests. The series ended in a 1-1 tie and all eyes shifted to a phenomenon.

Rahul led Royal Challengers Bengaluru in the inaugural season of the Indian Premier League. The IPL got off to an electrifying start, with Brendon McCullum blasting 158 for Kolkata Knight Riders against Rahul's 'RCB' in the opening game. RCB never quite recovered from the thrashing and finished seventh in the eight-team event.

India's tour of Sri Lanka in mid-2008 was another disappointment. Like most of his colleagues, Rahul struggled to comprehend the wiles of a 'mystery' spinner called Ajantha Mendis and India lost the series 1-2. A solitary fifty was all that he had to show. He scored 51 in the first of four Tests against Australia at the start of the 2008-09 season, but did little of note later. India won the series 2-0 to take possession of the Border-Gavaskar Trophy for the first time since 2004, but the triumph was tinged with sadness; Sourav Ganguly, who had strangely been left out of the Irani Cup game before being picked in the team for the first Test, had had enough of the uncertainty and 'selectorial whims and fancies.' He declared at the start of the series that it would be his last. Anil Kumble also bid farewell after the third Test at Delhi.

Rahul did not endear himself to the 'pundits' with scores of 3 and 4 in a Test against England at Chennai that India won after overhauling a target of 387. There were suggestions that he be 'put to pasture,' a cruel reminder of the ruthlessness of sport. Mahendra Singh Dhoni, who had taken over as 'Test' captain after Kumble's retirement, won the toss in the second Test at Mohali and elected to bat in nippy conditions. Sehwag fell with only six on the board and Rahul joined Gautam Gambhir. The veteran was playing for his career, if sections of the media were to be believed.

Gambhir and he played a waiting game. They let the England bowlers dominate but not dictate. As the minutes and hours ticked by, the bowlers lost their edge and the batters then asserted themselves. This writer happened to be in the President's Box at the venue, in his capacity as an employee of the BCCI. In the enclosure were some former cricketers and current and former administrators of the Board, but the cynosure of all eyes was a close associate of Rahul's. This individual stayed rooted to his seat through the day, even requesting that lunch and snacks be brought to him instead of his having to walk to the buffet table, in what was his attempt to bring Rahul some luck.

Unbeaten on 65 at the close, Rahul batted with a lot more freedom on the second morning. His tenacious 136 marked the end of his bad patch and the beginning of a period that was productive and replete with foreseen and unforeseen developments. Three fifties on the tour of New Zealand in early 2009 were followed by an entry in the record-books. Down 0-1 in the series and needing an impossible 617 to win the third Test at Wellington, the hosts were 30-0 when Tim McIntosh got an outside edge off Zaheer Khan. Rahul, standing at second slip, dived to his left to take the catch. It was his 182nd in Tests and it made him the most successful fielder in Test history, ahead of Australia's Mark Waugh.

> 'Rahul is the best "slipper" I have seen. Both Kumble and Harbhajan had immense faith in him. They trusted his "soft hands." Jacques Kallis comes the closest to Rahul in terms of slip-catching, amongst cricketers of the modern era. Individuals like Sachin, Rahul, Laxman and Anil epitomized professionalism. They did not have egos and they never abused the eminent status that they enjoyed. The youngsters respected them and they in turn respected and backed the youngsters. The affection was mutual. Sourav and later Dhoni benefitted greatly from the inputs provided by the seniors. I do not recall any incident that spoilt the atmosphere in the dressing room.'
>
> – Virender Sehwag

The members of the first Indian team to win a Test series in New Zealand since 1967-68, took off for South Africa soon after returning home. The organizers of the IPL tried their best to work the schedule of the tournament's second season around the General Elections, which were to be held at the same time. However, talks with the Government failed and the IPL was shifted across the Indian ocean.

Rahul was replaced as RCB's captain by Kevin Pietersen, who had been acquired by the franchise in the second players' auction. Pietersen returned to his international commitments after six games, as was decided earlier, and Anil Kumble took over and guided the side to the final, where they lost to Deccan Chargers. In a tournament in which some individuals who had excelled on flat pitches in the first season were exposed on the juicier wickets of South Africa, Rahul finished as his side's third-highest scorer—behind Jacques Kallis and Ross Taylor—with 271 runs from 13 games.

While the tournament was a success, the fact remained that the Indian players were an exhausted lot when they boarded the plane for England to defend their 2007 title in the ICC World T20 2009. They were eliminated in the first round.

The batting continued to be patchy on a short tour of the Caribbean, and the selectors, convinced that the only solution was to infuse the batting with stability, reversed the 'tough call' that the previous selection committee had taken the previous year. Rahul was recalled for a tri-series in Sri Lanka and the ICC Champions Trophy, which was to be played in South Africa. When asked for his reaction, he said that he would give his best. He delighted all those who had adored him for years by declaring that he had never played cricket to 'prove a point.' 'To me, it's about trying your best to be the best you can be, day after day, in whichever format you are playing and for whichever team you are playing,' he told the *Deccan Herald*.

It was obvious that the search for 'characters who could express themselves' had not yielded anybody who was half as malleable as him. His 47 in the league game against Sri Lanka prompted the team management to ask him to open with

Tendulkar in the final against the same team. Sehwag was missing due to injury and Dinesh Kartik, who had opened in the league games, hadn't clicked. Rahul struck a boundary off the very second ball and got his team off to a start for the first time in the competition. He fell for 39 after putting on 95 with Tendulkar, who went on to score a match-winning hundred.

India's Champions Trophy campaign began with reports that a member of the coaching staff had 'advised' the players to seek casual sex to boost their testosterone levels. Needing 303 to win their first game against Pakistan, India ran into a teenage prodigy called Mohammed Amir, who rocked the boat with early strikes. Rahul and Gambhir tried to resuscitate the innings before a misunderstanding resulted in the latter's run out. Rahul batted well until his hamstring acted up and he too was run out. His 76 was India's top score in a game that they lost by 48 runs. The next game against Australia was ruined by rain. The Indians went flat out in their last league game against West Indies, bowling the opposition out cheaply and then overhauling the target of 130 in 32.1 overs, but it wasn't enough to secure them a berth in the semi-finals.

Rahul's omission from the ODI squad for the next series, a seven-match tussle against Australia at home was as unexpected as his inclusion earlier in the year. To observers, it came across as a cruel way in which to treat a player of his stature; he was required in a country like South Africa, where the wickets had something in them for the bowlers, but he was not needed on the featherbeds at home, where the bowlers had little or no help and the younger batsmen could swing through, inside and across the line with impunity.

He did not say a word in public and let his bat do the talking in a three-Test series against Sri Lanka. An innings of 177 in the first Test at Ahmedabad was followed by 144 in the second Test at Kanpur. With Gambhir and Sehwag also scoring centuries, it was only the second instance of India's top three batsmen reaching triple figures in the same Test innings. India won the game by an innings and 144 runs and achieved another innings triumph in the final Test at Mumbai. Six of India's top seven batsmen, Rahul included, scored at least fifty. Virender Sehwag failed by only seven runs to become the first batsman in Test history to score three triple tons.

The country celebrated not only the series triumph, but also the team's ascent to the summit of the ICC Test Rankings for the first time. The side's consistency on foreign soil in the new millennium had played a critical role in this regard. One of those who drove the team to the top was an individual who had starred as batsman in all the notable 'away' wins in the first half of the 2000s and excelled as batsman/captain/senior statesman in most of the victories achieved in the second half.

Rahul began 2010 on an auspicious note with a hundred at Dhaka, in the second of two Tests against Bangladesh. He was on 111 and looking good for many more when he ducked into a bouncer by Shahadat Hossain and took his eyes off the ball. The lapse in concentration proved to be costly. The cherry thudded into the grille of his helmet and the impact was powerful enough to break his jaw. Rahul missed the remainder of the Test as well as the series against South Africa at home that followed.

The hiatus would have given him the time to introspect. He was 37 and had achieved a lot more than what he had set himself to do at the start of his international career. His ODI career was for all practical purposes, over (or so he and everybody else thought). The ICC Cricket World Cup 2011 was less than two years away and he and Laxman were not on the selectors' radar 'for the same.'

However, the pair that had rewritten the record-books at Kolkata and Adelaide still had a lot to play for. India were scheduled to tour South Africa, West Indies, England and Australia in the next eighteen months, and they had never won a series in South Africa and Australia. Experience, the veterans knew, would count in these countries. India had topped the ICC's Test Rankings, but the likes of Tendulkar, Laxman and Rahul were among those who believed that it was important to not merely scale the summit, but also stay there to prove that the ascension was not a fluke. They believed that they still had a lot to offer to Indian cricket and decided to carry on.

Rahul returned to action in the third season of the IPL, which made more news for tweets, income tax raids and a suspension, than the cricket. RCB reached the semi-finals, where they went down to Mumbai Indians. Rahul was his side's fourth-highest scorer, behind Jacques Kallis, Robin Uthappa and Virat Kohli, with 256 runs from 16 games.

He then struggled for the second successive time on a tour of Sri Lanka, not scoring a fifty in a series in which Tendulkar and Laxman were in cracking form.

Mohali, where he had ended his lean trot in 2008, brought out the best in him once again. His first-innings 77 against Australia was one of four half-centuries that enabled India to reach 405 in response to Australia's 423. The game turned out to be a thriller, with VVS Laxman, Australia's old nemesis, defying a bad back to take India from 124-8 to the target of 216. Ishant Sharma and Pragyan Ojha, India's numbers ten and eleven respectively, played their respective parts to perfection, as did Suresh Raina, who ran for Laxman for most of his innings.

India retained the Border-Gavaskar Trophy with a seven-wicket win in the second Test at Bengaluru. Rahul fell for just one in the first innings, the highlight of which was Tendulkar's second double hundred in four Tests. The 'Little Champion,' who like Rahul was on the wrong side of 35, had been on a roll for the past couple of seasons and was declared the ICC Player of the Year for his performances in 2009-10, on the eve of the Bengaluru Test. Laxman had also been among the runs. Rahul did not need to be told what was going on in the minds of the 'pundits.'

India needed 207 to win the game and Dhoni had at the back of his mind, the collapse at Mohali. With Laxman missing, the captain decided to space the seniors out and take the pressure off Suresh Raina and the debutant Cheteshwar Pujara. Accordingly, the team's most adaptable batsman was asked to bat at no. 5. Watchers were surprised when Pujara, who had scored four in the first innings, went in at the fall of the first wicket. The debutant got his eye in and essayed a fine innings. By the time he was third out for 72, the target was only 61 runs away. Rahul then went in and completed the formalities with Tendulkar.

He batted beautifully to score 104 in the first innings of India's next Test, against New Zealand at Ahmedabad. Leading by 28 in the first innings, the hosts had a scare when the Kiwis reduced them to 15-5 in the second essay. But Laxman staged another of his 'Houdini' acts in the company of Harbhajan Singh, who scored his maiden Test hundred. The Test was drawn, as was the second. India took the series with a massive innings win in the last Test at Nagpur. The batsman of the game was Rahul, who completed his 31st Test century and went on to score 191.

The Indians went on to have their most successful tour of South Africa. Rahul was not among the runs, but he made headlines nevertheless. After losing the first Test at Centurion, the visitors played exceptional cricket in the second Test at Durban. South Africa were in trouble at 103-6 in response to India's 205, when Dale Steyn played forward to Harbhajan and got a thick outside-edge. The cherry flew past Dhoni, but Rahul, standing at slip, judged it perfectly. He caught the ball with his outstretched left palm and held onto it as he fell to his left. The catch made him the first 'fielder' in Test history to complete a double century of catches.

Laxman's 96 in the second innings enabled India to set the hosts a target of 303. The Indian bowlers then went flat out and completed a victory by 87 runs. As their teammates celebrated, three members of the team—Rahul, Tendulkar and Laxman—would have remembered their subjugation for 100 and 66 at the same venue, fourteen years previously. A lot had changed in Indian cricket since. The senior statesmen were the catalysts of the transformation.

The series decider at Cape Town went India's way until Jacques Kallis took his team to safety with an unbeaten hundred in the second innings.

World Cup hysteria had taken over by the time the tour of South Africa ended. Sourav Ganguly, VVS Laxman, Anil Kumble and Rahul himself would never get to be part of a

World Cup winning team*, but the fact was that Dhoni and his team would not have achieved what they did at the Wankhede Stadium on the evening of 2 April 2011, had the icons not shown them the way at the start of the new millennium. More than the matches and series they won, the runs they scored, the wickets they took and the catches they held, the greatest contribution of the likes of Tendulkar, Ganguly, Kumble, Laxman, Srinath and Rahul was to steer Indian cricket out of the muck left behind by the match-fixing scandal and restore the credibility of the sport with their passion, perseverance and professionalism. In the process, they inspired the likes of Zaheer Khan, Harbhajan Singh, Virender Sehwag, Gautam Gambhir, Yuvraj Singh, Virat Kohli and of course, Mahendra Singh Dhoni, to follow their footsteps.

The World Cup was preceded by the fourth IPL Player Auction, in which Rahul's services were dispensed with by RCB. He was roped in by Rajasthan Royals, who had done little of note in the league after winning the title in 2008. Those who looked forward to seeing Rahul work in tandem with Shane Warne, RR's Captain-Coach, were disappointed as the team had another patchy season and failed to qualify for the Playoffs. Rahul had his best IPL season till that point, with 343 runs at an average of 31.18 from 12 games. His most memorable performance was an unbeaten 43 off 32 deliveries in RR's last league game against the Mumbai Indians, in which he and Shane Watson opened and knocked off the target of 134 by themselves.

The senior statesman continued from where he had left off at Kingston's Sabina Park in July 2006, in the first Test of the 2011

*as players

series against the West Indies at the same venue. He scored 40 and 112 in a game in which only three other batsmen crossed fifty. India won by 63 runs, but the victory was forgotten after the 'cop-out' in the final Test at Roseau. After occupying the driver's seat for most of the game, India were seemingly coasting to their second win of the series (the second Test was drawn) when something inexplicable happened. On the fifth afternoon, they were 94-3 and needed 86 more to win with a minimum of 15 overs. In the middle were Rahul and Laxman, batting on 34 and 3 respectively. Virat Kohli and Dhoni were slated to come in next. Reaching the target seemed akin to taking a stroll in the park. However, the West Indians were pleasantly surprised when the visitors called the match off. Duncan Fletcher, who had succeeded Gary Kirsten as India's coach after the World Cup, defended his team at the media conference, but he could not get the majority to alter its view that India's 'ceasefire' was unbecoming of a team that stood at the top of the Test Rankings.

Fletcher would surely have alerted his boys to the dangers of adopting a conservative approach during their next assignment. The Indians needed to be bold and belligerent to retain the Pataudi Trophy against an English team that had outclassed Australia in Australia a few months previously.

The Indians also needed a bit of luck. Zaheer Khan, their most successful bowler overseas since the previous tour of England, had taken the West Indies tour off to tend to a troubled ankle. Sreesanth, Gambhir and Yuvraj had also skipped the tour due to fitness concerns. All these players were declared fit for the England tour. Tendulkar was also back after being rested for the West Indies series and Sehwag, who was recuperating after a shoulder operation, was to join the team after the first two

Tests. Those who hoped that the players would be rejuvenated after their breaks had no inkling of what was in store for them.

Zaheer walked off the field with a hamstring 'strain' in the first session of the first Test and was subsequently ruled out of the entire series. There were many more injuries and indispositions thereafter. Weeks and months of incessant cricket had finally taken their toll.

As the players broke down, so did the team. England won all four Tests and ensured an inglorious end to India's reign as the Numero Unos of Test cricket. The first Test at Lord's was the 100$^{th}$ between England and India and the 2000$^{th}$ of all time. England won the toss and batted solidly to declare at 474-8. Rahul was among the first to see the writing on the wall, even as he held firm at one end while wickets fell at the other. The Indian batting was simply not good enough to counter the opposition.

In a landmark Test match being played on the cricketing world's grandest stage, one of the greatest cricketers of all time pitted his wits and wares against a formidable bowling line-up. It used to be said of Sunil Gavaskar that 'batting for him was not merely batting, but an intellectual exercise;' Rahul would prove over the next few weeks that he was his hero's kindred soul.

He came in at 63-1 and proceeded to delight the purists. His drives were fluent and his glides and clips delectable. The Indian supporters weren't the only ones relieved when Chris Tremlett beat him with a beauty that came within millimetres of taking the outside edge, but didn't. When the redoubtable James Anderson strayed in line and length, Rahul made him pay. The maestro was equally severe on spin; Graeme Swann was cut for four and when the offie served a rare long-hop, Rahul rocked back and thumped it through mid-wicket for another boundary. An imperious on-drive off the same bowler took Rahul to fifty.

It wasn't only his boundaries that had all of England's Test cricket-loving community enthralled; his defence was copybook and his judgement exemplary. He never ever took his eyes off the ball till he essayed a stroke or let the cherry pass through to the keeper. It was by no means a chanceless innings, but Rahul followed the old dictum of taking it 'one ball at a time.' His timing was precise and the ball always seemed to hit the middle of the middle of his bat. An on-driven two off Tremlett took him to a hundred, much to the delight of the spectators. He had come within five runs of a hundred in his debut Test, which was played at the same venue. Fifteen years later, he bettered that performance in what was certainly the last of his four Tests at cricket's HQ. His roar of delight when he completed his hundred, his 33rd in Tests, was more Kohliesque than Dravidesque; it was an outcome of his being as much pleased with the way he had batted as with the way he had battled for his team.

The visitors folded up for 286, with Rahul undefeated on 103. The hosts stayed in front for the rest of the game. Needing 458 to win, the Indians had a new opening pair in the second innings. Gautam Gambhir had taken a hit on the elbow while fielding and he could not come in to bat. Rahul opened with Abhinav Mukund and scored 36 before being caught behind off Anderson. India lost by 196 runs.

India began well in the next Test at Nottingham. Dhoni elected to bowl and England were reduced to 124-8 before the lower order took them to 221.

Rahul, the designated opener for the game with Gambhir tending to his elbow injury, lost Mukund, his partner, without a run on the board. In came VVS Laxman, who knew a thing or two about batting with Rahul and vice versa. With Laxman taking full toll of every bad ball—and some good ones as well—at one end, Rahul flowered at the other. The highlight of his innings was his duel with Stuart Broad. A delivery that made contact with Rahul's right glove fell short of the keeper only because the maestro had loosened his grip just before the moment of impact. It wasn't that Rahul was the only one dictating terms. Tim Bresnan hit him on the right forearm, necessitating the intervention of the physiotherapist. A delivery by Broad struck him on the back thigh and it appeared that Rahul was struggling. However, Indian fans stopped worrying when they saw what happened next; Rahul essayed a forward defensive stroke that was straight out of the coaching manual. It was a message to the bowler that he needed to do a lot more. Rahul then added insult to injury with two scintillating strokes—a clip on the leg-side, which he followed by going down on one knee to square-drive the cherry for four.

The spectators rose to Rahul when he completed his fifty with a straight 'tap' off Broad, which was so perfectly timed that the ball sped to the boundary. Laxman contributed 54 to a stand of 93 before he nicked Bresnan to the keeper. The artiste was gone, but the artisan carried on.

As Rahul batted and battled, there was a lot more to cheer for the connoisseurs of Test match cricket. Broad continued to give it everything he had, and at one point, he sat on his haunches after a delivery went past Rahul and missed the bails by a whisker. Rahul shook his head and willed himself to make the most of the reprieve. A paddle-swept boundary off Swann gave him his second century of the series. However, his 117, as also Yuvraj Singh's 62, went in vain. India took a first-innings lead of 67, but England amassed 544 in the second innings and their bowlers completed the job. India lost by 319 runs.

An Indian cricket-lover would rather the third Test at Birmingham was expunged from the record-books. Virender Sehwag got a king's pair in his 'comeback' game and Alastair Cook scored 294 for England. The hosts won by an innings and 242 runs and the 'glorious uncertainties' of cricket were forgotten as Indian fans geared up for another catastrophe in the final Test at the Oval. Their team was far too demoralized by then.

England won the toss and declared at 591-6, with Ian Bell and Kevin Pietersen scoring 235 and 175 respectively. India's gambit of flying R.P. Singh, who was holidaying in Miami, as a replacement for Zaheer Khan and playing him ahead of Munaf Patel, who was part of the original squad, backfired with the left-armer making a wayward start and eventually conceding 118 runs in 34 overs without taking a single wicket. India's 'Mr Adaptable,' who had returned to the number three spot at Birmingham, was shunted up the order again for the final Test, with Gambhir unavailable due to a head injury sustained at Birmingham.

Sehwag and Laxman fell early. Rahul's response to the situation was an imperious square cut off Anderson. He clipped the paceman to the mid-wicket boundary in the next over. He had failed at Birmingham with scores of 22 and 18, but at the Oval, he was 'in the zone.' This did not mean that the bowlers were not testing him, but he was always a couple of steps ahead of them and adept at erasing his errors from memory. Tendulkar kept him company in a partnership of 55, but those who came in later failed to make an impression.

Amit Mishra, who came in at 137-6, stayed in long enough to have the best view of a Batting Masterclass. He watched a master who was in love with his craft and displaying his proficiency in it, sans the slightest hint of arrogance or bluster. Many watchers viewed Rahul's batsmanship as a reflection of the struggle to ensure that the quest for excellence continued to be recognized in the 2010s, an age in which hubris and obnoxiousness were being considered synonyms of success, and mediocrity and short-cut approaches were being institutionalized across sectors.

The fall of wickets at the other end made no difference to Rahul, who continued flipping through the pages of the coaching manual and leaving even the opposition appreciating his technique, fortitude and footwork. However, never at any stage did he put technique over enterprise. Every scoring opportunity was seized upon and every attempt made to reduce his team's imminent deficit. He became more assertive as he neared his third hundred of the series and moved from 86 to 98 with three boundaries in a single Swann over. A lofted hit in the vacant deep mid-wicket region was followed by a late cut and an on-drive. He then almost committed hara-kiri, going for a single, but Broad's throw missed its mark. He was then struck on his left hand by Bresnan, but the impact did not sting all that much as he had loosened his grip in the nick of time. It was Test match batting at its very best.

A cut past the slips off Bresnan gave him two runs and his third hundred of the series. It was his 35th in Tests, taking him past Sunil Gavaskar's 34 and making him India's second-highest centurion after Sachin Tendulkar.

Mishra (43) and R.P. Singh (25) helped Rahul take India to their highest total of the series. When the final wicket fell at 300, Rahul was unbeaten on 146. He had batted for nearly six-and-a-half hours and faced 266 deliveries. Only two Indians—Sunil Gavaskar and Virender Sehwag—had carried their bat through a Test innings, before him.

> 'In England, you can get runs only if you are patient enough to spend time at the wicket and not be in a hurry to "settle down." His performances on the 2011 tour of England were extraordinary. I remember him opening the batting in the last Test at the Oval and carrying his bat through the innings to remain unbeaten on 146. We were asked to follow-on and he was back in the middle as an opener. The stadium gave him a standing ovation. It was a memorable moment for all of us. Like us, the spectators knew that one of the greatest cricketers of all time was in the twilight zone of his career and they needed to make the most of him while he was there.'
>
> – Virender Sehwag

Rahul's final innings of what had been a memorable series for him but a disastrous one for his team featured a reprieve, a life and then a sentence at the hands of the Decision Review System (DRS) that was being used in the series. He was on 7 when the English claimed a catch at short-leg off Swann. The umpire ruled Rahul out, but he asked for a review and the decision was overturned. One run later, Rahul nicked one that was dropped by Matthew Prior. He had moved to 13 when the umpire negatived another appeal for a catch at short-leg, but this time around, England asked for a review. An edge was detected and Rahul had to go.

England were frustrated by a partnership of 144 between Tendulkar and Mishra, but the innings disintegrated rapidly once both batsmen fell at the same score and India slid from 262-3 to 283 all out. Andrew Strauss and his team were awarded the sponsors' trophy, the Pataudi trophy and the ICC Test Championship Mace. The only silver lining at the presentation ceremony from an Indian viewpoint was the announcement of their Player of the Series. It was an easy choice for Andy Flower, the England coach, to make.

> 'This gentleman has been a pillar of strength and resilience throughout this series. His outstanding performances have further underlined what a true champion he is… As well as being one of the game's great batsmen, he is a great bloke and hugely respected by all in the England team…'
>
> – Andy Flower's message, as read out by Michael Atherton at the presentation ceremony.

Rahul was his usual decorous self in his post-presentation talk with Atherton, as he congratulated the England team and expressed his disappointment at the way India had played. When asked by the former England captain if he could 'put a finger' on why it was such a disappointing series for India, his reply was quick; 'It might take half an hour.'

He had scored 461 runs at an average of 76.83 from four Tests. In what was a remarkable coincidence, he had achieved exactly the same aggregate in the ICC Cricket World Cup 1999, which was also played in England. That performance, twelve seasons previously, had established his credentials as an all-format batsman. In 2011, there was nothing left for him to prove, but that was precisely what made his deeds special. That he was still able to keep going and bat the way he did, was testimony to his brilliance. The game, especially its traditional version, could not have asked for a greater ambassador.

A member of that Indian team, who had played a fair bit with Rahul, told this writer that Rahul, being a cricketing purist, loved playing in England, a country where cricketing traditions were valued. 'He loved the country. Whenever the team bus halted at a roadside café on our way to the next venue, Rahul would sit at one of the tables, book in hand, and sip a coffee. He would converse with the people who would approach the players. I don't recall him doing this during the 2007 tour, when he was the captain. He was more relaxed in 2011 and that showed in his batting,' the player said.

Even as they struggled to come to terms with the injuries to their players during the Test series, the Indian selectors did something unexpected between the second and third Tests. They picked Rahul in the squad for the solitary T20 International and five-match ODI series against England that was to follow the Tests. Considering that Rahul had been one of the players to be axed in January 2008 as part of what was a long-term plan for the 2011 World Cup, his recall to the squad just four months after India won the same tournament was ironic. He followed the announcement of the team with one of his own and declared his retirement from the limited-overs versions. He said that he had not informed the powers-that-be of his desire to focus 'solely on Test cricket' earlier, because he had not expected to be picked for ODIs after not being considered for two years. He signed off with an assurance that he was committed, as always, to India's interests in the upcoming series.

Rahul would not have been human to have not been hurt by the way he had been treated by the selectors and indeed, the team management, in mid-2009. In 2011, he would have experienced a feeling of déjà vu. India's next international assignment after the limited-overs series in England was another limited-overs series against the same team, but at home. One did not have to be a genius to anticipate what the selectors would do. He was entirely justified in not wanting to have the events of 2009 repeat themselves.

He scored 31 on his T20 International debut. He delighted the Indian supporters by hitting Samit Patel, the left-arm spinner, for three consecutive sixes. His first two strokes cleared the long-on boundary and he swept the third over square-leg. England won the game by six wickets and proceeded to dominate the ODI series against a team that was clearly a shadow of the one that had won the game's ultimate prize earlier in the year.

Rahul's best performance of the ODI series was 69 in the final game at Cardiff. He batted brightly, adding 170 with Kohli before he came down the wicket to Swann and went for a big hit, but missed. As he commenced the walk back to the pavilion for the last time as an ODI player, the bowler broke into a jog in his follow-through and shook Rahul's hand. The England players followed suit and the spectators then took over.

Should Rahul have gone the whole hog instead of retiring from two formats? Hindsight certainly suggests that the England tour ought to have been his last in all forms of the game, but then, he had Australia on his mind.

'Fundamentally, there are two types of batsmen. I belonged to the type that wanted to 'feel the ball.' Virender Sehwag was also a part of this club, which is why the opposition would aim to frustrate us by bowling just wide of the off-stump and try to make us reach out for the ball. Rahul belonged to the second category of batsmen—those who want to understand where their off-stump is. The more effective he was in terms of judging and ignoring deliveries pitched just outside the off-stump at the start of an innings, the better he would bat as he went along. Cheteshwar Pujara is like Rahul, in that he has loads of patience and is prepared to wear the bowlers down.'

– Sachin Tendulkar

16

# YESTERDAY, TODAY AND TOMORROW

'I have sometimes found myself in the middle of a big game, standing at slip or even at the non-striker's end and suddenly realized that everything else has vanished. At that moment, all that exists is the contest and the very real sense of the joy that comes from playing the game. It is an almost meditative experience, where you reconnect with the game just like you did years ago, when you first began, when you hit your first boundary, took the first catch, scored your first century, or were involved in a big victory. It lasts for a very fleeting passage of time, but it is a very precious instant and every cricketer should hang on to it. I know it is utterly fanciful to expect professional cricketers to play the game like amateurs; but the trick, I believe, is taking the spirit of the amateur—of discovery, of learning, of pure joy, of playing by the rules—into our profession. Taking it to practice or play, even when there's an epidemic of white-line fever breaking out all over the field. In every cricketer there lies a competitor who hates losing, and yes, winning matters. But it is not the only thing that matters when you play cricket. How it is played is as important for every member of every team because every game we play leaves a footprint in cricket's history. We must never forget that.'

– Rahul Dravid, Bradman Oration, 2011

It was around 9:15 pm on Monday, 7 March 2012. This writer, who was then the Manager—Media Relations and Corporate Affairs at the BCCI, received a call from Mr N. Srinivasan, the then President of the BCCI. The President came straight to the point; 'Rahul has decided to retire and he wants to announce the same in a media conference, a couple of days later.'

The Indian players outplayed the West Indies 2-0 at home in the winter of 2011. Rahul had another good series, with scores of 54, 31, 119, 82 and 33. Laxman and he scored hundreds in the second Test at Kolkata and Tendulkar came tantalizingly close to completing his 100th international hundred in the third Test at Mumbai, falling for 94. These knocks ensured that the three bulwarks of India's batting line-up were in just the right frame of mind on the eve of the tour of Australia. Some of the players, Rahul included, repeated what they had done before the start of the Test series in South Africa the previous year and flew to Australia early to acclimatize, while the others played in the ODI series against the West Indies.

His early departure meant that Rahul could not attend the fifth annual BCCI Awards Ceremony, where India's top performers of the 2010-11 season were felicitated. There was only one contender for the Polly Umrigar (Indian Cricketer of the Year) Award and his parents received it on his behalf.

The tour of Australia turned out to be as cataclysmic as the one of England, with the Indians being outplayed 0-4 for the second time in six months. Indian cricket appeared to have regressed within months of the World Cup victory.

Among the notable failures was Rahul. He scored 194 runs at an average of 24.25, quite a fall from his heroics in England. In what was most uncharacteristic of the man, he was bowled six times in eight innings. One of his teammates put this down to 'technical issues.' 'Rahul's head was falling and his left leg was going too far across. The Australian bowlers were good enough to exploit that chink in his armour,' the player told this writer.

His fans hoped that the season of 2012-13, in which India was to play as many as ten Tests at home, would provide the three bulwarks a platform that they could utilize to return to form before bowing out on a high. When the Australia series ended, Rahul was 39, Sachin a couple of months shy of 39, and Laxman 37. There was talk about the need for the BCCI to prepare an exit management plan, as the team could not afford to lose all three simultaneously.

In July 2012, this writer was at a Working Committee Meeting of the BCCI, where a senior administrator recalled a conversation with Rahul in March that year. The administrator told the gathering that when Rahul informed him about his decision to retire, he advised him to reconsider and told him that he would score heavily in the ten 'home' Tests of the forthcoming season. Rahul's response left him speechless. The stalwart said that while he *knew* that he had a good chance of doing well in the home season, he wanted to make way for a youngster. India were scheduled to make tours of South Africa, New Zealand and later, England and Australia, in the run-up to the 2015 World Cup. He reckoned that it would be better if a youngster was inducted into the team during the long home season, so that he would get attuned to Test cricket in familiar conditions, before travelling overseas.

That was Rahul Sharad Dravid.

> 'I would like to announce my retirement from international and domestic first-class cricket. It has been 16 years since I first played a Test match for India, and I feel that it is time for me to move on. Once, I was like every other boy in India, with a dream of playing for my country. I could never have imagined a journey so long and so fulfilling. I have had a wonderful time, but now, it is time for a new generation of young players to make their own history and take the Indian cricket team even further.'
>
> – RAHUL DRAVID at the Media Conference on 9 March 2012

Rahul thanked his teammates, coaches and physiotherapists at different levels, the KSCA and the BCCI, the selectors and the media, in his statement. He remarked that he would miss the 'joy of being part of a unit' more than anything else. He mentioned his parents, brother and wife, who had been pillars of strength, especially in tough times.

The main hall of the Chinnaswamy Stadium was bursting at the seams that morning. Members of the media, former international and first-class cricketers, administrators of the BCCI and the KSCA, as well as individuals who wanted to be there and somehow managed to get there, were in attendance. The crowd comprised an employee of the International Cricket Council (ICC), who had flown from Dubai to Bengaluru for a wedding in the family that was taking place the same day. 'I don't care if my family disowns me, I just had to be here for Rahul,' he told this writer. The preparations for the media conference were supervised by Javagal Srinath in his capacity as the Hony. Secretary of the KSCA. Anil Kumble, another former teammate of Rahul's, shared the dais with the BCCI President and Rahul himself, in his capacity as President of the KSCA.

Rahul with parents, Sharad and Pushpa

Rahul answered all the questions that came his way with aplomb for more than half an hour, after which, he, his family members and select attendees made their way to Kumble's room for lunch. It was then that this writer's phone buzzed; a senior cricket journalist, who had come all the way from Delhi, wanted to meet Rahul. He had attended the media conference but hadn't asked a question. This writer conveyed the message to Rahul, who agreed to step out immediately. The journalist looked straight into Rahul's eyes, and after ten seconds of silence, thrust out his hand. 'Thank you for everything,' he said to Rahul, shook his hand and walked away.

> 'Having played a key role in getting Rahul to bat at 'no. 3,' I was delighted when he ended his career with more Test runs at that position than any other batsman in the game—10,524. He was an ideal number three. The position demands solidity, patience and technique. Rahul ticked all these boxes. On most occasions, he was able to wear the opposition down, which helped those who followed him in the batting order.'
>
> —Sachin Tendulkar

The BCCI organized a Farewell in Mumbai, later that month. The Indian team, on its way to South Africa for a one-off T20 International, was in attendance, as were former India captains and current and former administrators. Eloquent and emotional speeches were made by Anil Kumble, Sourav Ganguly, VVS Laxman, M.S. Dhoni and Sanjay Jagdale, the Hony. Secretary of the Board. All of them could not thank Rahul enough for what he had done for Indian cricket. Among those who had a lump in their throat was the man himself. He began his speech by admitting that while he had decided not to cry at any function, 'that resolve of his was going to be tested.' However, he handled himself very well, as was only to be expected from someone who had constantly challenged himself and triumphed. The evening culminated with Rahul receiving a memento as well as the last standing ovation of his career as an international cricketer.

In his speech, Rahul mentioned one of the attendees 'whose dream he had lived.' Sharad Dravid, his father, was a compact top-order batsman who idolized Vijay Hazare and played a lot of cricket during his formative years in Gwalior in Central India. In later years, he was instrumental in building up a club team that played in the local league in Bengaluru. Sharad Dravid's long professional association with 'Kissan' led to his elder son being nicknamed 'Jammy.' Rahul and his younger brother Vijay would accompany their father to the Chinnaswamy stadium to watch cricket matches.

Dravid senior's recollections of Vijay Hazare, particularly those pertaining to the maestro's run-hunger and technique, left their mark on his son. The father would have been more pleased than the son when the latter scored 233 and an unbeaten 72 to take India to a historic win at Adelaide on the same ground where Hazare had scored twin hundreds against Bradman's 'lnvincibles' in 1947-48.

Sharad Dravid passed away in July 2013.

As supportive of Rahul was his mother Pushpa, a teacher and artist. She was a distinguished member of the Department of Architecture in Bengaluru's Vishveshwaraya College of Engineering from 1968 to 2001. She completed her PhD on `Professor Nicholas Roerich and his Himalayan Paintings' in 1999 and became the first lady from Karnataka to complete a PhD in Art. Rahul inaugurated an exhibition of her paintings in Kochi in March 2005, on the eve of an ODI between India and Pakistan in the same city. A couple of years later, she was requested by the KSCA to create murals of the twenty Karnataka cricketers who had represented India, in their headquarters at the Chinnaswamy Stadium. Among those whom she 'drew' on the KSCA walls was her own son.

Like the mother, the son specialized in using his hands to leave an indelible mark on canvasses of a different kind—those that had a lot of grass on them.

Rahul and Vijeeta have two sons, Samit and Anvay, who were born in 2005 and 2009 respectively. Samit has been making waves in junior-level cricket for quite some time now. The boys may or may not emulate their father by wearing the India cap, but their upbringing will ensure that they will epitomize all the qualities that were synonymous with Rahul, in whichever profession they opt for.

Rahul's parents were complemented by his teachers. One of them was Father Dennis Coelho, the Principal of St. Joseph Boys' School, Rahul's alma mater. When Rahul's parents were reluctant to let their soil travel to Vijayawada with the Under-15 Karnataka team, it was Father Coelho who assured them that he would take care of the youngster's studies. In any case, Rahul was so good in his studies that there were never any concerns on that front. Rahul made that trip to Vijayawada and never looked back.

'If you want to be a cricketer, look like one,' Keki Tarapore, who played Dronacharya to Rahul's Arjuna, would never tire of telling the youngsters under his charge. Rahul adhered to this principle for the entirety of his career. Not only did he always look like a cricketer, but he also never indulged in anything that was 'not cricket.'

> 'The fact that I am playing at this level, is due to the early training and the well-drilled basics that I got from Keki.'
>
> —RAHUL DRAVID, *The Hindu*, 28 July 2001

Tarapore passed away in July 2001, a few months after his pupil scored an epic 180 against Australia at Kolkata.

Rahul commenced a new innings in June 2015, with the

BCCI announcing his appointment as coach of the India 'A' and national under-19 teams. He was no stranger to 'mentoring,' having played that role for Rajasthan Royals in 2012 and 2013. However, the IPL was a seven-week tournament. Coaching, mentoring, motivating and travelling with those who constituted the future of Indian cricket demanded an extraordinary degree of commitment.

The 'Rahul effect' was immediate. India 'A' beat their Australian and South African counterparts in a tri-series and undertook successful tours of South Africa and Bangladesh in the 2015-16 season. The Under-19s also delivered. They were invincible in 2015-16 and even beat a 'senior' Board President's XI in the lead-up to the World Cup. The idea of making them play against a 'senior' side before the global tournament was their coach's. Ishan Kishan's team played well in the World Cup, but lost to the West Indies in the final.

The coach also partnered the management of the senior team to create a roadmap for the future. Quite a few of the India 'A' players whom he had mentored, made it to the senior side in the 2016-17 season and delivered.

> 'At the India 'A' level, it's not so much about technique. The large part is about where they are in their career: some close to a national call-up, some might have just come onto the scene. For us, it is about creating the best environment for them to do well. We give them what's required for them to feel relaxed and enjoy the game. We also challenge them. We push them a little bit and we demand high standards.'
>
> – Rahul Dravid, *The Times of India*, 8 August 2018

India's under-19 squad of 2017-18 went one step ahead of

its predecessor. India's fourth triumph in the under-19 World Cup was their most comprehensive till date.

> 'What can a youngster learn from Rahul Dravid? For starters, his discipline—waking up early, meditating and then working out and training. Rahul is one of the few legends of the sport to have taken to active and hands-on coaching. The under-19s and 'A' team cricketers could not have asked for a better mentor. While he values all three formats of the game, he is the kind of person who will stress on excellence in the traditional version. If you are a good Test cricketer, then you can easily become a good T20 cricketer, but it isn't quite the same the other way around. The boys will do well to imbibe this learning from him. He deserved the praise he got for his stand that if an under-19 cricketer is good enough to play the Ranji Trophy, then he should not play under-19 cricket. I liked the way he tried out more than 40 players in the lead-up to the under-19 World Cup. This idea of his was criticized, but he and his boys had the last laugh. His insistence that all members of the support-staff should get the same amount as a performance bonus, was typical of the man.'
>
> – Virender Sehwag

Rahul's pursuit of excellence was one of the reasons Indian cricket scaled hitherto unconquered peaks in the 21st century. As coach, he carried on in the same vein and encouraged his boys to aim high. They will do well to imbibe not only his many attributes, but also the zeal that made him one of the greatest match-winners in cricketing history.

Nice guys, they say, finish last. In an extraordinary career,

Rahul Sharad Dravid proved otherwise.

> 'I would like to thank the Indian cricket fan, both here and across the world. The game is lucky to have you and I have been lucky to play before you. To represent India, and thus to represent you, has been a privilege and one I have always taken very seriously. My approach to cricket has been reasonably simple. It was about giving everything to the team, it was about playing with dignity and it was about upholding the spirit of the game. I hope I have done some of that. I have failed at times but I have never stopped trying. It is why I leave with sadness, but also with pride.'
>
> – Rahul Dravid, Media Conference, Bengaluru, 9 March 2012

# ACKNOWLEDGEMENTS

I would like to thank the following individuals who helped me in various ways to write this book: Akash Chopra, Allan Border, Anant Gaundalkar, Andrew Leipus, Anshuman Gaekwad, Anuradha Prabhudesai, Ashok Mankad, B.P. Bam, Chandrashekhar Prabhudesai, Charu Sharma, Chinmay Prabhudesai, Clayton Murzello, Dilnaz Anklesaria, Gundappa Viswanath, Hanif Mohammed, Jonty Rhodes, Medha Prabhudesai, Mike Coward, Moin Khan, Mudassar Nazar, Murali Kartik, Navjot Sidhu, Paras Mhambrey, the PMG team, R. Kaushik, Raju Mehta, Ratnakar Shetty (Prof), Richie Benaud, Ritika Hiranandani, Robin Singh, Ruchi Kaushal, Sachin Tendulkar, Salil Ankola, Sandeep Patil, Sharda Ugra, Simon Willis, Sudhir Vaidya, Sumedh Shah, Sunil Gavaskar, Sunil Joshi, Syed Kirmani, Venkatapathy Raju, VVS Laxman, Virender Sehwag, Yajurvindra Singh, and R.K. Mehra, Air Marshal M. Baladitya, Kapish Mehra, Abhimanyu Prabhudesai, Ira Prabhudesai and Sonal Prabhudesai.

# THE RAHUL DRAVID FACTFILE

Name: Rahul Sharad Dravid

Date of birth: 11 January 1973

Specialization: Right-handed batsman, right-arm off-break, wicketkeeper

Major teams represented: India, Karnataka, South Zone, Rest of India, Kent, Scotland, Royal Challengers Bengaluru, Rajasthan Royals.

**Batting and fielding**

| | Mat | Inns | NO | Runs | HS | Ave | 100s | 50s | Ct | St |
|---|---|---|---|---|---|---|---|---|---|---|
| **Tests** | 164 | 286 | 32 | 13,288 | 270 | 52.31 | 36 | 63 | 210 | 0 |
| **ODIs** | 344 | 318 | 40 | 10,889 | 153 | 39.16 | 12 | 83 | 196 | 14 |
| **T20Is** | 1 | 1 | 0 | 31 | 31 | 31.00 | 0 | 0 | 0 | 0 |
| **First-class** | 298 | 497 | 67 | 23,794 | 270 | 55.33 | 68 | 117 | 353 | 1 |
| **List A** | 449 | 416 | 55 | 15,271 | 153 | 42.30 | 21 | 112 | 233 | 17 |
| **T20s** | 109 | 101 | 7 | 2,586 | 75* | 27.51 | 0 | 13 | 23 | 0 |

**Rahul Dravid, The Captain: Tests**

| Matches | Won | Lost | Drawn |
|---|---|---|---|
| 25 | 8 | 6 | 11 |

- In 2007, Rahul became only the third Indian captain after Ajit Wadekar (1971) and Kapil Dev (1986) to win a Test series in England.
- The year before, he became the second Indian captain after Ajit Wadekar (1971) to win a Test series in the West Indies.
- He was the first Indian captain to win a Test match on Pakistani soil (Multan, 2003-04).

**ODIs**

| Matches | Won | Lost | No-result |
|---|---|---|---|
| 79 | 42 | 33 | 4 |

The Indian team set a world record for the highest number of successful chases in a row—17—in the period from October 2005 to May 2006, with Rahul at the helm.

**Prominent distinctions:**

- The first batsman in Test history to score a century in every Test-playing nation of his time.
- The scorer of more Test runs at number three—10,524—than any other batsman.
- The first and till date, only Indian to score centuries in four consecutive Test innings.
- The first fielder to take 200 catches in Tests.
- Holds the world record for the maximum number of catches in Tests as a 'non-wicketkeeper'—210.

- The second Indian after Sunil Gavaskar to score centuries in both innings of a Test, twice.
- Coach of the Indian team that won the ICC Under-19 Cricket World Cup, 2018.

**Prominent Awards:**

- 1998: Arjuna Award
- 1999: CEAT International Cricketer of the World Cup
- 2000: *Wisden* Cricketer of the Year 2000
- 2004: Sir Garfield Sobers Trophy (ICC Player of the Year)
- 2004: Padma Shri
- 2004: MTV Youth Icon of the Year
- 2006: Captain, ICC's Test Team
- 2011: Lifetime Achievement Award—NDTV Indian of the Year
- 2011: The BCCI's Polly Umrigar Award for being India's cricketer of the year
- 2012: Don Bradman Award
- 2012: *GQ* Legend of the *Year*
- 2013: Padma Bhushan
- 2015: *Wisden* India's Highest Impact Test Batsman
- 2018: ICC Hall of Fame

**Orator:**

- The first non-Australian to deliver the Sir Don Bradman Oration (2011)
- The BCCI's MAK Pataudi Memorial Lecture (2015)

**Prominent brands endorsed:**

- Castrol
- Reebok
- Pepsi
- Bank of Baroda
- Kissan
- Hutch
- Samsung
- Skyline Construction
- Karnataka Tourism
- Max Life
- Citizen
- Gillette
- Sansui
- World Trade Center, Noida

**Social Commitments**

- Children's Movement for Civic Awareness (CMCA)
- UNICEF Supporter and AIDS Awareness Campaign
- Brand Ambassador, National Tobacco Control Campaign, Union Health Ministry

# BIBLIOGRAPHY AND REFERENCES


**ALMANACKS**

Wisden Cricketers' Almanack—1996 to 2004

**BOOKS**

Gulu Ezekiel, *Sachin,* Penguin Books India, 2002

Gulu Ezekiel, *Sourav,* Penguin Books India, 2003

Mike Coward, *Rookies, Rebels and Renaissance—Cricket in the 80s,* ABC Books.

Partab Ramchand, *India's Captains—From Nayudu to Ganguly,* Penguin Books India, 2004

Shane Warne, *Shane Warne, My Autobiography,* Hodder and Stoughton, UK, 2001

Vaibhav Purandare, *Sachin Tendulkar—A Definitive Biography,* Roli Books, 2005

Vedam Jaishankar, *Rahul Dravid, A Biography,* UBSPD, 2004

Vedam Jaishankar, *Casting A Spell—The story of Karnataka Cricket,* UBSPD, 2005

Devendra Prabhudesai, *Hero—A Biography of Sachin Ramesh Tendulkar*, Rupa, 2017

Sourav Ganguly, *A Century is not Enough*, Juggernaut Books, 2018

**NEWSPAPERS, MAGAZINES AND PERIODICALS**

*Cricket Today*

*Mid-Day*

The Hindu

The Indian Express

The Sportstar

Wisden Asia Cricket

*Wisden Cricket Monthly*

The Times of India,

Outlook

India Today

**TELEVISION CHANNELS**

ESPN-STAR

Ten Sports

**WEBSITES**

Cricinfo

Cricketforindia.com

Rediff.com

YouTube

Wikipedia

# INDEX

1983

Kaps

↓

Kapil Dev

↓

Roger binny

↓

Yashpal Sharma

↓

Srikkanth

↓

Dilip

↓

Ravi Shastri

" Like people once said

tongue wants more